Institutional Designs for a Complex World

Institutional Designs for a Complex World

Bargaining, Linkages, and Nesting

Edited by

Vinod K. Aggarwal

Cornell University Press

Ithaca and London

First published 1998 by Cornell University Press
First printing, Cornell Paperbacks, 1998

Printed in the United States of America

LIBRARY OF CONGRESS CATALOGING-IN-PUBLICATION DATA

Institutional designs for a complex world: bargaining, linkages, and
    nesting / edited by Vinod K. Aggarwal.
        p.   cm.
    Includes index.
    ISBN 0-8014-3460-2 (alk. paper). — ISBN 0-8014-8464-2 (pbk. :
alk. paper)
        1. International agencies—Social aspects.   2. Organizational
change.   3. Organizational behavior.   4. Negotiation.   I. Aggarwal,
Vinod K.
    JZ4850.I57   1998
    302.3'5—dc21   98-18839

Cloth printing   10 9 8 7 6 5 4 3 2 1

Paperback printing   10 9 8 7 6 5 4 3 2 1

Contents

Contributors

VINOD K. AGGARWAL is Professor in the Department of Political Science, Affiliated Professor in the Haas School of Business, and Director of the Berkeley APEC Study Center (BASC) at the University of California, Berkeley

BENJAMIN J. COHEN is Louis G. Lancaster Professor of International Political Economy at the University of California, Santa Barbara

BEVERLY CRAWFORD is Lecturer in the Political Economy of Industrial Societies Program and Research Director of the Center for German and European Studies at the University of California, Berkeley

CÉDRIC DUPONT is Assistant Professor at the Graduate Institute of International Studies, Geneva

STEVEN WEBER is Associate Professor in the Department of Political Science at the University of California, Berkeley

Preface

Understanding the creation of international institutions has long been central to the study of world politics. By contrast, less attention has been paid to the problem of how existing institutions are modified and how new and old institutions might be reconciled. These questions are particularly important in the context of Europe, with its long history of institutionalization and current efforts to adapt and build new arrangements. As institution building proceeds in other parts of the world, insights from the European experience may help shed light on this process.

This book could not have been written without the generous financial support of the Center for German and European Studies at the University of California. The Center's recent director, Richard Buxbaum, and its current director, Gerald Feldman, provided guidance and encouragement throughout the project. Going beyond the call of duty, Gerald Feldman attended two workshops at Berkeley in December 1994 and December 1995 and provided intellectual stimulus for the participants. The staff of the center, particularly Gia White, greatly facilitated the management of the project. Beverly Crawford, research director of the center, not only supported the intellectual thrust of the project but agreed to contribute a chapter to the volume. At the Berkeley workshops, several scholars provided valuable comments on earlier drafts of the papers. Christopher Ansell, Ole Røste Bjørn, Eileen Doherty, Elizabeth Kier, Jonah Levy, and Paolo Guerrieri served ably as discussants and stimulated valuable revisions. The contributions of additional colleagues are acknowledged in each of the chapters.

Earlier versions of these chapters were presented at roundtables in September 1995 at the annual meeting of the American Political Science Association and in April 1996 at the annual meeting of the International Studies Association. The essays also appeared in 1996 in the Working Papers series of the UC Center for German and European Studies.

As editor of the volume, I have benefited from the research and organizational support of several research assistants, including Nikolaos Biziouras, Kristine

Davidson, Sylvia Donati, Laboni Hoq, David Kang, Gregory Linden, Trevor Nakagawa, Jacob Okun, Rose Razaghian, and David Stuligross. I am grateful to the participants in the project who greatly contributed to the overall design and execution of this work. My introductory and concluding essays are considerably richer for their comments and criticisms. I am especially thankful to Cédric Dupont for spending so much time with me to reconceptualize and tighten the theoretical framework. The book as a whole has also benefited greatly from two anonymous reviewers whose comments both I and the authors found of immense usefulness.

Roger Haydon, editor for Cornell University Press, has been especially helpful. He ensured that the manuscript received a prompt external review, advised me on revising it, and has ably shepherded it through the publication process.

On a personal note, I thank my family for their continuing support. My parents, Om and Saroj Aggarwal, have worked hard to encourage my research and take on tasks that would facilitate my ability to concentrate on my academic work. Sonia, my seven-year-old daughter, has developed into an able research assistant and encourages me to publish by keeping a dust jacket of my last book on her desk. I have been especially fortunate to have the moral support of my wife, Nibha Aggarwal. Her own grueling work schedule while she completed her MBA has been an inspiration. I dedicate my contributions in this volume to her for making our home a happy nest.

VINOD K. AGGARWAL

Berkeley, California

Abbreviations

APEC	Asia-Pacific Economic Cooperation
ASEAN	Association of South East Asian Nations
BDF	Banque de France
BIS	Bank for International Settlements
CAP	Common Agricultural Policy
CDU	Christian Democratic Union
CFSP	Common Foreign and Security Policy
CMEA	Council of Mutual Economic Assistance
CPR	Common Pool Resources
CSCE	Conference on Security and Cooperation in Europe
EAEC	East Asian Economic Caucus
EC	European Community
ECB	European Central Bank
ECJ	European Court of Justice
ECU	European Currency Unit
EEA	European Economic Area
EEC	European Economic Community
EFTA	European Free Trade Area
EMM	European Monitoring Mission
EMS	European Monetary System
EMU	European Monetary Union
EPC	European Political Cooperation
ER	Exchange Rate
ERM	Exchange Rate Mechanism
EU	European Union
FDI	Foreign Direct Investment
FSF	Financial Support Fund
FTAA	Free Trade Area of the Americas
G-7	Group of Seven Industrial Nations

G-10	Group of Ten Industrial Nations
GATT	General Agreement on Tariffs and Trade
GEMU	German Economic and Monetary Union
GNP	Gross National Product
HDZ	Croatian Democratic Union
HLNG	(Joint EC-EFTA) High-Level Negotiating Group
IBRD	International Bank for Reconstruction and Development
IEA	International Energy Agency
IFOR	Implementation Force
IMF	International Monetary Fund
ITO	International Trade Organization
JNA	Yugoslav National Army
MERCOSUR	Common Market of the South
MFA	Multi-Fiber Arrangement
MFN	Most Favored Nation
MTFA	Medium Term Financial Assistance
NAFTA	North American Free Trade Agreement
NATO	North Atlantic Treaty Organization
OECD	Organization for Economic Cooperation and Development
OPEC	Organization of Petroleum Exporting Countries
OSCE	Organization for Security and Cooperation in Europe
PD	Prisoner's Dilemma
RPR	Rassemblement Pour la République
SDR	Special Drawing Rights
SEA	Single European Act
SFF	Supplementary Financing Facility
SPD	Socialist Democratic Party
STMS	Short Term Monetary Support
UN	United Nations
UNCTAD	United Nations Conference on Trade and Development
UNHCR	United Nations High Commission for Refugees
UNPROFOR	United Nations Protection Force
VSTF	Very Short Term Financing Facility
WEU	Western European Union
WTO	World Trade Organization

Institutional Designs for a Complex World

CHAPTER ONE

Reconciling Multiple Institutions: Bargaining, Linkages, and Nesting

VINOD K. AGGARWAL

International institutions are rarely created in a vacuum. When new institutions are developed, they often must be reconciled with existing ones.[1] One approach to achieving such reconciliation is the nesting of broader and narrower institutions in hierarchical fashion. Another means of achieving harmony among institutions is through a division of labor, or "parallel" linkages. The challenge of institutional reconciliation is not, however, unique to the creation of new institutions. In lieu of creating new ones, policymakers may modify existing institutions for new purposes. When doing so, they must also focus on issues of institutional compatibility. Moreover, bargaining over institutional modification is likely to be strongly influenced by existing institutions.

The post–Cold War era is likely to increase the difficulty of crafting and reconciling international institutions. As in the 1940s and 1970s eras of changing relationships among major powers, current power shifts in the international system have created stresses for a variety of institutions. In particular, changing

For financial support, I am grateful to the Center for German and European Studies at the University of California. Some of the theoretical ideas were developed while I was a Visiting Fellow at the East-West Center in Honolulu, whose hospitality I greatly appreciate. For comments on earlier versions, I am especially indebted to Cédric Dupont, and thankful to Muthiah Alagappa, Pierre Allan, Christopher Ansell, Benjamin Cohen, Beverly Crawford, Paolo Guerrieri, Ernst Haas, Guy Holburn, Robert Keohane, Sumner La Croix, Aija Leiponen, Jeff Macher, Steven Weber, and Yaacov Vertzberger. Kristine Davidson, Sylvia Donati, Nikolaos Biziouras, and Trevor Nakagawa provided able research assistance.

[1] I use the term "institution" to refer to the combination of a meta-regime and a regime. For a discussion of these terms, see the first section of this chapter.

power relationships in the international security system, marked by the demise of the Soviet Union and the rise of China, have challenged the post–World War II consensus among Western powers. The future role of NATO and its relationship to the United Nations and European institutions have become a subject of controversy. Within the Asia-Pacific area, the role of the United States and the possible need for security institutions have become matters of debate. In the economic realm, long delays in the negotiation of the Uruguay Round and the creation of regional accords in trade such as NAFTA and APEC have fostered concerns about undermining the World Trade Organization. In the heavily institutionalized European arena, efforts to move toward monetary union have created dissension in the European Union. In short, the problem of institutional reconciliation, particularly through nesting, is likely to become an increasingly important issue in international bargaining. Understanding this process is the central task of this volume.

In the first section of this chapter, I discuss some basic concepts related to the understanding of institutions and provide examples of different modes of institutional reconciliation. I then develop the notion of an "institutional bargaining game" in the second section. Specifically, I suggest that we can construct these bargaining games based on three elements: (1) the types of "goods" that are involved in the issue-area of concern; (2) the "individual situation" of actors—defined by their international power position, domestic coalitions, and politicians' beliefs, which influence actors' national positions;[2] and (3) the presence or absence of institutions within which bargaining takes place. By drawing on and developing theoretical ideas from different schools of thought about institutional change, I then show how these three elements will determine the structure of the bargaining game.

Set in motion by varying stimuli, these institutional bargaining games will generally result in differing payoffs for actors. Faced with undesirable payoffs, some actors may attempt to modify the bargaining game in which they find themselves. The methods and results of these attempts provide the focus for the third section, where I show how actors can use power resources to manipulate the three elements (goods, individual situations, and institutions) that define the institutional bargaining game. In this book our primary focus will be on actors' efforts to change the institutional games—rather than their efforts to manipulate goods or individual situations directly.

Whether actors create new institutions or only modify existing ones, they must decide on the characteristics of the institution (multilateral versus bilateral, as well as the strength and nature of the arrangements) and also on a bargaining

---

[2] See Aggarwal 1989 and 1996 on both the concepts of individual situations as well as parallel and nested linkages (discussed below).

route to establish these characteristics. Drawing on existing schools of thought about institutional change, the fourth section provides a theoretical rationale for the actors' choices, and it asks the key question of how actors choose appropriate forms of institutional linkages. Actors must decide if some institutions (or issues) will be subordinated to others, or if they will be reconciled by a division of labor among institutions.

In view of our emphasis on bargaining in the context of existing institutions, the fifth section reviews the book's empirical cases. These cases all have a European-related focus.[3] Europe has a history of institutional richness, beginning in the post–World War II era with the European Economic Coal and Steel Community, which then, over time evolved into the complex European Union. In particular, Steven Weber's chapter examines questions of institutional constraints and institutional deepening in the context of the crisis of the European Monetary System. He looks at how the nested nature of institutions in this area prevented a collapse of this system. Institutional challenges have also arisen from the problem of integrating new members into the community, either on a case-by-case basis, or in a broader effort such as the European Economic Area (EEA). Cédric Dupont examines this failed institutional effort to bring together the EC and EFTA. In the security area, we have seen an active role by NATO as well as the Conference on Security Cooperation in Europe (CSCE) and the Western European Union (WEU). How these different institutions might work together in coping with crises has yet to be resolved; they provide the subject of Beverly Crawford's chapter on the Bosnian crisis. Finally, Benjamin Cohen's study focuses on the interaction of the United States and European countries in the context of a combined economic and security crisis—the 1973–74 Oil Crisis. In particular, Cohen examines the difficulty of creating new institutions to address this crisis in the context of existing financial arrangements. In view of our concern with institutionalized areas, the European arena provides an ideal setting to examine cases of institutional modification and reconciliation.

THE ANALYTICAL FRAMEWORK: AN OVERVIEW

We begin with an overview of the institutional bargaining process to get a better grasp of the specific question of institutional reconciliation. Figure 1.1 depicts the elements of the institutional bargaining problem. Starting with the center of the chart, we can distinguish between two aspects of institutions: meta-regimes

[3] For an insightful discussion of the prospects for European institutions after the Cold War see Keohane, Nye, and Hoffman 1993.

[4] See Aggarwal 1985. Zacher (1987 and 1996) uses the distinction developed in this work in his analysis of regimes.

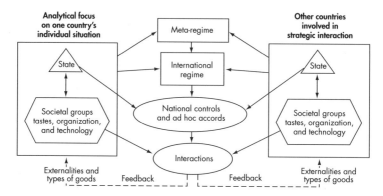

FIGURE I.I.   The institutional bargaining problem

and regimes.[4] Whereas the term *meta-regimes* represents the principles and norms underlying international arrangements, the term *international regimes* refers specifically to rules and procedures. Regimes can be examined in terms of strength, nature, and scope. "Strength" refers to the stringency of the multilateral rules that regulate national behavior; "nature" (in an economic context) refers to the degree of openness promoted by the accord; and "scope" refers to both the number of issues incorporated in the regime—issue scope—and the number of actors involved (bilateral or multilateral)—institutional scope. In this book, we focus primarily on institutional scope.

International regimes, whether multilateral or bilateral, are developed to regulate the actions of states. The term *national controls* can include unilateral actions or ad hoc bilateral or multilateral accords. These measures in turn affect the types and levels of *interactions* that we observe in particular issue areas. Examples of interactions, which primarily result from nongovernmental activities by private actors, include trade, investment, or short-term capital flows.[5] These actions are affected by changing technology, tastes, and modes of organization. Such elements provide the driving factors behind the changing supply and demand of products and services as well as the interaction that results from exchange among private actors within states.[6] In an apolitical world, we could imagine a closed loop with societal actors engaging in interactions without the presence of any types of governance structures—be they national controls, ad hoc agreements, or institutions—to influence these activities.

[5] In security matters, for example, we could examine weapons flows, the movement of fissionable materials, and so on.

[6] This emphasis on private actors does not, of course, rule out the direct exchange of goods and services by states themselves, but merely reflects the primary mode of exchange at this level.

Changes in interactions will influence state and societal actors. Bargaining among states is generally stimulated by some type of impetus, which occurs through significant changes in existing patterns of interaction as a result of changes in governance patterns or economic changes.[7] This often creates some type of *externality* or affects the provision of *goods;* states then respond to these changes in light of what I have termed their *individual situations.* The result is a bargaining game among states that takes place in either an institutional or non-institutional setting. As noted earlier, our focus in this book is on cases of bargaining where institutions already exist. Thus, the next step concerns states' decisions on whether to use or adapt existing institutions, or whether to create new ones.

Regardless of whether institutions are adapted or newly created, our primary focus is on understanding how they might fit with existing institutions (see figure 1.2.). Actors must decide on how the institutions they adapt or create will be reconciled with existing arrangements—that is, through nesting or by parallel connections.

A few examples will illustrate these ideas. One can think about the problem of reconciling institutions from both an issue-area and a regional perspective.[8] Nested institutions in an issue-area are nicely illustrated by the relationship between the international regime for textile and apparel trade (the Long Term Arrangement on Cotton Textiles and its successor arrangement, the Multifiber Arrangement) with respect to GATT. In the 1950s, continental European protectionist measures in textile and apparel trade were inconsistent with GATT's objectives and eroded American efforts to bolster an open multilateral trading system. At the same time, in the early 1960s, President John F. Kennedy faced strong protectionist lobbying efforts from the cotton textile and apparel industries. In view of Kennedy's desire to promote a new round of tariff reductions, the U.S. government found itself in a quandary. To cope with these competing pressures, it promoted the formation of a sector-specific international regime under GATT auspices. This "nesting" effort ensured a high degree of conformity with both GATT's principles and norms as well as with its rules and procedures.[9] Although the textile regime deviated from some of those norms in permitting discriminatory treatment toward developing countries, it did adopt and adapt the most-favored nation norm, treating all developing countries

[7] Societal actors can, of course, also affect other states directly, but I have not shown these links here so as to simplify the charts and presentation.

[8] See Oye 1992 for a good discussion of regionalism. Also see Gamble and Payne 1996 and Lawrence 1996, among others.

[9] See Aggarwal 1985 for a discussion of nested systems and institutions in the context of sectoral arrangements. Also see Aggarwal 1994 for analysis of institutional nesting in a regional context in North America and the Asia-Pacific region as well as an analysis of APEC's options. The term nesting has been used by Barkun (1968) to examine hierarchical systems.

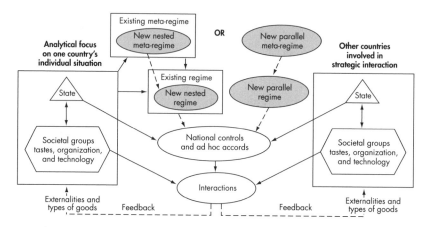

FIGURE 1.2. Reconciling multiple institutions

alike. Moreover, while allowing protection against imports, the textile regime remained at least partially consistent with GATT norms that fostered trade openness by calling for the gradual liberalization of restrictive measures.

For an example of the nesting of regional institutions, we can turn to the development of the Asia-Pacific Economic Cooperation grouping (APEC) in 1989 and its relationship to GATT. APEC's founding members were extremely worried about undermining GATT and sought to reconcile these two institutions by focusing on the notion of "open regionalism." In justifying this accord, APEC members saw "open regionalism" as a better alternative than the use of Article 24 of GATT, which permits the formation of free trade areas and customs unions. Although the interpretation of "open regionalism" continues to be contested, the idea behind this concept was that while the members of APEC would seek to reduce barriers to goods and services amongst themselves, they would do so in a GATT-consistent manner. The ways to achieve this consistency include dealing with non-GATT issues or pursuing unilateral liberalization measures that would be open to all GATT signatories—whether or not they are members of the APEC grouping.

An alternative mode of reconciling institutions would be to simply create "parallel" institutions that deal with separate but related activities, as exemplified by the GATT and Bretton Woods monetary system. In creating institutions for the post–World War II era, policymakers were concerned about a return to the 1930s era of competitive devaluations, marked by an inward turn among states and the use of protectionist measures. As a consequence, they focused on creating institutions that would help to encourage trade liberalization. By promoting fixed exchange rates through the IMF and liberalization of trade through GATT (following ITO's failure), policymakers hoped that this parallel institutional division of labor would lead to freer trade. Also on an issue-area basis, one example of institutional modification and reconciliation involves the shifting roles of the International Monetary Fund (IMF) and the International Bank for Reconstruction and Development (IBRD, the World Bank). Whereas the two institutions had a clearer division of labor based on short-term versus long-term lending as originally formulated in the 1940s, more recently this division has become fuzzier and a potential source of conflict.

Finally, on a regional basis, one can see the development of the European Economic Coal and Steel Community and the Western European Union as parallel organizations. The first was oriented toward strengthening European cooperation in economic matters (with, of course, important security implications), while the second sought to develop a coordinated European defense effort.

We now turn to a more specific discussion of the concept of an institutional bargaining game, which we will consider as an approach to the process of institutional transformation and reconciliation.

Specifications of the Institutional Bargaining Game

The key task of this section is to describe the elements (goods, individual situations, and institutions) that constitute an institutional bargaining game and then to show how they fit together to yield game payoffs. (See figure 1.3A.) This figure serves as the basic framework to set up bargaining games for the empirical chapters.

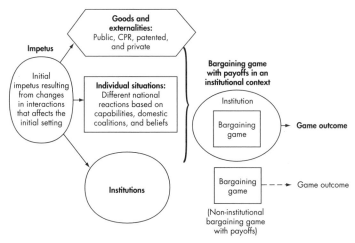

FIGURE I.3A. The institutional bargaining game

The Initial Impetus

In general, an initial impetus significantly alters the preexisting bargaining context. Examples include the Oil Shock of 1973, the breakdown of the Bretton Woods system in 1971, and the end of the Cold War following the collapse of the Soviet Union. An impetus can also come from both endogenous and exogenous changes that are less dramatic, such as actions by currency speculators or electoral victories that shift actors' individual situations. These changes, which can be either directly related to the issue at hand or affect the broader institutional context within which an issue is being negotiated, will create differing incentives for actors.

Goods and Externalities

Initial shocks may either create a positive or negative externality on actors who are not immediate participants in the precipitating event. Alternatively, economic or political changes may stimulate or impede the provision of some type of goods, namely public goods, common pool resources (CPRs), inclusive club goods (or what I have termed "patented goods"), or private goods.[10] Differences among goods can be characterized along two dimensions: jointness, which refers to the extent to which goods are affected by consumption; and the possibility of exclusion, which refers to whether noncontributors to the provision of goods can be kept from consuming them.[11]

In the case of public goods (e.g., national defense), actors face a collective action dilemma because all can benefit from their joint nature. However, because exclusion is not possible, beneficiaries need not contribute to their creation or maintenance. In such cases, analysts have focused on the incentives for differently situated states to provide public goods. The classic representation of the provision problem for public goods is the n-person prisoners' dilemma: in such cases, cooperation can potentially help all players, but actors' dominant strategy is to defect, in which case, the goods may not be provided.[12]

Common pool resource goods include global commons concerns such as fishery resources or goods where exclusion of noncontributors from consumption of the goods is not feasible.[13] In such cases, providers of goods risk being exploited

---

[10] For a discussion of these four types of goods and actors' motivations to provide them, see Aggarwal 1996. On common pool resources in particular, see Ostrom 1990. For an earlier insightful discussion of types of goods see Snidal 1979. The best summary of the literature on goods is by Cornes and Sandler 1996.

[11] See Snidal 1979.

[12] Hardin 1982.

[13] For a good discussion of CPRs and international institutions, see Keohane and Ostrom 1994.

since they will not only end up paying for the cost of the goods, but will also suffer from free riding that will diminish the goods. Thus, at least in principle, the provision of such goods will be a more severe form of the prisoners' dilemma.

Inclusive club goods, or "patented goods," refer to the type of goods that exhibit jointness (i.e., those that are not diminished by use), but where exclusion is possible. Two examples of this type of good are the provision of satellite transmission of television and the use of scrambling technology to prevent noncontributors from accessing certain broadcasts. Because of the benefits of having additional consumers, we might expect that, in the case of international institutions, actors would compete to have their institutional approach adopted as the standard by all participants to maximize their revenue possibilities.

Private goods, which reflect the possibility of exclusion but not jointness, refer to goods that are diminished by use. Individual actors will have an incentive to produce these goods and to charge according to the marginal cost of extension of these goods.

To better understand the implications of this basic characterization of these various types of goods, we also need to consider the effects of actors' individual situations and the institutional context within which interaction takes place. Put differently, goods only give us a first cut into understanding the type of problems that actors face and their incentives: knowledge of the types of goods involved in bargaining does not allow us to adequately determine specific payoffs because the position of national actors or the institutional setting may alter the bargaining problem.

Individual Bargaining Situations

States are likely to have varying interests in the issue-area within which bargaining takes place. While the factors that might affect actors' interests (and hence their payoffs) are nearly endless, the most significant influence on national responses can be narrowed down to (1) an actor's international position, as defined by its issue-specific and overall capabilities; (2) its domestic coalitional stability; and (3) elite beliefs and ideologies. The first of these elements refers to both the actors' position in the overall international system as well as to its relative capabilities in the specific issue-area under discussion. These factors will influence a state's objectives as well as its ability to secure its desired outcomes. The second element, a state's domestic coalitional stability, focuses on the incumbency expectations of government decision makers. This variable taps into decision makers' discount rates. For example, in debt rescheduling negotiations, domestically unstable governments are more reluctant to undertake sharp economic adjustment measures for fear that they will be ousted. Finally, elite beliefs and ideologies about the causal connections among issues and the need to handle problems on a multilateral basis will also influence the payoffs and actors' responses.

In earlier work, I have examined the influence of certain factors—issue capabilities, overall capabilities, and domestic coalitional stability—on actors' basic goals.[14] I have constructed preference orderings for actors in order to set up games of strategic interaction in a noninstitutional context, and I have solved these games for equilibria to predict the likely outcome of bargaining. In the essays in this volume, the authors do not formally specify a complete preference ordering for each actor in order to construct bargaining games. But they do systematically consider how these factors influenced state preferences and choices in setting up the initial bargaining game.

The Institutional Context

As states attempt to secure their preferred outcomes, they will interact strategically, possibly in the context of one or more institutions. Institutions should influence how actors interact, and may provide either focal-point solutions for coordination games or may help states to overcome collective action problems.[15] Institutions are also likely to have important distributive consequences and may influence actors' bargaining behavior by tying the hands of both other international actors and domestic ones.[16] More significantly, some analysts argue that international institutions may lead to fundamental changes in actors' basic interests and possibly facilitate greater cooperation.[17]

Constructing Institutional Bargaining Games

We can now attempt to combine the three elements, goods, individual situations, and institutions, to gain insight into different types of institutional bargaining games. Understanding how such games are constituted will also give us insight into the strategies that actors might subsequently pursue in an attempt to change the games in which they find themselves. It is worth noting that an exact a priori specification of the effect of the three elements on game payoffs—absent a specific empirical issue—is a difficult if not impossible task; instead, the discussion below focuses on some general considerations of the effects of different elements. Before examining specific hypotheses with respect to game construction,

[14] See Aggarwal 1989 and 1996.

[15] See Stein 1983, Snidal 1985a, Axelrod and Keohane 1985, and Martin 1992, among others.

[16] See Aggarwal 1985 and below on the use of institutions to control other actors. For additional discussions, see Krasner 1991 and Knight 1992.

[17] See, for example, Haas 1980.

it is useful to briefly review some of the standard schools of thought on the development of institutions.

Hegemonic stability theorists suggest that institutions reflect power balances and argue that the demise of global-level institutions is an inevitable result of the relative decline of the United States in the international economic system.[18] The focus of this approach—which I label neorealist institutionalism to differentiate it from realists who see no role for international institutions—is on the distributional consequences of international regimes or arrangements.[19]

In contrast to neorealist institutional approaches, neoliberal institutionalists suggest that institutions will be more robust. Based on transaction cost approaches, they theorize that because global accords help to foster cooperation among states and provide them with ongoing benefits, cooperation "after hegemony" can be sustained.[20] The essence of this argument is that states are able to reduce organizational and information costs through the use of institutions, particularly when "issue-density" is high. One of the key functions of regimes is to reduce the costs that would come from having to negotiate a host of bilateral agreements with other states.[21] Moreover, regimes also help to provide information to the participants, with their secretariats or staff keeping track of the actions of member states.

Finally, institutional innovation and change has been examined with a focus on the role of expert consensus and the interplay of experts and politicians.[22] New knowledge and cognitive understanding may lead decisionmakers to calculate their interests differently. For example, politicians may use linkages to create new issue packages in international negotiations to form international regimes.[23] This focus on types of linkages, combined with the ideas developed here, helps us to significantly increase our understanding of the dynamics of institutional change.

Turning now to the specific question of game construction in relation to goods and individual situations, the neorealist institutionalist school hypothesizes that hegemonic powers will be willing to provide public goods and allow free riding because of purely economic calculations (as when an owner of a large number of ships pays for a lighthouse). Put differently, we should expect actors'

---

[18] There is an extensive literature on this subject. See, among others, Kindleberger 1973, Gilpin 1975, and Krasner 1976.

[19] I have not seen this term used before. Moravcsik (1992) does point to the difference between realist and liberal conceptions of institutions, but does not use the term neorealist institutionalism.

[20] *After Hegemony* is the title of a book by Robert Keohane (1984) that provides the best exemplar of the neoliberal institutionalist perspective. Keohane draws upon the work of Williamson (1975) in discussing transaction-cost approaches.

[21] Keohane 1982 and 1984.

[22] See E. Haas 1980 and P. Haas 1989, among others.

[23] E. Haas 1980.

payoffs to vary as a result of their differing positions, possibly changing the nature of the game as initially suggested by the goods involved. Lisa Martin presents an example of this by showing how a prisoner's dilemma game turns into a "suasion" game when a hegemon is present.[24] Because of this transformation resulting from differing individual situations, the outcome of the game will be a unilateral provision of public goods by the hegemon. Hegemons might also be willing to make economic sacrifices because of linkages to overall security concerns.

Alternatively, rather than a benevolent hegemon which provides public goods, we might also see aggressive powers that form institutions to monitor against potential shirkers or that simply use power directly by threatening free riders. The provision of public goods might also be possible with small numbers of actors, rather than with only one in cases of hegemony.[25] What might the public goods provision game look like with two players? While one might argue that the game would still remain a prisoners' dilemma, it seems more reasonable, given the jointness of the good, to consider the game as one of chicken: each actor would like the other to pay for the good, but the joint nature of the good means that free riders will not impair one's own consumption. The exact form of the game in this case will depend on the size of each of the two players in comparison to the overall cost of providing the public good.[26]

In the case of common pool resources, as noted above, the problem of provision and maintenance of such goods is more severe than for public goods because of the lack of jointness. Following the logic of the relationship between individual situations and public goods, we would expect the resulting hegemonic and bipolar provision games in the CPR case to mimic those in the case of public goods discussed above. However, in view of the lack of jointness, both the suasion and chicken games will have worse payoffs both for cooperation and defection, thus potentially making it more difficult for actors to come to agreement on the development of such goods. Yet this pessimism may not be fully warranted. While the lack of jointness inherent in CPRs makes it less likely that a hegemon would be willing to provide the good, this very "crowding" may actually stimulate the provision of CPRs. Hegemons in CPR cases will be more likely to encourage joint provision of goods through coercive means. Thus, possible free riders may be brought into the fold since their nonparticipation in providing a good has direct consequences for the supply. If they are then forced to pay for the good in question, the hegemon's initial investment and maintenance costs will be lower.

Drawing on neoliberal ideas, I maintain that CPRs in an institutionally thick context should clearly stimulate group activity in monitoring and possibly sanc-

[24] Martin 1992.

[25] See, for example, Snidal 1985b.

[26] See Aggarwal and Dupont (forthcoming) on a more formal treatment of the relationship between goods, individual situations, and institutions.

tioning because of the negative implications involved in free riding. Thus, it is likely that there will be *more* active participation by all members, and therefore, less likely that the good will be eroded over time. And finally, drawing on a cognitive perspective, actors may redefine their interests in view of the potential benefits of cooperation and be less likely to shirk in the provision of CPR goods.

With respect to private versus patented goods, I would hypothesize that the strong benefits that accrue to actors from the provision of patented goods will stimulate competition to provide the good. Thus, in an institutional setting, if benefits can be gained by "selling" the good to possible new members of an institution, we should see competition among groups of states to encourage nonparticipants to join their arrangement. The game in this case would look much like a coordination game, with each party vying to have its own institutional form adopted. In the technology standards area in a private setting, attempting to set up one's own standard as the national or global standard parallels this institutional hypothesis.

In sum, as suggested in this section, bargaining among actors—based on the games defined by goods, individual situations, and institutions—yields payoffs that are likely to vary for the actors involved in the initial negotiating game. For example, as Cohen's chapter notes, France and the United States responded quite differently to the 1973 Oil Shock because of differences in their individual national situations. Initially, they split over how the crisis should be addressed. Subsequently, as Cohen's chapter notes, they also disagreed over the appropriate type of institutions and the relationships among them that might be used to cope with this shock.

To this point, we have considered the factors that interact to create a static bargaining game. Faced with the payoffs that result from their initial strategic interaction, states may simply accept the outcome of their bargaining. But the game may not simply end at this point: indeed, actors are likely to make efforts to alter the bargaining game in which they find themselves in order to improve their payoffs in a new game structure.[27]

ACTORS' OPTIONS AND INSTITUTIONAL OUTCOMES

When will actors make efforts to promote game change? Logically, they consider the existing payoffs in the current bargaining game and compare these

[27] See Aggarwal 1996 for a discussion of game change efforts in debt rescheduling. For applications to other issue-areas, see Aggarwal and Allan 1994. While from a game theoretic standpoint, the choices that actors make in subsequent bargaining rounds are simply choice points in an elaborate extensive bargaining game, the notion of "game change efforts" provides a useful metaphor. This idea allows us to distinguish between the repeated play of the game within existing constraints, and efforts to improve one's payoffs by modifying the constraints themselves.

with their projected payoffs from instituting some form of game change. To make this calculation, states evaluate their ability to secure more favorable outcomes by assessing their own power resources in light of their own individual situation and that of their opponent or opponents. The relevant power resources that they might use include material capabilities (either issue specific or overall), appeal to like-minded allies, and institutions as a power resource.[28]

Figure 1.3B identifies the choices that actors might make in the initial bargaining game in an effort to improve their payoffs, and serves as the basis for examing game change in the empired chapters. Actors have three options. First, they can attempt to directly manipulate the types of goods involved in negotiations, say by forming an alliance that excludes other actors. Second, they can alter either their own or their opponents' individual situations. These could include such efforts as overthrowing governments, building up one's own capabilities in specific issue-areas, or attempting to change the views of decision makers in other countries. Third—the primary focus of this book—they can change the *institutional context* within which actors are operating. It is worth keeping in mind that such institutional change strategies may indirectly influence the goods involved in the negotiations and may well change actors' individual situations.

Given our emphasis on institutional strategies to alter games and influence bargaining outcomes, actors seeking to make game changes must make several additional decisions. Specifically, they must (1) decide if they would be better off by creating a new institution or modifying existing ones; (2) choose the characteristics of the institution that they want, specifically, the institutional scope; (3) select the bargaining route they want to follow; and (4) decide whether to engage in issue linkages, and if so, the type and nature of these linkages.

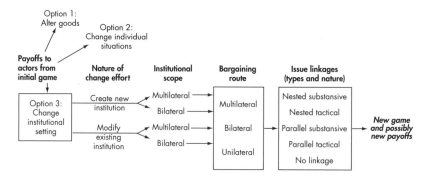

FIGURE 1.3B. Institutional game change efforts

[28] For a discussion and use of these power resources in different bargaining situations, see Aggarwal and Allan 1983, Allan 1984, and Aggarwal 1996. From a neorealist perspective, Waltz (1979) discusses the options of self-help and appeals to alliances as options for states.

Nature of Change Effort

When faced with unsatisfactory payoffs, states may seek to develop a new institution. For example, as noted, when several states in the Asia-Pacific became worried about the prospects for a successful conclusion to the Uruguay Round of trade negotiations, but at the same time did not wish to undermine GATT, they decided to pursue the formation of APEC within a GATT umbrella. Actors could, of course, decide that a new institution is not warranted. In this case, they may bargain within the context of the existing institutions of the initial bargaining game and promote modifications through, for example, the development of new linkages.

Characteristics of Institutions: Institutional Scope

If a state decides to pursue the formation of a new institution, it must decide on its institutional scope: bilateral (such as the Canada–U.S. Free Trade Agreement) or multilateral (such as APEC). It must also decide on the institutions' specific characteristics with respect to the strength and nature of the arrangements. But if a state decides that a new institution is undesirable, it could still work to modify it, possibly by changing its institutional scope (as with the expansion of the Canada–U.S. Free Trade Agreement to include Mexico). The next stage in the process is to decide on an appropriate bargaining route.

Bargaining Route

As indicated in figure 1.3B, states may choose to bargain multilaterally or bilaterally or take unilateral actions to achieve their ends.[29] Turning first to the bargaining route within an existing institution, although multilateral negotiations in a multilateral institution are common, states can also pursue bilateral and unilateral strategies—despite the existence of a multilateral institution. For example, even though the United States was involved in the Uruguay Round trade negotiations, it continued to discuss specific issues with Japan on a bilateral basis and took unilateral actions with respect to other states using specific GATT provisions.

What about the use of different bargaining routes for the creation of a new institution? In the case of multilateral arrangements, multilateral strategies can include coalition-building efforts. States can also use bilateral and unilateral strategies by imposing agreements on other states through either bipolar cooperation or hegemonic imposition. By contrast, if the institution in question is a bilateral one, it is less obvious theoretically how states might pursue a multilateral bargaining route. An example of this could be where actors engage in multilateral

---

[29] On the use of unilateral, bilateral, and multilateral approaches, see Diebold 1952, 36.

negotiations and then decide on an appropriate bilateral regime for a subset of the states involved. The emerging regime guiding relations between the PLO and Israel, resulting from negotiations in a multilateral forum, fits this notion.

Issue Linkages and Institutional Reconciliation

The final decision node in figure 1.3B concerns actors' decisions to link either issues or institutions in negotiations. In addition to choosing whether or not to engage in linkage formation, they must also make two other choices, so as to establish the type of linkage (nested or parallel) and the nature of the linkage (tactical or substantive).[30]

We have already given detailed consideration to the concepts of nested and parallel linkages. This distinction taps into one key dimension of the linkage issue. Will parallel linkages among issues or institutions be perceived as forced, owing to power plays, or as a logical division of labor that ensures compatibility among issues or institutions? And will a hierarchy of institutions be driven by power considerations or an accepted ranking of goals among the participants? To address this latter consideration, we must look at the nature of linkages. By considering the nature of linkages, we highlight the intellectual basis of the connection between issues. If two issues are seen to be unrelated but become tied together in negotiations, this can be considered a power-based connection or tactical link. By contrast, if the issues exhibit some intellectual coherence, then the linkage can be labeled substantive. Table 1.1 presents the alternatives under different conditions.

Substantive linkage will likely result in the creation of a stable issue-area and most likely a stable institutional arrangement. This outcome arises from bargaining whereby one actor convinces another (the target) of the impact of externalities involved in a particular set of negotiations and is able to convince its counterpart that issues are logically packaged. As we shall see, substantive linkages should lead to more stable institutions because actors are more likely to accept this type of issue packaging as a logical connection between or among issues.

The second type of manipulated linkage, failed substantive linkage, is more complicated. Here, even though experts agree that two issues are interconnected (such as access to markets for trade and the ability to service debt), policymakers in the target country do not recognize the issues as substantively linked. Instead, they perceive the issues as only tactically related.[31] Without changes, even though

---

[30] For a discussion of tactical and substantive linkages, see Oye 1979, Stein 1980, and E. Haas 1980, among others. Building on Haas's contributions in particular, I elaborate on the nature of linkages in Aggarwal 1996 from which a portion of the following discussion is drawn.

[31] Haas (1980) refers to what I term "failed substantive" and "failed tactical" linkages as "fragmented" linkages but does not distinguish between the two different types identified here.

TABLE I.I. The dynamics of issue linkage

Linkage type	Objective reality	Target decision makers' perceptions	Basis for issue connections	Outcome
Substantive link	Connected	Connected	Knowledge	(1) Stable issue-area
Failed substantive link (perceived as tactical)	Connected	Unconnected	Power	(2) Temporary solution to externalities
Tactical link	Unconnected	Unconnected	Power	(3) Unstable issue-area
Failed tactical link (perceived as substantive)	Unconnected	Connected	Misunder-standing	(4) "Contingent" (to unstable issue-area if consensual knowledge changes)

the target actor treats the issues as connected, this will prove to be only a temporary solution to the externalities problem. Such a situation may provide hope for the actor, or "linker," trying to establish the link. When the policymaker's initial reaction is a rejection of substantive connections among issues, experts in both countries may play a prominent role in swaying decision makers' opinions. Thus, over time, with changed causal understanding, we may see a move to substantive-linkage-based institutions.

The third type of link, tactical linkage, may foster even greater conflict. This method of connecting issues is a pure power play. If it is used as a positive inducement, it can diminish conflict. But if used as a stick, tactical linkages will create sharp conflict in negotiations and will most likely lead to unstable agreements or institutions.[32]

Finally, in the last case, that of misperceived tactical linkages, policymakers in the target country see the issues as substantively linked—even though they are only linked tactically. Although the target decision makers' own experts will attempt to dissuade their policymakers from accepting the linkage, the decision makers may come to some type of joint agreement and consider the issues in question as a package. Clever manipulation by the linker could produce considerably more favorable outcomes than might otherwise be the case. But because it is based on a misunderstanding, this is an unstable situation and will lead to unstable institutional formation. Indeed, if and when the target comes to realize that the connection was tactical in nature, the bargaining connection will shift to a potentially unstable one that will only endure as long as the linker maintains its superior power.

[32] See E. Haas 1980 for a discussion of this type of outcome.

Institutional Outcomes

We can now look at the possible outcomes resulting from efforts, on the one hand, to either (1) modify existing institutions (2) or create new institutions and reconcile them with the old ones and efforts, on the other hand, to understand the types and nature of linkages.[33] In each of the two rows in table 1.2, the top entry reflects a convergence of perceptions on linkages, whereas the bottom entry reflects a divergence of perceptions.

Modifying Existing Institutions. If we focus now on the first major row—the decision to modify existing institutions—we see there are three possibilities that we must consider: nested linkages, parallel linkages, and no linkages.

The first category in the table concerns nested substantive linkages. Under that category, the top entry refers to a case of convergence of perceptions. The relationship of issues in the IMF under the Bretton Woods system was clearly ordered. Fixed exchange rates were the crucial concern. Within that context, gold provided the basis for backing the dollar. The dollar played several key roles including the *numeraire*, the intervention currency, and the like, and there was widespread agreement on this structuring. The Germans and some others see the EMU convergence targets for debt, government spending, interest rates, and inflation as a natural economic connection between the higher-level objective of monetary union and the subordinate goals necessary to achieve smooth progress toward fixed exchange rates in the Union. By contrast, as noted in the bottom entry of that cell, some Southern European members of the EU have exhibited considerable skepticism about this claim, viewing the connection as a tactical effort by the Germans and other Northern Europeans to control their economic policies. In this case perceptions clearly diverged.

Under the category of tactical nested linkages, example (3) once again illustrates convergence of perceptions. Almost all states in the United Nations recognized that the decision-making structure there, with the Security Council dominating the General Assembly, was a tactical consideration based on the power of the major players in the system. An example of divergence of views in tactical nested linkages (4) is the aid to Lomé convention members for commodity price stabilization. From the perspective of the poorer members, this agreement is a substantive connection to stabilize markets. But from the perspective of many EC members it is simply a tactical exchange tied to political and economic interests in maintaining the Lomé agreements.

Moving across the chart to cases of parallel linkages, the relationship between the IMF and World Bank (1) provides a good example of parallel substantive

---

[33] For ease of presentation, I have avoided discussion of two elements, the type of institution and the bargaining strategy that actors might pursue to accomplish their ends.

TABLE 1.2. Linkage bargaining and institutional adaptation

	Linkage type				
	Nested linkage		Parallel linkage		No linkage
	Substantive	Tactical	Substantive	Tactical	
Use or modify existing institution or institutions					
	1. Stable hierarchical link between issues within an existing institution or between institutions *Role of dollar, gold, and exchange rates in IMF*	3. Contingent, hierarchical link between issues within existing institution(s) (to independent issues or in conflict with power change) *Security Council's role vs. General Assembly's role in the UN*	1. Stable, intra- or cross-institutional link between related issues *IMF and World Bank*	3. Contingent, intra- or cross-institutional link between issues (to independent issues or in conflict with power change) *Voting power and economic standing criteria in IMF*	Institutionally based negotiations on single issue *GATT dispute-settlement body*
	2. Temporary hierarchy between issues within existing institution(s) (target perceives link as tactical link) *Southern Europe's view of EMU convergence criteria*	4. Unstable, hierarchical link between issues within existing institutions(s) (if target perceives link as substantive link) *Commodity fund aid within Lomé convention*	2. Temporary, intra- or cross-institutional solution to externalities (target perceives link as tactical link) *Services and manufactures in Uruguay Round (LDC view)*	4. Unstable, intra- or cross-institutional link between issues (target perceives link as substantive link) *Special and differential treatment for developing countries in GATT (LDC view)*	

TABLE 1.2. Continued

	Linkage type				
	Nested linkage		Parallel linkage		No linkage
	Substantive	*Tactical*	*Substantive*	*Tactical*	
Create and reconcile new institution with old institution or institutions?					
	1. Stable, hierarchically compatible institutions created to deal with related issues *WTO-APEC*	3. Contingent, hierarchically compatible institutions created to deal with related issues (to independent issues or a conflict with power change) *APEC-EAEC connection*	1. Stable, compatible inter-institutional link for related issues *IMF and BIS connection*	3. Contingent, inter-institutional compatibility with related issues (to independent issues or in conflict with power change) *GATT vs. UNCTAD role in global trade negotiations*	Independent institutions (no concern for compatibility) *World Health Organization and ITU*
	2. Temporary, hierarchically compatible institutions created to deal with related issues (if target perceives link as tactical link) *MFA within GATT (LDC view)*	4. Unstable, hierarchically compatible institutions created to deal with related issues (if target perceives link as substantive link) *Global Environmental Fund and World Bank (LDC view)*	2. Temporary, inter-institutional compatibility between issues (target perceives link as tactical link) *GATT-UNCTAD Trade Development Center (LDC view)*	4. Unstable, inter-institutional compatibility with related issues (target perceives link as substantive link) *Financial Support Fund and the International Energy Agency (French view)*	

connections with respect to financial assistance. In the Bretton Woods system, the IMF was designed to engage in short-term lending to help countries facing balance of payments difficulties to economically adjust. Meanwhile, the World Bank would provide longer-term loans to help improve the functioning of countries' economies. The second case (2), the connection between services and manufactures in the GATT Uruguay Round, provides an example of differing views involving negotiations within an existing institution. Whereas the United States saw this connection as a substantive one, many developing countries argued that it was merely a tactical ploy and that services had no place in GATT negotiations. In the end, the negotiation proceeded on two separate tracks, but there was an implicit connection between the two.

Moving to tactical parallel linkages, the notion of weighted voting is clearly seen as a power based decision (3). In the IMF, countries are allocated voting shares based on economic criteria. While the indicators of economic wealth have come under increasing challenge, there is little question that this linkage is tactical in nature. Finally, in this set, calls for special and differential treatment for the developing countries (4) have been seen as a tactical concession to facilitate trade liberalization by the developing countries. Thus, developed countries have repeatedly made special provisions in negotiating rounds—dating back to the Kennedy Round and now in the Uruguay Round—that allow for delays in the implementation of WTO rules. By contrast, this effort has been viewed by many developing countries as a substantive logical connection deriving from their relatively uncompetitive position.

In this row, the last example reflects a case of no linkage. The GATT dispute-settlement body provides a forum for the resolution of issues without linkages to other concerns. In an ideal setting, these institutional mechanisms are to deal with the specific issues brought up for resolution by member states without connections to other issues.

Reconciling New and Old Institutions. We next turn to the second half of table 1.2. The first example (1), that of nestested substantive linkages illustrate, a case of convergence. I have already discussed the WTO and APEC connection as one that explicitly argued for a new arrangement in the Asia-Pacific that would be consistent with actors' higher-level concerns about continuing trade liberalization through GATT. The example given at the bottom of this first cell (2) presents a case of what some view as substantive nesting being perceived by others as tactical, a case of divergence of perceptions. The nesting of the MFA within GATT was seen by developing countries to be a tactical ploy to restrict their imports, and the claims of GATT consistency were argued to be a sham.

In the next column, we have cases of tactical linkages. In the first example (3), the connection between APEC and the East Asian Economic Caucus (EAEC), all parties recognize that this linkage exists because of pressure by Malaysia to create a separate grouping that would exclude North America and Oceania. Although some lip service is paid to the notion that this grouping is substantively connected, no one really thinks this is a credible view, and nearly all see this as a tactical connection.

As an example of a tactical link being perceived as substantive, we can consider the case of the Global Environmental Fund and its connection to the World Bank following the Rio environmental summit (4). From the developing countries' point of view, the promise of aid was a natural logical connection to broader financial aid organizations such as the World Bank. But developed countries have a more jaundiced view of this linkage and generally see it as a tactical payoff to get developing countries to reduce harmful emissions.

The third column in this row addresses the use of parallel substantive linkages. Consider the first example (1). When the IMF was created in 1944, there was initially seen to be conflict with the BIS. But within a few years, the relationship between the two stabilized in a division of labor that actors have accepted as logical. The situation is different in the second example (2). Consider the cooperation between The United Nations Conference on Trade and Development (UNCTAD) and GATT on trade enhancement. In this case, GATT's interest in trade liberalization was compatible with UNCTAD's focus on promoting exports—at least in the minds of developed countries. These two institutions have been partially reconciled through the formation of a Trade Development Center,[34] although developing countries remain more skeptical about this connection and perceive it more as a tactical linkage.

The fourth column examines the case of parallel tactical linkages among institutions. The decision to create UNCTAD and its relationship to GATT in the various trade rounds, example (3), has been seen by all countries as a tactical development resulting from developing countries' pressure to create a forum for their interests. While negotiations continue in GATT, UNCTAD often serves as a forum in which developing countries can get advice on how to improve their bargaining skills and obtain information about the issues involved. The fourth case concerns an example of a parallel tactical link that is perceived as substantive. As the chapter by Benjamin Cohen notes, when the United States proposed the Financial Support Fund as a tactical linkage to encourage development of the International Energy Agency, the French saw this as a substantive link connected to helping countries that faced balance of payments difficulties.

Finally, the last column in the table presents an example in which no effort was made to reconcile institutions, a case of the persistence of independent in-

---

[34] Another example, mentioned earlier in this chapter, is the parallel substantive link between the IMF and World Bank.

stitutions. Here we consider the World Health Organization and the International Telecommunication Union, which traditionally have dealt with quite disparate issues.

The discussion of possible outcomes as a result of linkage types and institutional formation is now complete. We now consider the causal factors that explain bargaining paths and outcomes.

HYPOTHESES ON GAME CHANGE EFFORTS AND INSTITUTIONAL RECONCILIATION

What factors will determine decision makers' choices on whether to pursue institutional change strategies to influence bargaining games? And how will these decision makers decide if institutions should be reconciled? Because of the considerable overlap between the arguments about modifying versus creating new institutions, I discuss the hypotheses with respect to institutional innovation, institutional scope, bargaining strategies, and reconciliation through different forms of linkages.

Modifying Existing Institutions versus Creating New Ones

One of the key issues in choosing whether to alter existing institutions or create new ones relates to the goods that are involved in the negotiations. For example, to prevent free riding that might take place with public and CPR goods, neorealist institutionalists point to the possible role of institutional strategies in altering the nature of the goods, as when the major powers decided to prevent developing countries from free riding due to the MFN norm of GATT. Thus, in the Tokyo Round, only those countries who signed onto specific codes (subsidies, government procurement, and so forth) were given the benefits of liberalization entailed by these codes.[35]

Focusing on transaction costs, if an existing institution is providing valued goods, it might be possible for actors to link the provision of goods in one arena with the provision of goods in another arena. Thus, given the organizational and informational benefits of an existing institution, actors may be reluctant to "free ride" in another area for fear of undermining the existing institution. With respect to new institutional creation and reconciliation, particularly in a nested context where goals in the new institution are subordinate to higher-level concerns in a broader institution, a similar incentive for actors to work together to provide public goods or CPRs may exist. That is, in view of their higher-level

---

[35] See Krasner 1979 and Grieco 1990 on this issue.

objectives, actors may be willing to risk cooperation in light of possible defection because of their concerns about meeting their higher-level goals.

Cognitive perspectives do not directly address the problem of overcoming collective action problems to secure provision of public goods or CPRs. Instead, cognitivists point to the possibility that as a result of learning, it may be possible to achieve some convergence of interests. Of course, such convergence is hardly guaranteed; states might simply better understand that their interests are in conflict! But we might extend cognitive thinking on how institutions might be used to deal with the provision of goods. How might growing cognitive convergence overcome the problem of free riding that is inherent in the provision of public goods—even when actors have common interests? I would argue that we can think of this problem in the context of thick interactions among states. In such a case, the convergence of interests would likely facilitate cooperation among states along standard neoliberal lines. A second cognitive effect on the provision of goods is the possibility that changes in knowledge may lead to changed understanding of the goods involved: this might mean that states could better understand how to exclude free riders, or that their initial estimate of the type of goods involved in the negotiations were not really of the type that they initially thought. Such changes do not a priori point to a greater likelihood of cooperation in the provision of goods. As noted above, actors may simply realize that the supply problem was more difficult than they had initially estimated and, therefore, be less likely to cooperate.

Excluding the creation of an institution de novo and noninstitutional bargaining, actors can either use or modify existing institutions or develop new ones and reconcile them with existing arrangements. Simple inertia would lead us to expect that actors' first instinct will to be to utilize or modify an existing institution to their advantage rather than to pursue development of a new institution—this is true both from a neorealist and neoliberal institutionalist perspective.[36] New institutions are expensive to create. Thus, if actors can achieve their objectives by simply modifying an institution, this will likely be the preferred course. Of course, if the institution has repeatedly failed to "deliver the goods"—even with modifications, then institutional innovation will be the logical option.

Beyond these standard arguments, we can hypothesize that an important constraint on the innovation of new institutions will be the degree to which existing institutions in which an issue might be resolved are deeply embedded among other institutions. Thus, if actors see existing arrangements in which negotiations might take place as substantively connected to other arrangements, either in nested or parallel fashion, this will influence prospects for new institutional creation.

---

[36] On this issue, see Keohane 1984 and Haggard, Levy, Moravcsik, and Nicolaïdis 1993, 181.

Institutional Characteristics: Institutional Scope

Institutional characteristics will be affected by several factors.[37] First, with respect to our interest in examining the issue of multilateralism versus bilateralism, we would expect different predictions from neoliberals and neorealists. Neoliberals would expect that multilateralism would be the preferred avenue to reduce transaction costs and provide the widest dissemination of information. By contrast, from a neorealist perspective, unless an actor is exceptionally strong, it might prefer bilateral over multilateral arrangements to maximize its leverage.[38]

Second, the choice of a multilateral versus a bilateral institution will be affected by the type of institutions that already exist. Thus, for example, I have argued that the norm of multilateralism in GATT strongly constrained the formation of the Short and Long Term Cotton Textile Agreements in 1961–62. This outcome can be explained as the result of actor concerns about institutional nesting and fear that bilateral and unilateral actions would undermine this GATT norm—*independent* of the benefits of reducing transaction costs through a multilateral arrangement.[39] By contrast, without strong substantive linkages among issues, the decision between a multilateral or bilateral institution will be more influenced by transaction and control considerations.

Third, the question of the choice between a multilateral or bilateral approach to institutional formation can be considered from a more cognitive perspective. In a volume edited by John Ruggie, a number of scholars argue that this choice derives from the preferences of states who fundamentally believe in the value of organizing the world system on a multilateral basis.[40] Thus, they are not concerned with the number of states involved in an activity, but rather with examining state commitments to norms of collective action. As a result of such concern, these analysts go beyond the neoliberal institutionalist view of multilateralism as simply a means for reducing transaction costs.

Bargaining Route

To achieve their ends, actors can pursue either a unilateral, bilateral, or multilateral route. The classic argument in this regard is a neorealist institutionalist one that views hegemonic states as being tempted to develop regimes. Other work in from this perspective has shown that like-minded states may be able to

---

[37] For a discussion of the factors that influence the strength and nature of regimes, see Aggarwal 1985.

[38] For a discussion of these ideas, see Diebold 1952, Keohane 1984, and Gilpin 1987, among others.

[39] Aggarwal 1995.

[40] See Ruggie 1992.

cooperate on a bilateral or multilateral basis to secure regimes and need not always fall victim to dilemmas of collective action.[41]

Less has been directly written about reconciling international institutions. Although we would expect power considerations to be still important, the usage of material power in these situations is constrained by existing institutional power resources. Appeals to norms and rules can play a significant role in this instance, particularly when actors agree upon the substantive nesting of issues. In addition, the presence of a highly institutionalized regime also constrains actors' efforts to develop a new institution for bureaucratic reasons. The bureaucracy and secretariat of extant organizations will be likely to oppose the formation of a new institution. In addition to direct resistance from the bureaucracy, states often have vested interest groups that benefit from the organization. These pressure groups and domestic bureaucratic groups are also likely to resist institutional innovation.

Linkages and Institutional Reconciliation

With respect to linkages, specifically parallel versus nested ones, I propose several hypotheses. Within an existing institution, from a cognitive perspective, decisionmakers' choices will depend on their understandings of the relationships among issues. For example, if they perceive inherent spillovers and connections among issues and believe that there is a hierarchical relationship among them, they will seek to make nested connections. Without such interconnections, it is easier to cope with spillovers through a division of labor—that is, through parallel connections.

In reconciling new and old institutions, or significantly modifying old ones, the choice of whether to support parallel or nested institutions will depend on the existing institutional environment. If institutions already exist, actors contemplating institutional innovation must decide how important it is to reconcile institutions. If one is developing narrow issue-area or region-based accords, and an issue's salience is low relative to broader issue-area or regional arrangements, actors will make strong efforts to nest the new institution within the broader one—even if there is no clear substantive connection among issues. Thus, we should also expect to see consistent goal ordering, and hence, nested institutions, when the threat is high. By contrast, if issue-area or regional institutions are crucial to actors, they may be willing to risk conflict with other institutions by developing parallel arrangements.

Turning to substantive versus tactical linkage issues, when actors do not share a cognitive consensus on the relationships among issues, tactical linkages will be

---

[41] See Snidal 1985b.

related to power-based efforts to assert the superiority of some issues or to deny the hierarchical ordering of connections proposed by other actors. Furthermore, on the specific question of differences between modifying existing institutions versus creating wholly new institutions and reconciling them with old ones, we should expect it to be more difficult to achieve a clear cognitive consensus in the latter case. Whereas in the case of minor institutional modification the question of cognitive consensus only applies to connections between individual issues, in the case of new or significantly modified institutions, actors must actually agree on the relationship between different institutions. This may turn out to be a more difficult problem because of the number of issues involved, which would suggest that the nesting of wholly-new and old institutions is more difficult than simply modifying old arrangements.[42]

This section has presented several hypotheses concerning the evolution of institutional bargaining games. In drawing on existing approaches to understand institutions, as well as elaborating on undeveloped strands of thinking, my objective has been to explore choices about institutional creation, institutional scope, and bargaining routes. Ultimately, my focus is on trying to tap into the logic of decision making that underlies actors' thinking about reconciling international institutions, either through nesting or parallel connections. Taken together with the ideas on construction of institutional bargaining games presented in the second section, the empirical chapters that follow explore the utility of this approach, providing a better understanding of the development and reconciliation of institutions in practice.

The Case Studies

While the case studies that follow are not a scientific sample, they do provide sufficient variety to examine the plausibility of the approach discussed here and the insight gained from it. Two of the chapters, the one by Steven Weber on the EMS and the EU, and the other by Beverly Crawford on the interplay of security institutions in the Bosnian case, focus on examples of modifying relationships among existing institutions. They also illustrate relative success and relative failure in reconciling different institutions. The other two chapters, by Cédric Dupont on EC-EFTA relations and Benjamin Cohen on the Financial Support Fund, consider how efforts were made to create new institutions and reconcile

---

[42] One could argue that institutions may facilitate the tight and accepted integration of issues. If this is the case, then the problem may be no more difficult than in the case of new institution creation.

them with existing arrangements, and they also show the difficulty in successful reconciliation of institutions, particularly on a nested basis. In total, these four studies provide ten cases in the sense of separate identifiable bargaining efforts. They also focus on both regional and issue-area concerns to more fully capture these two aspects of the institutional reconciliation problem.

Each of the cases follows a similar format. The authors begin by examining the impetus that stimulated bargaining efforts. They then consider the initial game that the relevant actors found themselves in and then turn to game change bargaining efforts through the use of international institutions. In examining the process of institution formation, the authors consider and weigh the role of the theoretical elements that influence the process of bargaining. Each author concludes by drawing some lessons about the bargaining process in terms of the formation or modification of institutions and specifically examines the pitfalls in efforts to nest institutions.

Steven Weber's chapter examines the evolution of the EMS. He focuses on the 1993 crisis when both the British pound and the Italian lira left the EMS. Weber argues (in contrast to the majority of other scholars' accounts of this crisis), that the deep nesting of the EMS within the EC, exemplified by the nested substantive linkage to Maastricht, prevented the EMS from undergoing total collapse. He shows how options to end the EMS through a free float of EC currencies, or a bilateral French-German fast track EMU, were rejected in favor of continued exchange rate coordination through the EMS. Ironically, the end result of the crisis from Weber's viewpoint was not a weakening of the EU, but rather its strengthening as member states successfully overcame the exchange rate crisis.

The chapter by Beverly Crawford deals with the response of European states to the end of the Cold War and the subsequent civil war in Yugoslavia. She shows how the weakness of the meta-regime underlying existing European security institutions prevented them from coping with the break-up of Yugoslavia and the war in Bosnia. As a result, Germany pursued a policy of unilateral recognition of Croatia and Slovenia, which undermined joint European coordination efforts. The end result was the entry of the United States, Russia, and NATO as key actors in the Bosnian crisis—culminating in the Dayton Plan and an institutional division of labor. She argues that the fragility of this effort lies in the lack of consensual agreement among the Western powers on any norms beyond the procedural one of multilateralism. The chapter thus highlights the difficulty in modifying relationships among existing institutions when the broader institutions themselves are poorly institutionalized.

Cédric Dupont's chapter considers the interaction between the EC and the EFTA countries as they sought to create a new institution—the European Economic Area—to address the dual challenge of rising competition on world markets and dramatic political and economic changes in Central and Eastern Europe. The new institution was supposed to give EFTA countries better access to the Single Market (that is, to private goods) to preserve the EC "inclusive club good" from crowding-out effects, and it was also supposed to take care of pan-regional stability in Europe, a common pool resource. Dupont shows why the EEA failed to fulfill its initial mandate. He argues that although there was a strong basis for establishing a substantive nested linkage of existing institutions inside the new institution, the salience of the EC precluded such smooth nesting. EC countries resisted giving too many privileges to EFTA countries, forcing the development of an asymmetric institution that EFTA countries, under severe domestic pressure, had no reason to stick with. Without their support, the new institution could not provide the common pool resource of pan-regional stability, leaving the EC with not only growing demands from Central and Eastern Europe but with almost all EFTA countries knocking at their door.

The last empirical chapter, by Benjamin Cohen, also examines the eventually unsuccessful efforts to develop a new institution—the Financial Support Fund (FSF). This fund was promoted as part of a broader American effort to form the International Energy Agency as a countercartel to the OPEC oil cartel. The case highlights the differing views of the United States and France with respect to the appropriate response to the oil crisis. It shows how the United States used tactical linkages in an effort to secure its preferred outcome and then managed to negotiate an agreement to create the FSF as an OECD facility that was to be firmly nested within the IMF system. Cohen then discusses how changing economic conditions, combined with a lack of domestic consensus and growing conflict between the IMF and OECD, led to a stillborn FSF. The end result, for reasons elaborated on in this chapter, was a failure to nest this new institution within the existing IMF system.

An important message clearly emerges from the empirical studies: the substantive nesting of institutions can be highly desirable to provide institutional stability and diminish conflict. Yet as the chapters show, it is not easy to achieve such nesting, particularly in the context of the development and reconciliation of wholly new institutions. Thus, decision makers will probably be forced to cope with increasingly difficult challenges in the post–Cold War era as existing institutions come under stress. Our hope is that this volume will help to better clarify some of the obstacles that decision makers will face in the future.

REFERENCES

Aggarwal, Vinod K., 1985. *Liberal Protectionism: The International Politics of Organized Textile Trade* (Berkeley: University of California Press).
———, 1989. "Interpreting the History of Mexico's External Debt Crises." In Barry Eichengreen and Peter Lindert, eds., *The International Debt Crisis in Historical Perspective* (Cambridge: MIT Press).

————, 1994. "Comparing Regional Cooperation Efforts in Asia-Pacific and North America." In Andrew Mack and John Ravenhill eds., *Pacific Cooperation: Building Economic and Security Regimes in the Asia-Pacific Region* (Sydney: Allen and Unwin).

————, 1996. *Debt Games: Strategic Interaction in International Debt Rescheduling* (New York: Cambridge University Press).

Aggarwal, Vinod K., and Pierre Allan, 1983. "Evolution in Bargaining Theories: Toward an Integrated Approach to Explain Strategies of the Weak." Paper presented at the American Political Science Association meeting, Chicago, September.

Aggarwal, Vinod K., and Cédric Dupont, forthcoming. "Goods, Games, and Institutions," Unpublished ms.

Allan, Pierre, 1984. "Comment négocier en situation de faiblesse? Une typologie des stratégies à disposition." *Annuaire Suisse de Science Politique* 24.

Axelrod, Robert, and Robert Keohane, 1985. "Achieving Cooperation under Anarchy: Strategies and Institutions." *World Politics* 38 (October).

Barkun, Michael, 1968. *Law without Sanctions: Order in Primitive Societies and the World Community* (New Haven: Yale University Press).

Cornes, Richard, and Todd Sandler, 1996. *The Theory of Externalities, Public Goods, and Club Goods* (New York: Cambridge University Press).

De Melo, Jaime, and Arvind Pangariya, eds., 1993. *New Dimensions in Regional Integration* (Cambridge: Cambridge University Press).

Diebold, William, 1952. "The End of the I.T.O." *Princeton Essays in International Finance*, no. 16 (October).

Frankel, Jeffrey, Ernesto Stein, and Jan Wei, 1995. "Trading Blocs and the Americas: The Natural and the Supernatural." *Journal of Development Economics*, 47 (June).

Gamble, Andrew, and Anthony Payne, eds., 1996. *Regionalism and World Order* (New York: St. Martin's Press).

Gilpin, Robert, 1975. *U.S. Power and the Multinational Corporation* (New York: Basic Books).

————, 1987. *The Political Economy of International Relations* (Princeton: Princeton University Press).

Grieco, Joseph M., 1990. *Cooperation among Nations: Europe, America, and Non-Tariff Barriers to Trade* (Ithaca: Cornell University Press).

Haas, Ernst, 1980. "Why Collaborate? Issue-linkage and International Regimes." *World Politics* 32, no. 3.

Haas, Peter, 1989. "Do Regimes Matter? Epistemic Communities and Mediterranean Pollution Control." *International Organization* 43 (Summer).

Haggard, Stephan, Marc Levy, Andrew Moravcsik, and Kalypso Nicolaïdis, 1993. "Integrating the Two Halves of Europe: Theories of Interests, Bargaining, and Institutions." In Robert Keohane, Joseph Nye, and Stanley Hoffmann, eds., *After the Cold War: International Institutions and State Strategies in Europe, 1989–1991* (Cambridge: Harvard University Press).

Hardin, Russell, 1982. *Collective Action* (Baltimore: Johns Hopkins University Press for Resources for the Future).

Keohane, Robert, 1984. *After Hegemony: Cooperation and Discord in the World Economy* (Princeton: Princeton University Press).

Keohane, Robert, and Joseph Nye, 1977. *Power and Interdependence: World Politics in Transition* (Boston: Little, Brown).

Keohane, Robert, Joseph Nye, and Stanley Hoffmann, eds., 1993. *After the Cold War: International Institutions and State Strategies in Europe, 1989–1991* (Cambridge: Harvard University Press).

Keohane, Robert, and Elinor Ostrom, 1994. "Local Commons and Global Interdependence: Heterogeneity and Cooperation in Two Domains." *Journal of Theoretical Politics* 6 (October).

Kindleberger, Charles P., 1973. *The World in Depression, 1929–1939* (Berkeley: University of California Press).

Knight, Jack, 1992. *Institutions and Social Conflict* (Cambridge: Cambridge University Press).

Krasner, Stephen D., 1976. "State Power and the Structure of International Trade." *World Politics* 28 (April).

———, 1979. "The Tokyo Round: Particularistic Interests and Prospects for Stability in the Global Trading System." *International Studies Quarterly* 23 (December).

———, 1991. "Global Communications and National Power: Life on the Pareto Frontier." *World Politics* 43 (April).

———, ed., 1983. *International Regimes* (Ithaca: Cornell University Press).

Lawrence, Robert, 1996. *Regionalism, Multilateralism, and Deeper Integration* (Washington, D.C.: The Brookings Institution).

Martin, Lisa, 1992. "Interest, Power, and Multilateralism." *International Organization* 46 (Autumn).

Moravcsik, Andrew, 1992. "Liberalism and International Relations Theory." Paper presented at the Program in Politics, Economics, and Security. (PIPES), Chicago.

Ostrom, Elinor, 1990. *Governing the Commons: The Evolution of Institutions for Collective Action* (New York: Cambridge University Press).

Oye, Kenneth, 1979. "The Domain of Choice." In Kenneth Oye, Robert Lieber, and Donald Rothschild, eds., *Eagle Entangled: U.S. Foreign Policy in a Complex World* (New York: Longman).

———, 1992. *Economic Discrimination and Political Exchange* (Princeton: Princeton University Press).

Oye, Kenneth, Robert Lieber, and Donald Rothschild, eds., 1979. *Eagle Entangled: U.S. Foreign Policy in a Complex World* (New York: Longman).

Ruggie, John, 1993. *Multilateralism Matters* (New York: Columbia University Press).

Snidal, Duncan, 1979. "Public Goods, Property Rights, and Political Organization." *International Studies Quarterly* 23 (December).

———, 1985a. "Coordination Versus Prisoners' Dilemma: Implications for International Cooperation and Regimes." *American Political Science Review* 79 (December).

———, 1985b. "The Limits of Hegemonic Stability Theory." *International Organization* 39.

Stein, Art, 1980. "The Politics of Linkage." *World Politics* 33 (October).

———, 1983. "Coordination and Collaboration: Regimes in an Anarchic World." In Stephen D. Krasner, ed., *International Regimes* (Ithaca: Cornell University Press).

Waltz, Kenneth, 1979. *Theory of International Politics* (Reading, Massachusetts: Addison-Wesley).

Williamson, Oliver, 1975. *Markets and Hierarchies: Analysis and Anti-Trust Implications* (New York: The Free Press).

Zacher, Mark, 1987. "Trade Gaps, Analytical Gaps: Regime Analysis and International Commodity Trade Regulation." *International Organization* 41 (Spring).

Zacher, Mark, with Brent Sutton, 1996. *Governing Global Networks: International Regimes for Transportation and Communications* (Cambridge: Cambridge University Press).

CHAPTER TWO

Nested Institutions and the European Monetary System

STEVEN WEBER

One way to think about social-political systems is to envision each as a set of nested institutions. For our purposes two important questions follow: how does the nesting of institutions take place, and how or when does this resolve conflict.

The rationale for thinking about nested institutions when considering issue-areas is clear. Even "pure" markets are wound up tightly in many tiers of institutional infrastructure. Property rights systems nest within information exchange systems which nest within systems that store and exchange value, and so on. In discussing regions, the rationale is less obvious. Part of the problem is the need to agree first on what it is that constitutes a region. Geography is plastic, or at least it is plastic in the way that human minds construct maps. It might be possible to develop objective and easily measured delineators to mark off regions, but this has not yet been successfully done, despite repeated attempts.[1] What if we were instead to conceive of regions as clusters of nested institutions? This might very well be compatible with "transaction density" measures, since most people agree that institutions surround transactions even when there is a difference of opinion over the direction of the arrows of causality that run between them. Two things, then, are worth knowing:

This chapter was partially prepared while the author was a Fellow at the Center for Advanced Study in the Behavioral Sciences. I am grateful for financial support provided by the National Science Foundation, Grant No. SBR-9022192, and by the University of California at Berkeley Center for German and European Studies. Participants in the convenor group that led to this volume provided very helpful comments and suggestions.

[1] These unsuccessful attempts include attempts to measure transaction densities, phone call densities, and bundles of externalities, among others.

Density and Boundaries: How densely institutionalized is the region, and what are its boundaries (that is, where does density of a "nest" fall off)? It is easy to talk casually about these things and exquisitely difficult to measure them.

Principles and Logic of Organization: A set of nested institutions will share, at a minimum, principles and norms, which Vinod Aggarwal (chapter 1, this volume) sees first as cognitive factors. Beyond these principles (which are sometimes hard to isolate) are rules and procedures or systemic factors, all of which I prefer to think of as logics of organization, standard ways of doing things, and patterns of authority and obligation. Harry Eckstein's classic work on Norway argues that "congruence" between these patterns of authority, at different levels of social and political structure, is the major explanation for the surprising stability of a conflict-ridden society.[2] Focusing on the principles and organizational logic of a nested system might clarify how the system itself came to be; or it might not. But it will almost certainly help to illuminate what kinds of conflict can be resolved, under what conditions, with what means, and—perhaps—with what outcome.

This chapter examines the 1992–93 crisis in the European Monetary System (EMS). I argue, contrary to standard opinion, that the EMS did not collapse in this crisis. Instead, it was sustained in its essentials and was restructured so that it could be reconciled with changes in market conditions. It remains as a central part of the nested institutional structure that makes up the European Union (EU). It survived because the EU as an institutional cluster supports principles and logics of organization that can provide for the provision of certain kinds of goods—in this case, common property resources or CPRs—in "unconventional" ways.[3]

The EMU

In March 1979, the European Economic Community (EEC) launched a bold experiment in monetary cooperation aimed at creating a "zone of monetary stability" among its member states.[4] Two major economic issues drove this project. The first issue was increasing concern over exchange rate instability among EEC currencies that had developed with the collapse of Bretton Woods, the Oil Shocks, and other developments of the 1970s. The second issue was a perceived opportunity, to use exchange-rate stability as a mechanism for driving forward

[2] See Eckstein 1966.

[3] To be precise, in ways that standard social science arguments about collective action would judge unconventional.

[4] Helmudt Schmidt used this phrase, quoted by Cameron 1995, 6.

convergence of economic policies and trends among member states. The central (but by no means only) objective of that convergence would be price stability: to narrow and to lower the range of inflation rates in community economies. In the minds of some European leaders, the European Monetary System was aimed also at promoting longer range goals of monetary union and perhaps political union as well.

Fifteen years later, the EMS seemed in disarray. A series of crises (or perhaps one long crisis) rocked the system from the summer of 1992 through the autumn of 1993. The pound and the lira left the exchange rate mechanism (ERM). Many remaining currencies devalued against the German mark. In the summer of 1993, the EC decided to widen the bands within which currencies fluctuate from 2.25 percent to 15 percent. To many observers this signaled the effective demise of the system, papered over by a thin veneer of constraints more cosmetic than real.

When the EMS "collapsed," economists argued that this outcome was ultimately preordained given the logic of money and markets arrayed against the system. It is a basic axiom of international economics that states cannot sustain at once capital mobility, fixed exchange rates, and autonomous monetary policies. The standard story was that EMS had evolved into a system quite close to that triad and that something had to give way. What gave way according to most observers, was the system itself. The question became, what would come next? Mainstream prescriptions from the economics community and from many political scientists as well were to replace what they saw as an inherently unstable EMS, either with monetary union (abolishing autonomous policies) or a de facto float (abolishing fixed exchange rates).[5]

What does it really mean for an institution to fall apart? The answer depends substantially on what we think the institution is or ought to be. I argue in this chapter that the EMS can be understood as something like a voluntary organization for the management of a common property resource (CPR). The CPR in this case is credible exchange rate stability and the economic "goods" that come along with it. Seen in this light, the EMS did not fall apart during the crises of 1992–93. Rather, the system was sustained in its essentials according to two basic criteria.[6] The first is that adaptations made to accommodate the impact of exogenous shocks and endogenous developments, which together may destabilize the day-to-day workings of an institution, are carried out in accord with the nested system's higher order collective choice rules. In other words, the inevitable renegotiation of imperfect contracts in an imperfect world happens in

---

[5] Reintroducing some kind of exchange controls was a much less popular notion because of presumed effects on the single market and the technological and legal difficulties of doing so effectively. A partial exception was the Eichengreen/Wyplosz idea of a tax on open foreign currency positions.

[6] See Shepsle 1989. Shepsle recognizes that in the real world, institutions will not meet the criteria for subgame perfect equilibria.

ways that adhere to (and reinforce) the "meta-regime."[7] The second criteria is that the institution continues to provide the essential goods that members expected of it before the shock.[8]

I argue in this chapter that the EMS meets both these criteria for survival. The system came to a crisis because of exogenous shocks (principally German reunification) and endogenous developments (principally political pressures, accentuated by Maastricht, to avoid realignments). Although the stage was set nicely, the bleak predictions of standard collective action arguments do not apply here. With two notable exceptions that I consider later, EC member states made adaptations to the system's specific operational rules in conformity with higher order rules about collective choice processes. In Aggarwal's terms, member states chose to change the institutional context by modifying an existing institution. Months after the rash of devaluations and the move to wider bands, the system was delivering the goods—relative monetary stability—nearly as effectively as before the crisis began. States demonstrated in rhetoric and in costly behaviors a continued commitment to the EMS.[9] These commitments are being taken seriously by governments and by the markets, which is a substantial change from preponderant expectations in the immediate wake of the "final" crisis phase of August 1993. Europe has not deteriorated into a continent of competitive devaluators, and the negative political spillover from the crises has generally been contained. The outcome of the crises do not look like the probable product of an n-person prisoner's dilemma game where the most powerful and most important player chose to defect. Instead, it looks more like a successful adaptation of a valued institution. As of this writing, alternative interpretations—most importantly, variants of the argument that Germany simply did what it wanted to do and others followed along without any real choice—don't stand up to scrutiny, and I don't think that future developments will change that assessment.

THE EMS: A SHORT SELECTIVE HISTORY PRIOR TO THE CRISES OF 1992

Monetary coordination within the EEC goes back at least in principle to the Treaty of Rome, which called for consultation among member states on short

---

[7] See Aggarwal 1985.

[8] Another possibility is that the institution adapts so that it (intentionally or not) starts to provide a different set of goods. This may not seem a failure per se but neither does it signal the survival of an institution; it is probably better to think of the outcome as a new institution that is serving different purposes.

[9] The two members that left the system at that time now take different positions. Britain has no intention of rejoining the system any time soon. Italy, on the other hand, consistently declared its aim to reenter the ERM as soon as practicable and did so in late 1996. I discuss the reasons behind these positions later.

term macro policies and raised the possibility of mutual assistance for balance of payments disequilibria. It also established a Community Monetary Committee, "an advisory body of national Treasury and Central Bank Officials," to serve as a permanent institutional locus for discussions. Exchange rates were to be considered "a matter of common concern," but national monetary policies would not be subject to any binding constraints.[10] There was at the time no convincing reason to do more than this, since the single market was still a long way off, and the Bretton Woods system was working reasonably well. Indeed, Germany was wary of any European monetary arrangements that could have been interpreted as discriminating against or competing with the dollar. The French were the most vocal but certainly spoke for others when they expressed opposition to sacrificing any substantial degree of national control over monetary policy to some supranational EEC authority.

These conditions changed gradually over the course of the 1960s as the Bretton Woods system showed increasing strain. Once DeGaulle left office, monetary coordination came back on the agenda. At their 1969 Hague Summit, and in the wake of a franc devaluation and mark revaluation, EEC leaders agreed in principle that monetary union would be a goal for the Community. This was a diffuse agreement that did not extend to a consensus even on a general strategic approach. The French argued for what was then called a "monetarist view," that states should force themselves toward policy convergence by fixing exchange rates up front. The "economist view," favored by Germany, was that states should first coordinate policies and only later fix exchange rates after greater convergence had been achieved.[11] These attitudes followed (at least in part) from obvious calculations of who would bear the costs of adjustment in each case. Under the monetarist plan, the Bundesbank, as guardian of the strongest currency in the system, would have been impelled to support weaker currencies and thus pay some of the costs of convergence that it would avoid if states fought their way toward convergence on their own.

By 1971 the weakening dollar was putting more pressure on Europe. The Smithsonian Agreement (December 1971) not only devalued the dollar and the pound but also widened to 2.25 percent the bands within which currencies could fluctuate against the dollar. In Europe, this meant an effective tripling of the possible divergence between any two EEC currencies since the range within which they could move against each other was now about 9 percent. That was a problem for trade flows but, even more, a problem for the Common Agricultural Policy (CAP) whose costs were already taking a substantial portion of the community's budget. If EEC currencies could fluctuate this widely it would be impossible

---

[10] Treaty of Rome, Articles 105 and 108.
[11] See Tsoukalis 1977, 91–97.

to forecast the real cost of the CAP and thus to budget effectively. This led to the idea of establishing a European "snake" in a Bretton Woods "tunnel."

The snake, a German-led initiative introduced in April 1972, lined up European currencies in a bilateral parity grid of 2.25 percent bands. This effectively cut in half the fluctuation range of "member currencies," but it was a very weak arrangement. Participation was not limited to EEC members—Britain, Ireland, Sweden, and Norway joined—and there were no formal mechanisms for joint interventions or negotiated realignments. The snake was a statement about targets or a declaration of intentions, and it didn't work. States held firmly to their divergent monetary policies. In particular, the Bundesbank ran a much more restrictive policy than did France and Italy, leading to recurrent pressures for revaluation. In March 1973, the "tunnel" itself disappeared when the EEC countries suspended defense of their currencies against the dollar. By the end of 1978 the snake looked more like a de facto D-mark zone than it did any real EEC currency stabilization scheme.

In its second phase European monetary coordination began to take on more substantive institutional elements. German Chancellor Helmudt Schmidt was still reluctant to "sideline" the Americans, but he saw both continued weakness in the dollar at the end of the 1970s and upward pressure on the D-mark as a real threat to the export-dependent German economy.[12] He found a willing partner in French President Valéry Giscard d'Estaing, who was pushing a "franc fort" policy to beat inflation and knew that he could increase the credibility of that policy with an effective D-mark peg. French-German bilateral talks on the subject began in February 1978. Notably, Paris was represented at the talks by the governor of the Banque de France (BDF), Bernard Clappier, while the Germans sent Horst Schulmann, an economic adviser to Schmidt and not a Bundesbank official.[13] In April the talks expanded to include other EEC states. By the end of the year, a detailed plan for the EMS was agreed on.

The EMS differed from the snake in several important respects, which I will discuss in more detail later. While it retained the snake fluctuation range for most currencies, the system's exchange rate mechanism was now limited to EEC members.[14] The ERM created a community fund for joint intervention and a specific set of rules under which central banks would be obligated to intervene.

---

[12] Schmidt's worries were reinforced by doubts about the quality of American leadership. See Story 1988.

[13] See Ludlow 1982, 84–85. Schmidt was anticipating reluctance at the Bundesbank, and he certainly encountered it later.

[14] States that entered the EMS later were given wider fluctuation bands; Italy was later given a wider band as well. Central rates for Italy, Ireland, and France were derived from market prices. The UK did not participate but was given a notional central rate for the purpose of calculating the divergence indicator (which I discuss later).

Monitoring of the system and negotiation of any realignments was delegated to the EEC monetary committee. These changes were substantial moves toward creating an EMS with mechanisms for provision, monitoring, and enforcement.

One clear signal of this is that the Bundesbank took a much more serious attitude toward the EMS negotiations than it had taken toward the snake. The Bundesbank "dragged its heels" on the EMS when it was first endorsed by Schmidt.[15] Held at arms length by the German government early in the negotiations, the Bundesbank later demanded assurances from Bonn that obligations to the EMS effectively come second, after its obligation to defend the D-mark. Before Germany signed the December 1978 act establishing the EMS, an exchange of letters between Otmar Emminger (Bundesbank governor) and the German government said that if intervention obligations should threaten the value of the D-mark, the Bundesbank will start from the premise that, if need be, the German government will safeguard the Bundesbank from such a situation of constraint, either by a correction of the exchange rate in the EMS or, if necessary, by discharging the Bundesbank from its intervention obligations.[16] Economics Minister Otto von Lambsdorff confirmed this understanding before the Bundestag in December 1978, saying that the government would be responsible for managing appropriately any necessary realignments and that "the Bbank has the responsibility to intervene, *and the option not to intervene if it is its opinion that it is not able to do so.*"[17]

This would prove prophetic in later crises, but it does not diminish the importance of the normative change taking place here. The EMS was not a formal arrangement for fixed exchange rates, but it was also not just a low-cost wish list or a set of voluntary targets. It was a substantial (if still contingent) commitment by member states to take concrete steps toward creating a "zone of monetary stability" within the EEC.[18]

The EMS came into existence on March 13, 1979. The system needed two realignments that year, despite substantial currency interventions that central banks carried out in accord with the obligations to defend values set out in the agreement.[19] Both realignments were negotiated and agreed to by Finance Ministers and Central Bank Governors of member states meeting under Community auspices. There were no realignments in 1980, but the European Council that year did note growing instability within the international monetary environment, which suggested a need for further refinement of the mechanisms of the EMS. That observation turned out to be prescient.

[15] See Funabashi 1989, 122.

[16] Emminger (1986, 361 ff.) describes the letter in his memoirs.

[17] Italics added. Quoted in Eichengreen and Wyplosz 1993, 109.

[18] Schmidt, quoted in Cameron 1995, 6.

[19] In September the D-mark was revalued by 2 percent and the krone devalued 2.9 percent; in November the krone was devalued an additional 4.8 percent.

In March 1981, after a prolonged period of pressure on the lira, Italy devalued its currency by 6 percent. This was a unilateral move decided without prior consultation, and it caused considerable consternation among other EMS states whose export competitiveness would suffer from the Italian action. The fallout from this episode led to an agreement that future realignments should be collective decisions taken at or, at least, through the forum of the monetary committee. The next seven realignments were carried out, for the most part relatively smoothly, in accordance with this rule. And as the doctrine of monetary neo-orthodoxy spread among European capitals during the 1980s, a more elaborate set of standard practices connected with realignment developed and became an expected part of the consultation procedure within the committee.[20]

I summarize these in the language of norms. A country seeking realignment should present a domestic economic reform package that demonstrates to other EMS members its commitment to greater policy convergence. The Monetary Committee should discount requests for realignment, placing relatively more of the burden of readjustment on the EMS laggard. Lastly, realignments should be kept small so that market rates fall within the new bilateral central rates and not above them.

Often consistent with what countries generally wanted to do on their own, the steady practice of these seemingly diffuse norms nonetheless represented a progressive institutionalization of the EMS that member countries took as meaningful. There is clear qualitative evidence that the EMS did figure into state calculations about monetary policy during these years and that EMS commitments were instrumentally useful to governments that wanted to make difficult and painful economic choices in a politically credible way. EEC member states by the mid 1980s considered the EMS to have made a contribution to the reduction of exchange rate fluctuations within the system and to the convergence of national economic policies, which was one of the reasons why serious discussions of moving on to some kind of EMU were revived in the lead-up to the Single European Act (SEA) in 1985. And at least in some EEC member states, the EMS increasingly took on the mantle of being a central part of the general process of European integration.[21]

That connection would become more evident during an exchange rate "crisis" in 1987. Some of the events of 1987 are strikingly similar to the crisis of

[20] See Goodman 1992, 197–98.

[21] For an example, see Goodman 1992, 199–201. Discussing the "French turn" of 1983, Sachs and Wyplosz (1986, 294–95) write, "unlike the much looser commitment under the European Snake in the 1970s, which France abandoned on two occasions, membership of the EMS has been invested with enormous political importance at the very highest levels of government. That is why the debate over leaving the EMS was treated as synonymous with the debate over abandoning other spheres of cooperation in Europe, including participation in the Common Market."

1992–93, but the most important common feature is that in both cases the immediate preferences of certain states came sharply into conflict with each other and with EMS rules and norms. The events of 1987 took place against the backdrop of major changes in the sophistication of capital markets and foreign-exchange trading along with a declining dollar, sliding rapidly from its height of 1985. Under pressure from an appreciating D-mark, the franc dropped through its floor despite concerted central bank intervention of about $8 to $10 billion in about a week.[22] The realignment that followed did not happen smoothly, in part because the French accused the Germans of intransigence while the Germans accused the French of running irresponsible policies that permitted the franc to drop too far and too fast. It was only after thirteen hours of "acrimonious talks" in the monetary committee that officials reached an agreement on realignment. Despite the official German position that "on the basis of economic fundamentals there was no reason for realignment" the Bundesbank stood hard for that option (as it would again in 1993–94).[23] The alternative was to reduce German domestic interest rates but the Bundesbank ruled that out firmly until after the elections on January 25. If there had been any doubts about Bundesbank priorities this should have put them to rest: German monetary policy came first, everything else second.

Or so it might have seemed. Unfortunately, the January 12 realignment did not end the crisis. Instead, the French bond market soared on expectations that interest rate reductions were imminent. This along with continued dollar weakness brought new strains on the franc. The Bundesbank gave way, albeit in a manner that others interpreted as belated and half-hearted. Overriding its earlier commitment, the Bundesbank on January 22 cut its discount rate fifty basis points.[24]

The EMS survived its 1987 crisis, but with substantial criticism particularly from Paris. French Finance Minister Edouard Balladur reproached the Bundesbank specifically for its reluctance to intervene adequately not only at the obligatory level but earlier, on a voluntary basis, when it became clear that a crisis was imminent.[25] Balladur had a point, but his criticisms ignored the fact that the Bundesbank had taken same action. It did choose to make a "political interest rate cut" for the sake of the EMS in January of 1987. It did so ten days after a broad realignment and in the face of a firm commitment not to act, because of domestic political factors. When the Bundesbank cut rates, it did so primarily in support of the EMS not in response to German domestic conditions. Bundesbank support came grudgingly and reluctantly, but it came nevertheless.

---

[22] See Funabashi 1989, 123. The Dutch guilder and the Belgian and Luxembourg francs were driven up along with the D-mark.

[23] *Financial Times*, 13 January 1987.

[24] See Funabashi 1989, 124.

[25] See Balladur 1987.

In any case, European leaders recognized that EMS mechanisms needed some work. Capital mobility within international financial markets was changing certain parameters. The Basle-Nyborg agreement of September 1987 responded in a modest way by altering some EMS rules, in particular, by extending credit facilities for longer term loans in support of intervention and thereby making it possible for states to draw credit for intramarginal intervention as well. The agreement also suggested the practical value of making small and frequent realignments rather than allowing pressure to build behind differential inflation rates in Community economies.

This last recommendation made a great deal of economic sense but it was submerged in the political momentum behind the single market project and, later, Maastricht. For reasons that I discuss in detail later, the political stigma as well as the real costs attached to realignment increased dramatically over the next few years. There were no realignments after the 1987 crisis until January of 1990, when the lira was devalued at the same time as it was "graduated" to a regular fluctuation band of 2.25 percent. And Britain joined the ERM in October of that year. Overall, the system seemed to be working rather well even in the face of capital liberalization (capital controls in most EC countries were essentially eliminated by the beginning of 1990), massive growth of foreign exchange trading, and external shocks, the most dramatic of which was the Gulf War.

Eichengreen and Wyplosz argue that the apparent success of the EMS created "self-validating expectations of continued stability."[26] But it is also true that the ERM found itself in a world of nearly free capital movements with what had become de facto fixed exchange rates, but with member states still running "autonomous" monetary policies. Inflation differentials were building up behind currency values like water behind a dike.[27] The monetary fallout from German unification, the strict convergence criteria written into Maastricht, and the Europe-wide recession that would boost unemployment in Europe to historic levels in 1992 and 1993 (events, each of which I consider later) made the system more brittle by creating spectacular conditions for speculative attacks that could be just as self-fulfilling as earlier expectations of stability.[28]

---

[26] See Eichengreen and Wyplosz 1986, 59.

[27] Eichengreen and Wyploz argue that the data convincingly shows only Italy as suffering a substantial decline in competitiveness resulting from higher inflation; for Spain and Great Britain, some indicators point to a competitiveness problem but the evidence is not as clear. So it appears that this effect was not significant or immediate enough to cause a crisis of this magnitude on its own (albeit left unresolved, it could eventually have done so).

[28] Eichengreen and Wyploz (1993, 52) explain the logic: Briefly, one of the things countries wishing to qualify for EMU had to do, was to maintain their currencies within the EMS bands for at least two years without severe tension. The political and economic incentives for qualifying were high. Governments were willing to pay costs to achieve that goal, including high interest rates and resulting higher unemployment despite the Europe-wide recession. But a speculative attack that forced

When the crash came in 1992, political officials in the Community and member states bemoaned their bad luck, bad circumstances, and bad timing of Maastricht referenda. But in retrospect there is a greater sense of inevitability to what happened, since the system had come to rest on expectations that could be easily shattered. This raises two questions: What would member states sacrifice to sustain the system? And why would they desire to do so?

EMS LOGIC

I will answer those questions in four steps. The first step is to assess the goods: what it is that the EMS provides to states, that they would wish to sustain it. The second step is to look at the logical structure of provision and appropriation for those goods. I argue here that the EMS has characteristics of a CPR. Third, I consider standard solution concepts—the leviathan and privatization models—and how they apply to the EMS. Finally, I examine the EMS "rulebook" and standard operating procedures to see what kind of an institution the EMS actually is.

In essence, there are CPR elements within the EMS but the institution follows a logic different from the standard solution concepts. Instead, the EMS has characteristics that make it more like a voluntary organization, "a binding contract [among the players] to commit themselves to a cooperative strategy that they themselves will work out."[29] My analysis of how the EMS works and how it survived the crisis of 1992–93 illustrates what the above statement means in practice and what role the nesting of European institutions plays in the explanation.

The generic good that the EMS provides to states is exchange rate stability, and four analytic arguments provide a complete description of the nature of this good. The *transactions argument* says that a single market works better with one currency that enhances the usefulness of money as a medium of exchange, as a unit of account, and as a store of value, and it does this mainly by reducing transaction costs. The *inflation argument* says that countries with a history of relatively high inflation can enhance the credibility of a promise to lower inflation rates in the future by linking currencies to a country with a long history of price stability. A tangential part of the inflation argument is that the EMS should help countries avoid any moves toward competitive devaluation of currencies.[30] The

---

devaluation would also take away the biggest incentive for a country to pursue high interest rates and other austerity policies aimed at achieving charter membership in EMU. That point was not lost on domestic political forces. Thus speculation could prove self-fulfilling.

[29] See Ostrom 1990, 15.

[30] The idea here is that in a relatively low-inflation but high-unemployment world, a state might be tempted to devalue its currency and tolerate a bit more inflation for the sake of increasing export

political argument says that movement toward a single currency is more than just an economic act—it is a prominent symbol of constructing a polity, since control over money is still generally understood to be a central sovereign right.[31] The *budgetary argument* focuses on the value of placing boundaries around exchange rate risk that the EU has to hedge against in its own internal budgets, particularly with CAP expenditures.

The credibility that attaches to states' promises to defend relative exchange rates and the benefits that financial markets extend to that promise have many characteristics of a CPR. CPRs are nonexcludable but subtractable goods. They are generally joint in provision as well. Individual actors then have incentives to overappropriate and lack sufficient incentives to contribute to provision of the good. The "tragedy of the commons" is the standard result.

A priori, the dilemmas connected to exchange rate (ER) stability look familiar in this context. ER stability within the EU is practically nonexcludable, in the sense that it would be very difficult for EMS member states to expel one of their own. There are in fact no formal mechanisms for doing so. On a more general level, involuntary expulsion from the EMS during the 1980s would have been nearly tantamount to expulsion from the community as a whole. This was outside the range of acceptable options and almost inconceivable given the implications for the community's broader agenda and plans.

At the same time, ER stability is a rival good. If appropriators take too much too quickly, credibility can easily be depleted. The amount of stability in the system is neither fixed nor inexhaustible. Credibility needs to be supplied, repaired, defended, and replenished by the behavior of the members of the EMS. But unless there exist providers whose interest it is to supply and replenish the good

---

competitiveness and creating jobs. Since other states are similarly tempted, the stage is set for a competitive race to devalue. Such a competition would tend to be even more unproductive on aggregate in Europe than elsewhere. The reason is that devaluation "works" (that is, it boosts competitiveness) in part by causing a real pay cut for workers who, following devaluation, have to pay a higher price for imported goods. If workers demand and receive higher wages that fully compensate them, then the competitiveness gain is lost and what is left is inflation. In Europe workers are likely to demand higher wages because a relatively high percentage (much higher, for example, than in the United States) of what they buy is imported. Thus devaluation more visibly and quickly raises their costs of living. They are also more likely to receive some of their demands since real wages are far less flexible (at least in the downward direction) in Europe than in the United States, in part due to more effective labor unions.

[31] The EMS is not a single currency, of course, but the level of monetary cooperation within the system has represented an important part of political commitment to Europe. Britain's decision to join the ERM was interpreted broadly as a sign of significantly increased commitment to Europe. In Germany the official government stance turns this argument on its head by claiming that political cooperation or "union" is the price that reluctant EU partners must pay for greater monetary cooperation or "union." It may be hard to measure, but political symbolism and commitment to the EU project overall (even if defined vaguely) is certainly an important part of the EMS.

regardless of what others do or do not supply or regardless of how much they appropriate, provision is going to be a joint activity subject to the standard problems of making commitments, monitoring performance, and sanctioning putative providers who do not do their share.[32] In other words, provision is either a story about hegemonic stability, or it is a collective action story.

As for appropriation, countries that draw on ER stability within the system to bolster the credibility of their own currency commitments diminish the supply that is available for others to draw on.[33] Put differently, the confidence that financial markets place in the EMS is a subtractable good that easily can be overappropriated. This problem is tricky for both analysts and actors. It is hard to know just how much of the credibility resource appropriators can "use" in a sustainable way, because so much depends upon aggregate expectations. Italy, for example, draws from the CPR when it runs a substantial budget deficit over time, yet is able in the long term to borrow money at a lower cost than it would have been able to if it were outside the EMS. Other appropriators are tempted to and can do the same, drawing on the credibility of the system to their individual benefit. This sets up a classic commons dilemma because the costs are diffused over the entire community. Unless provision keeps up with appropriation, the CPR is going to be depleted and the credibility of the EMS run down.

Rendering this in different language clarifies the specific problem that developed within the EMS. As the system evolved toward a semifixed ER at the end of the 1980s, it became more difficult for individual countries to run de facto independent monetary and fiscal policies without placing great strains on the ERM. Several other options were closed off. Central bank intervention was becoming increasingly feeble compared to foreign exchange. And the EC lacked adequate alternative mechanisms for adjustment, particularly the large transfer payments that states use to cope with regional differences in economic performance. This meant that the burdens of adjustment would, on first rendering, fall heavily on weaker economies, and the question was whether governments would bear the strains of those costs.

The obvious temptation for governments was not to do so. Instead, the stark individual incentives favored the choice of appropriating credibility from the EMS "commons," by running looser monetary policies and more expansive fiscal policies while shifting at least some of the costs of adjustment to "the sys-

---

[32] Provision is also a problem of designing institutions, which often has elements of a second order collective action problem (but see Kreps et al. 1982). The relationship between provision and appropriation also matters here. Hegemonic stability posits a provider whose interest it is to provide a collective good regardless of whether or not others provide one as well. To the extent that this really happens in world politics, it is much less likely if the collective good is subtractable and subject to depletion by overappropriators.

[33] And they diminish, as well, the supply for themselves to draw on in the future.

tem"—that is, to the other member states. For most of EMS history, those incentives tempted mainly the weak currency countries. Realignments within the EMS did shift and diffuse the costs of adjustment—but it did so in a compromise balance according to a set of norms that I discussed earlier in the context of the Monetary Committee. In general, the costs did not fall as heavily on stronger economies (in particular Germany) as the weaker currency countries might have wished, but they did fall there somewhat more than the Germans wanted.

There are two standard solutions to CPR dilemmas. Centralized control, the equivalent of the leviathan solution, is what happens within a state. There is a central bank and/or a central government that sets the rules (in this case, the value of the currency). It manages adjustment by various measures including transfer payments. In the EC the equivalent solution would have been monetary union, the move to a single currency for all member states.[34] A new institution would conduct monetary policy for the community and (presumably) moderate the adjustment burden for poorly performing regions via the usual mechanisms. There are always substantial costs—monitoring, administering rules, sanctioning, and so forth—associated with the leviathan solution. And the political barriers to reaching it in this case would have been immense. Nonetheless it was one of the options raised as a possible answer to the EMS dilemma, and in a sense, it would have "worked." That is, monetary union would indeed have solved the CPR problem in the EMS.

The other standard solution concept is to privatize the good. Putting resources into private hands means aligning incentives and responsibilities with firm property rights. The analogy here is to floating exchange rates. Each state runs its own monetary policy, and adjustment of exchange rates takes place through the market. Governments might still intervene to moderate exchange rate movements that worked against their preferred economic growth and adjustment strategies. But intervention would be unilateral in the sense that no government would be obligated to intervene on behalf of another's currency. And intervention would matter only so far as it represented a part of supply-demand curves, or expectations about those curves held by other players in the market.

Privatization would also solve the CPR problem in the EMS, in effect by abolishing the system and leaving the market (in place of the ERM) as the main interlocutor for individual countries trying to run an economic policy. There are obviously costs here as well, although the purely economic costs are hard to measure. Given the historical context, the political argument matters greatly here, because a decision to abolish the EMS in 1992–93 would have struck an

---

[34] In principle, a system of permanently fixed exchange rates managed by a central authority would do the same thing, although there is no purely economic reason to think that this would happen.

enormous blow to the evolution of the Community. Member states were anxious not to have that happen.

Elinor Ostrom's argument about "voluntary organizations" suggests another kind of possibility for managing CPRs. The basic feature of a voluntary organization is "a binding contract [among the players] to commit themselves to a cooperative strategy that they themselves will work out."[35] Of course, the small-scale environmental concerns that Ostrom looked at are different from a currency exchange rate mechanism between nations. But if the generic logic of the problem, as well as the nature of the constraints and incentives facing the actors are similar, then the basic functional requirements for voluntary organization to succeed should be similar as well. A set of institutions that will support this kind of solution would have to deal with three generic challenges: supply, commitment, and monitoring. I consider them separately here, although in modified order because the first and third seem less problematic for the EMS than does the second.

Supply in this context means the supply of new institutions. It may be that a particular set of institutions, once they are in place, can solve or at least help to solve collective action problems. But how do those institutions come to be in place? Someone or something must supply them. If that is itself a collective action problem (as it frequently seems to be) then the dilemma has merely been pushed back one frame in the picture.[36] But the EMS "supply game" did not take place in an institutional vacuum, where stark cost-benefit calculations by autonomous actors might be the strongest determinants of the shape (or nonexistence) of new institutions. Instead, the game was itself nested within a well-developed and established institutional network, the EC.[37] This institutional environment sets forms and standards of legitimacy which new organizations strive to meet. There is a rough organizational template available. These conditions change the incentives facing would-be self-organizers who try to construct new institutions for collective action. The point is simply that EC member states, living in an already densely institutionalized environment, face incentives that are different from those they would face in a less densely populated environment— where "technical" criteria of efficiency and input-output rationality play a larger role. To supply a new institution within the EC means creating a rationale for its existence. The rationale may include technical elements but can draw heavily, as

---

[35] See Ostrom 1990, 15.

[36] See Bates 1988, esp. 394–95. One way to deal with supply is to introduce uncertainty, which makes possible a number of equilibria (some of which would include the supply of new institutions). Uncertainty is part of the EMS story, as it undoubtedly is for all real world institutions, but it is not the whole story and may not be the most important part of it for the EMS.

[37] For arguments about the importance of nesting in other contexts, that do not make use of organizational theory in this way, see Aggarwal 1985.

well, on institutional legitimacy, which is not subject to the same kinds of efficiency calculations that lie at the heart of collective action arguments writ in rational choice terms.[38] While "supply" may not be easy, within a densely nested institutional system it is certainly possible and is (at a minimum) one of many potential equilibria for the system as a whole.

Monitoring by comparison is relatively straightforward. EC member states have access to enormous information about each other's economic policies and performance. The challenge facing these states lies not in gathering data, but in understanding what the data precisely means in the context of a CPR-type situation. What is a sustainable level of appropriation? The answer is not always clear. It may also matter what the motivations are of an appropriator who seems to be testing the limits. Not all defections are the same and EC members know this. An institution that can support the kind of monitoring necessary to achieve that level of information and understanding (or can link itself to other institutions that do it) should be less brittle, particularly if graduated sanctions can then be matched to the circumstances.

The most difficult challenge is *commitment*, but this too may be different in a densely nested institutional environment than in an isolated game. If the EMS stood on its own, it is hard to see how it would happen. The problem is simply that once the EMS is set up and working, appropriators will be tempted by high immediate returns and by diffused and delayed costs to break the rules and over-appropriate. Reasoning backward logically unravels the institution. If players in the game know that they will later be faced with these temptations and that others will as well, they would not agree to join it in the first place. What is needed is a way to align incentives so that a contingent commitment, something like "I will stick to the rules if others do as well," can be sustained.

This is not a problem solved easily through abstraction. It is certainly possible to envision models that would claim to solve it.[39] But the question still remains how the critical problems actually do or do not get solved in real world interactions. The institutional structure of the EMS suggests some answers.

INSTITUTIONAL STRUCTURE OF THE EMS

Institutions can be seen as sets of agreements nested one within another. In *Governing the Commons* Ostrom lays out a three-tier framework for analytically

---

[38] See Weber 1994.

[39] These models are generally deficient in that they rely on summary variables, things like "long term expected net benefits," to drive their conclusions. The question then becomes, How do actors estimate, measure, or anticipate these benefits? And that is not a question that can be answered deductively.

disentangling this kind of layering.[40] *Operational rules* govern the day-to-day workings of the institution—the bands, the intervention rules, and so forth. *Collective choice rules* delineate who can change the operational rules and how they can do that. Together they make up what Aggarwal calls "rules and procedures." Both nest within a set of *constitutional rules*, which concern the identity of the actors and the basic nature of relationships among them—like Aggarwal's "principles and norms."

I have already made the point that a change in operational rules does not always signal a failure or collapse of an institution, so long as change comes about for purposes and via processes that fit within the higher-order rules. At the same time, it is important to remember that states do not respect analytic categories and are free to choose in which arena or arenas they pursue their interests. When the EMS came under pressure in 1992, there was room for action at all three levels. Member states could have gone so far as to break out of the constitutional rules that make up the EU's institutional environment—for example, by unilateral imposition of capital controls or unrestrained currency devaluation. Or they could have broken out of the collective choice rules—for example, if France and Germany had agreed in private bilateral negotiations to a fast-track franc–D-mark union. Member states chose neither of these kinds of options, but instead confined themselves for the most part to changing operational rules in a manner consistent with maintenance of the institution's higher order elements.

If this suggests that the EMS survives in essential equilibrium, then it also suggests that the bleak predictions of standard collective action theory do not fit comfortably here. I will offer a different explanation in two steps: first, by examining elements of the EMS rulebook that could contribute to the explanation; and second, through a focused narrative account of how those mechanisms (and others) "managed" the crisis of 1992–93.

EMS Rules

Concrete Obligations, and Burden Sharing. The snake was more a statement of intentions and a rudimentary information-sharing mechanism than a substantive institution. The EMS went considerably further than this even in its early years, although it remained optional—Britain chose not to join in 1978, and Greece chose not to participate when it joined the Community in 1981. When the ERM was established, each currency was assigned a "central rate" denominated in European Currency Units (ECUs).[41] The ratio between two ECU central rates is

---

[40] See Ostrom 1990, 52–53.

[41] Rates for snake member countries were based on snake rates. Rates for Ireland, Italy, and France were taken from the market. Although the UK did not join, a notional central rate for sterling was established based on the market rate at the time.

the bilateral central rate for the two currencies; linking these all together gives the parity grid for the system as a whole.[42] Member states agreed to maintain exchange rates within fixed bands around the central rate; those bands started at 2.25 percent on each side (with an exceptional 6 percent band for the lira).[43]

The EMS rulebook prescribes two separate stages of intervention to support these rates. The first stage is set off by the *divergence indicator:* when a currency moves outside 75 percent of the bandwidth of its ECU central rate. This carries a "presumption" to intervene and adjust domestic economic policy, but no obligation to do so. In practice the divergence indicator has had little direct impact on behavior. Intervention at this level has been rare. And while states often adjust domestic policies as currencies fall toward the 75 percent level, it would be hard to develop evidence that those adjustments were driven in any meaningful sense by the divergence indicator per se.[44]

Intervention becomes mandatory when a currency hits the boundary of a bilateral parity agreement. The issuing bank of the stronger currency purchases the weak one, while the issuing bank of the weak currency sells the strong currency (if necessary, after borrowing it from the other's central bank).

This can sometimes be expensive. But the use of ECU central rates (directly in the case of the divergence indicator and indirectly in the bilateral grid) and the central role of the ECU (not national currencies) in the settlement of borrowings made to support intervention, amount in effect to a Community burden-sharing scheme that spreads out the costs. Because the value in a national currency of debts and claims will be affected by the behavior of all the currencies that make up the ECU "basket," settlement in ECU spreads out the exchange rate risk for both debtor and creditor countries in interventions. It also allows a de facto larger divergence spread for smaller countries (whose currencies make up a smaller part of the ECU).[45]

Three separate financing facilities that member states can use in support of intervention make up another kind of burden-sharing scheme. The Very Short Term Financing Facility (VSTF) is essentially a network of mutual credit lines among central banks that are run according to a set of community-wide rules.[46]

---

[42] See Goodman 1992, 192.

[43] Spain and Britain were also given 6 percent bands when they joined the system in 1989 and 1990, respectively.

[44] Goodman 1992, 194.

[45] This was actually a compromise ("the Belgian Compromise") between states that wanted an ECU-based intervention obligation, and others that preferred intervention driven by bilateral parities. The technical arguments are reviewed in Koeune and van Ypersele 1985, 48–49.

[46] In principle, VSTF lines of credit are unlimited. Borrowing was originally for forty-five days. This was extended in 1987 to seventy-five days from the end of the month during which intervention took place (with two three-month renewals possible). Repayment must be at least 50 percent in the borrowed currency with the remainder in ECUs.

Short Term Monetary Support (STMS), also administered by the central banks, is aimed at temporary balance of payments problems and acts as a kind of "mini-IMF" for the EU. It includes a set of debtor and creditor quotas that can be waived under special circumstances by mutual agreement. The third facility, Medium Term Financial Assistance (MTFA), is something like a micro–World Bank. MTFA is administered by the Council of Ministers and provides longer term financing that is part of the more general set of EU allocation schemes favoring the less prosperous member states.[47] This burden-sharing scheme still involves an order of magnitude less regulation than the intricate redistribution regimes characteristic of single states. But it is considerably more than a privatized market for currencies in which stabilization and its costs are the sole responsibility of the individual states.

Monitoring, Collective Choice, and Conflict Resolution. In practice the EMS is a central part of political life within the European Union. The natural consequence is that many EU institutions are involved in monitoring and discussion of its operations although one specific institution, the Monetary Committee, is the primary arena where operational rules and some changes in collective choice rules are played out. Each member state appoints two representatives to the Monetary Committee. These are usually a top official from the Economics or Finance Ministry, and a first or second deputy governor of the Central Bank. The Commission also appoints two members.[48] Since the 1981 flap over the unilateral Italian devaluation, consultations within the Monetary Committee have been the standard procedure for negotiating realignment. And as discussed earlier, a set of norms about procedures and outcomes of realignments have generally been sustained through this process.

The Monetary Committee is also the central focus for the Union's multilateral monetary surveillance exercises, biannual since 1990. The mandate for these surveys is quite broad, extending from national statistics on employment, regional development, interest rates, and the like, to a review of budgetary policies including the size and proposed funding of deficits. The Monetary Committee does the work and drafts a report which serves as the basis for discussions at the Council. The Council, in turn, is entitled to make economic policy suggestions and issue country-specific recommendations with the concurrence of the Commission.[49]

---

[47] MTFA is denominated in ECUs, and loan terms are generally two to five years. There are agreed limits for each country.

[48] Personal Communication with Michael Shackleton, European Parliament, February 1994. Under special circumstances, other high officials from the Commission have joined committee meetings.

[49] See Council Decision of 12 March 1990, on the attainment of progressive convergence of economic policies and performance during stage 1 of economic and monetary union, *Official Journal of the European Communities*, 90/141/EEC, no. L 78/23, 24 March 1990.

None of this is binding, of course. But member states are obliged to "bring the results of the multilateral surveillance to the attention of their national parliaments so that it can be taken into account in national policy making." The European Parliament is also involved: it can call the President of the Council to appear before several committees to report on recommendations, and it is supposed to receive from the Council periodic reports on the progress made through the multilateral surveillance procedure. Again, there is nothing approaching leviathan here, but there is much that goes beyond a private market.

EMS Collective Action

These institutions make it easier for states to monitor each other's policies and activities that affect the common resource pool of exchange rate stability in the EMS. Label this activity "information provision," and it fits comfortably within the familiar conceptual framework of an "international regime." More interesting for my argument here is the contribution these institutions make toward contingent commitments with behavioral consequences that go beyond what the standard notion of regimes will support.[50]

How does this work? Ostrom found through close examination of many cases that successful voluntary organizations seemed to share a number of "design principles" which failures were less likely to have.[51] Several of these design principles have analogies in the EMS. The system has clearly defined boundaries, which distinguish common property from open access. It has collective choice arrangements, which allow all of the states affected by operational rules to participate in modifying those rules, at a reasonable cost, along with realistic dispensations for the more powerful states and particularly Germany. The high degree of interdependence in the EU boosts the private benefits of monitoring, since knowing what other states are doing is important to each member state's strategic decisions about its own monetary and fiscal policies. States have easy access to a dense network of conflict resolution mechanisms, and there are a set of norms about legitimate procedure that point to particular institutions as the appropriate (not necessarily efficient) place for conflicts to be worked out.

---

[50] This is a subtle claim that I will expand upon in detail in the conclusion. I do not say that the behavior of states in a voluntary organization is inconsistent with the notion of an international regime, but I do argue that it stretches that notion to a higher level of organization and compliance than "regime" usually represents.

[51] To be clear, Ostrom does not claim (and neither do I) that these are necessary conditions for success. And it is obvious that they are not sufficient conditions. They are simply generalizations induced from case studies, not definitive arguments or "explanations." Since each condition is backed up with a logical argument as to why it should matter, I feel comfortable treating them as working hypotheses—no more and no less.

The two most important features of the EMS in this context are "graduated sanctions" and "nested enterprises." What is important about graduated sanctions is the range of means by which member states can respond to noncompliance. Robert Axelrod tells a different story about decentralized cooperation in *Evolution of Cooperation* (1985). Tit-for-tat is an exemplar "trigger strategy" model, but one that is extremely "brittle," easily affected by defection or noncompliance. In Axelrod's stark model all defections are de facto the same—no matter who defects, or when or why the defection occurs. And all defections call up exactly the same response. It is obvious that the EMS (like most real world institutions) does not work that way, but it is much less obvious precisely how contingent cooperation *does* work once we introduce differentiated measures of behavior for both the "defector" and the "responder."

The term "graduated sanctions" captures the intuitive idea that in successful, real world organizations, all defections are not the same and that there exist ranges of possible responses—which together make cooperation less brittle than in Axelrod's world. The logic of compliance in this kind of system is less stark than in a trigger strategy model.[52] Two general beliefs support compliance. The first is the belief that the system to which one is contributing will, on the whole, deliver the collective goods one is helping to pay for. The second is the faith that most other members of the system will also contribute their share. The history of the 1992–93 crisis shows a similar logic of "quasi-voluntary" compliance operating in the EMS. The details in the next section of this chapter show the central importance of two shared beliefs: that the system will continue to provide exchange rate stability, and that others will contribute a fair share to that end by titrating interest rates and adjusting economic policies over the longer term.

There is a flip side to these beliefs. If someone seems not to be contributing, the relevant question in the EMS is Why not?—since in a highly interdependent and densely institutionalized system with a comparatively small number of players, it may be possible and cost-effective to try to differentiate among defections. A particular defection might very well be a baldly opportunistic grab for unilateral benefits, but it might also represent a genuine disagreement over management decisions (particularly given the level of uncertainty about sustainable yields from the CPR) or over the quality of existing rules that are supposed to govern appropriation. Another possibility is that a state with a strong reputation for compliance will be plunged into unexpected circumstances by an external shock, and succumb in an isolated instance to strong temptations.

---

[52] See Levi 1988, particularly chap. 3.

These differences should matter greatly to participants in a voluntary organization, both in terms of making decisions about whether and how to sanction the violator—or, more importantly for the EMS, whether to sustain their own contribution to the system or to withhold it, in which case the system itself would collapse. What is not possible to do in the institution-free world of Axelrod's thought experiment—to appreciate the significance of a defection—may very well be possible in the densely institutionalized environment of the EU. This can create "wiggle room" on compliance and sanctioning that would be central to the maintenance of the system in the face of external shocks. And that, essentially, is what happened in 1992-93.

Nested institutions play an important role in making this work. The norms and criteria of legitimacy that frame the EU's institutional environment set boundaries on what is legitimate and appropriate to do in collective choice mechanisms and operational rules. As in other institutional environments, congruence among the several levels stabilizes the entire structure and reinforces the historical trajectory of development that characterizes EU institutions.

These are abstract statements that will take on more specific meaning in the next section when I discuss the crisis. But it is worth pointing out now how nesting makes the EMS different from the snake. The snake was more an ancillary arrangement than an integral part of European integration, and that was true both institutionally and cognitively.[53] The EMS is different on both scores. National leaders and community officials publicly and consistently tied the success of the EMS first to the SEA and later to the more elaborate integration plans within Maastricht. Whether or not a single currency was technically necessary or even beneficial to either scheme was not the central argument around which decisions were taken (although such arguments were of course part of the debate). As the 1980s moved forward, it became increasingly difficult for national leaders to oppose the EMS and at the same time paint themselves in favor of European integration, whatever the technical merits of such a position might have been.[54] The debate over "multi-speed" Europe in the run-up to Maastricht clearly demonstrated that a country unable or unwilling to be a part of the EMS risked sacrificing legitimacy as a full member of the EU or in terms of whatever other institutional arrangements might come out of the negotiations. Such a position might have made sense substantively in a technical environment, but it simply did not make sense within the EC.

---

[53] As Jeffery Frieden (1993, 18) put it, "there was never any sense that the snake was an essential component of the EC; neither national politicians nor Community leaders had staked much political capital on the arrangement."

[54] See for example Garrett 1993.

EMS Under Crisis: 1992–93

The Build-up

The basic economics that brought about a crisis in the EMS is simple. Lurking in the background as an underlying impetus of change was the fact that the system had become brittle. There had been no major realignment since 1987, but member states continued to run economic policies that led to differential inflation rates among them.[55] At the same time, capital mobility was increasing rapidly both because of the formal lifting of most controls and the astounding growth of the foreign exchange market generally in the later 1980s and 1990s. The EMS seemed to be, de facto, much like a fixed exchange rate system in a world of capital mobility and among countries with supposedly "independent" monetary policies. While Eichengreen and Wyplosz argue that only Italy was suffering definite competitiveness problems as a result of currency "misalignment" (the data are less clear for Spain and the UK), pressures on currencies were certainly starting to build up. And although "real" economic forces from "fundamentals" might not have caused a crisis in 1992–93 on their own, the situation was certainly ripe for an external shock of sufficient magnitude to come along and do that.

German economic and monetary union (GEMU) was an enormous shock. As the de facto anchor currency of the EMS, the D-mark's interest rates set an effective floor for rates throughout the system and had done so for much of the 1980s. In late 1987 with domestic inflation rising moderately in Germany, D-mark interest rates had already began a gradual upward climb that carried rates throughout Europe somewhat higher. But the real shock came in 1990, when the Kohl government at the outset of GEMU decided (largely for political reasons) to exchange ostmarks for D-marks at a 1:1 ratio up to a very generous limit and to make enormous transfer payments to the eastern *Länder*, payment that were financed largely through deficit spending.

The effect of "ostmark diplomacy" was to expand the German money supply at a rapid rate and to create an enormous surge in public and private spending, particularly in the East, but without an immediate corresponding supply-side response. German inflation was a predictable result. In fact, the Bundesbank anticipated this dynamic as early as 1989 and tried to head it off by arguing for a D-mark realignment at that time. Standard economic reasoning clearly favored an appreciation of the D-mark.[56] This would make goods from other EC countries

---

[55] To be exact, there was a small realignment in 1990.

[56] Indeed, the D-mark did appreciate about 8 percent in real terms against the dollar and the yen between late 1989 and mid-1990. During the same period, German long-term rates rose more than 200 basis points to carry them above U.S. long-term rates (which were on the decline) by early 1990.

more competitive in Germany, so that the surge in German demand could be met by supply from all EC countries. Diffusing the demand spurt around the EC would have insured that output (and by implication, inflationary pressures) would rise in like manner throughout the Community rather than in Germany alone.

The problem, of course, was that suggesting an "upward realignment" of the D-mark was simply another way of suggesting a "downward realignment" or devaluation of other currencies within the system. By the end of the 1980s, devaluation had become a difficult and nearly unacceptable option for EC countries. This was in part because of the symbolic nesting of the EMS within other EC institutions and the commitment to a united Europe that exchange rate stability had come to represent. But it was also in part a result of important links to domestic political concerns and strategies. The Italian government, for example, argued that exchange rate stability was critical to its ongoing efforts to restructure public finances in Rome and to push through budget reforms aimed at reducing the country's enormous deficit. Rome saw devaluation of the lira as signaling a loss of credibility that it could not afford at such a crucial time.[57] The British government argued similarly that a devaluation of the pound so soon after it had entered the EMS would undermine the credibility of its monetary strategy. In France, the long-standing domestic political significance of the "franc fort" policy had been, if anything, magnified by German reunification and the changes in Franco-German relations that this was certain to bring. So when the Bundesbank suggested realignment in 1989 as a prophylactic measure against a crisis that had not yet materialized, it is not surprising that the idea was turned back firmly.[58]

Figure 2.1A captures the logic of the game at this point. Member states shared much common knowledge about the economics of GEMU and its ramifications for the EMS, but did not agree on what to do about it. As Eichengreen and Wyplosz explain, the necessary adjustments might have been made without a formal decision to revalue immediately, through several possible recipes combining differential inflation rates. Three general possibilities include:

(1) Substantial German inflation, stable prices elsewhere
(2) Stable German prices, substantial deflation elsewhere
(3) Moderate German inflation, moderate deflation elsewhere

Presumably, neither the French, the British, nor other EC states with relatively high unemployment would support option 2. And hardly anyone could have

[57] See, for example Balls 1993, 12.

[58] Wayne Sandholtz, in a colloquium presentation at the University of California at Berkeley in April 1994, added that Germany, not wanting at the time to appear domineering in any EC context, may not have pushed the issue quite so hard against the objections of its neighbors. See also Marsh and Marsh 1993, 3.

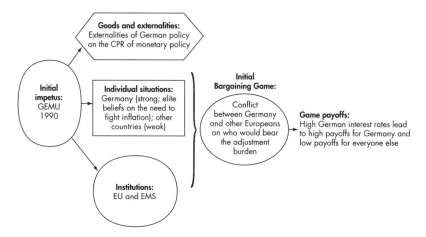

FIGURE 2.1A. Responses to German unification and GEMU

believed that the Bundesbank would stand for option 1. This left option 3, per-haps the best of the bad choices; but it still depended on the Bundesbank ac-cepting a certain amount of German inflation. What seems likely, is that other states believed that if realignment were indeed ruled out, the Bundesbank would take a responsible "European" perspective on the situation and compromise on a more expansionary German monetary policy than it unilaterally would have preferred.

They were wrong, at least at the beginning of the crisis. The Bundesbank stood by its domestic policy commitment to low inflation in Germany and boosted interest rates ten times, for a total of 600 basis points, between Decem-ber 1987 and September 1992. Central banks in other EMS countries found themselves with no real option but to raise their own rates to stem a flow of cur-rency into D-marks. In effect, the Bundesbank was choosing something close to option 2: the export of deflation, which contributed to recession and a rise in un-employment around the Community (from a GDP-weighted average of under 10 percent in EMS countries other than Germany in 1990, to over 11 percent by the same measure in 1993).

This would have made the necessary economic adjustments—but it was vul-nerable politically. Anyone living in Paris or particularly in London during 1992 would have witnessed the bizarre spectacle of a country in deep recession and with high and rising unemployment *raising* its interest rates more or less in lock-step with a central bank in another country.

What made the system even more brittle were some ironic follow-on effects from the "convergence criteria" agreed to under the Maastricht Treaty in December 1991. In addition to strict guidelines for budget deficits and inflation, Maastricht made exchange rate stability within the narrow band of the ERM a necessary prerequisite for two years for a state that wanted to enter stage three of European monetary union. Despite some room for discretion in applying the convergence criteria, this action made realignment an even more noxious idea to most member states.[59] To be cut out of monetary union would not only deprive a state of a position in a European Central Bank; it would be tantamount to accepting second-class citizenship in the EU. Figure 2.1B illustrates the logic of what was generally seen as a nested substantive linkage by most member states. Ironically it was that linkage that partly set the stage for crisis: "unable" to realign, unable to control capital flows across borders, and unable to convince the Bundesbank to moderate its anti-inflationary bias, member states in effect were locking themselves into deflationary monetary policies in the midst of recession.

To cast the story against the theoretical framework of a CPR problem, Germany did exploit the system here. Germany expanded its money supply in a flash and tried to transfer some of the costs of that decision to others. German behavior can be viewed as a kind of opportunism that is available to monetary pseudohegemons and is certainly not unique to Germany.[60] But in this case the special presence of the Bundesbank changed the logic of the situation. Instead of accepting inflation at home, the iron discipline of the Bundesbank turned the game around, to one of deflation abroad. This brought the EMS to a vulnerable

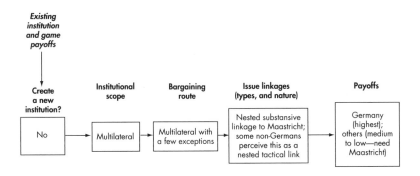

FIGURE 2.1B. The link to Maastricht

[59] On this point, see Alesina and Grilli 1993, 145–65.

[60] After all, the United States did something mildly similar during the Vietnam War and undermined (through inflation) the Bretton Woods accords.

point where the system for organizing provision and appropriation of the CPR—exchange rate stability in Europe—was on the brink of collapse.

The crisis of 1992–93, as I see it, is essentially a story about how change was "organized" to avoid collapse. The next section argues that the EMS survived in its essentials as I proposed at the beginning of this chapter. Its reorganization followed to a considerable degree the logic of a voluntary organization, which leads to some interesting questions. Which "design principles" turned out to be important causes? What other factors were important in holding the EMS together? And what does this suggest about the future of EMU?

The Crisis: Phase 1

In mid-summer 1992 historically low interest rates in the United States and much higher rates in Germany were driving money out of dollars (as well as out of pounds and lira) into D-marks. The inflow of money into Germany further increased the growth of its money supply and of inflation, and put additional upward pressure on German rates. At the same time, the pound and the lira fell near to their floors within the ERM, forcing the Bank of Italy to raise its discount rate to 13 percent in mid July. At the end of August, the Bank of England intervened massively in currency markets to support the pound. The Bundesbank raised the realignment issue again in early September but was turned back firmly by Italy and Britain with the support of France.[61] Additional intervention in support of the pound and lira (financed largely through borrowing from the VSTF and additional sources) along with another jump in the Italian discount rate to 15 percent barely managed to keep the pound and the lira above their floors.

When finance ministers and Central Bank governors met in Bath, England, during the first week of September, they knew the ERM was being sorely tested. The Italian treasury minister said that Italy would consider devaluing the lira if it were done in the context of a broader realignment, but that idea was still opposed strongly by both France and Britain. Both countries argued that the EMS problem was not about misaligned currencies, but about German interest rates. Bundesbank president Helmut Schlesinger disagreed but did offer up the possibility that the Bundesbank might lower its rates if the ministers could agree on a general realignment. His compatriots demurred and the meeting ended with only a continued commitment to support existing exchange rates and intervene as necessary. Figure 2.2A illustrates the logic of the game at this point.

Economists and other observers have since harshly criticized the Bath meeting for not acting more aggressively, but many of these criticisms do not take sufficient note of the stakes and the nature of the disagreements that were on the

---

[61] Cameron (1995, 23) provides detail on this.

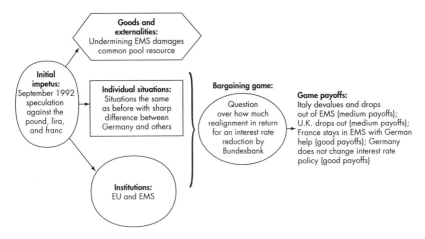

FIGURE 2.2A. The role of currency speculators

table. The Bundesbank position was not shared by other central banks, in large part because no one wanted to be the only country or one of only a few countries to devalue for the reasons I discussed earlier. The French in particular felt that a broad realignment also had to be ruled out, at the very least until after the French referendum on Maastricht, which was scheduled for September 20. With August opinion polls showing French public support for the treaty dropping below 50 percent, the French government argued that a realignment just before the referendum would embarrass the government's Europe policy and turn the vote into an almost sure defeat. From this perspective, the pressure was on Germany to make a sacrifice for the sake of Europe rather than the other way around. But the Germans still did not see it that way.[62]

During the following week the pound hovered barely above its floor and the lira slipped beneath its floor, despite intervention of around $16 billion to support it.[63] On September 11, Schlesinger and Bundesbank vice president Hans Tietmeyer met with the chancellor and his top finance aides to press the case within the German government for ERM realignment. Despite pressure from France, Kohl was won over by Schlesinger's arguments about the costs of continued intervention and its probable effect on the German money supply and the inflation dilemma.[64] They agreed that the government would support a

[62] A different perspective on this might suggest that the Bundesbank, unhappy with EMU plans under Maastricht, preferred to see the treaty defeated in the French referendum and held to its position with this in mind. Such a view represents an alternative argument to the entire case, which I will deal with in the final section of this chapter.

[63] *Financial Times,* 15 September 1992, 1.

[64] Ibid; see also Norman and Barber 1992, 2.

broad realignment, for which Schlesinger offered in return an interest rate cut linked to the size and extent of the realignment.

Tietmeyer and Horst Kohler (State Secretary of the Finance Ministry) arrived in Paris the next morning, to brief French government officials on the realignment/interest-rate-cut message they were about to carry to Rome. The Germans met with Finance Minister Michel Sapin and Jean-Claude Trichet, the director of the tresor—who was also at the time chair of the EC Monetary Committee. According to the *Financial Times,* Tietmeyer and Kohler told Sapin and Trichet that Germany wanted a broad realignment within the ERM but did not specifically request a meeting of the Monetary Committee to negotiate such a move. And Trichet did not call for a meeting, perhaps because he thought the British would block realignment and/or because his own government wanted desperately to make it past the Maastricht referendum (just one week away) with the franc intact. The Germans went on to Italy, where they agreed in bilateral negotiations with the Italians on a 7 percent lira devaluation to be answered with small reductions in the Bundesbank discount rate (0.5 percent to 8.25 percent) and in the Lombard rate (0.25 percent to 9.5 percent). In a mostly pro forma move the next day, ERM member states gave their approval to the German-Italian deal.[65]

This small and single devaluation was in some ways the worst of all possible worlds for the ERM. Not enough to shield the lira from pressure, it acted as a reminder and a signal that realignments could and did happen. This only whet the appetites of currency speculators, at least in their projections for the lira and the pound.

On Monday, September 14, Schlesinger and Tietmeyer said publicly that the Bundesbank had indeed asked Kohl to push for a broad realignment. The next day, the pound predictably fell to just above its floor against the D-mark. That evening, the *Wall Street Journal* and *Handelsblatt* released summaries of an interview with Schlesinger in which the Bundesbank president indicated clearly his own strong preference for a broad realignment. Regardless of whether Schlesinger had approved the precise language, this public revelation acted as another signal to currency traders.[66]

"Black Wednesday" (September 16) brought disaster to the pound. Britain, however, did not surrender the pound without an unprecedented fight. Over the course of the day, the Bank of England spent approximately 15 billion pounds (about half of total available reserves) to support the pound. The Bundesbank,

---

[65] Norman and Barber (15 September 1992) report also that the British considered joining the Italians in the devaluation but decided against it.

[66] *Financial Times,* 15 September 1992, 1; and 16 September 1992, 1. Norman and Barber (1992) describe the reaction in London.

the Banque de France, and other ERM members spent an additional 5 billion pounds. All told, this was probably the largest one-day central bank intervention in currency markets ever.[67] In addition, in the midst of a painful recession, Prime Minister John Major authorized two interest rate hikes, first from 10 to 12 percent at 10:30 in the morning of Black Wednesday, and later from 12 to 15 percent at 2:15 that afternoon. This represented the will to sustain a savage shock to the British economy and an enormous blow to John Major's already faltering popularity.

None of this would save the pound from its fate at the end of the day, but the outcome was, of course, not known to the actors who made the decisions when they made them. What seems clear is that the British government was willing to pay substantial, even unprecedented, costs both financial and political to keep the pound in the ERM. The alternative argument of some observers, that these were only theatrical moves prior to pulling out, has little evidence to support it and is not logically compelling. To what audience would this play? Certainly the government did not help its domestic position by raising rates for a few hours, raising them yet again, and then dropping out of the ERM and reducing rates at the end of the day. The British press and public reacted sourly to the whole affair, which (in part because of the interest rate moves) looked much more like a massive defeat for the government than a reasoned policy choice. The general sentiment among the London elite was that changing interest rates three times in one day was no way for a serious government to run a monetary policy.[68] But if the maneuver had worked to support the pound, the domestic picture for the government might not have been much better—as Major would have been stuck more or less with blistering interest rates and no politically acceptable way to lower them at least in the short run.

David Cameron characterizes Britain's action as an "exit"; but this is incorrect in my view. It simply ignores the fact that there was a price that Britain was willing to pay to sustain loyalty to the EMS. Another way to put it, is to ask if this series of events represents the abject failure of the EMS as an institution, and I think the answer to that question has to be a measured "No."

The system certainly failed to deliver the goods. Why? The story does not seem to be one of complete defection or free riding—certainly not by the British, and arguably not by the Germans either. A better characterization is that faulty management decisions made earlier left a nearly unsalvageable situation in September. Seen in that context, what is striking about this story is how much the states were willing to sacrifice in order to salvage what they could. The failure of the EMS to deliver the goods under these peculiar and unforeseen circumstances demanded a

[67] Estimates reported in *Financial Times,* 19–20 September 1992, 6.
[68] Personal observation and discussions.

change in operational rules. How those changes would be made—and the subsequent implications for the EC—are the important issues.

Major's government could not and did not accept defeat lightly, particularly insofar as it had staked so much of its domestic prestige on an economic policy that put ERM at the center. But in the mid-afternoon when the interest rate hike failed to push the pound up above its floor, the Bank of England had exhausted all its realistic options. Major called both Kohl and French prime minister Pierre Beregovoy to inform them that his government would withdraw from the ERM. The British Cabinet met after the close of the London markets, and at 7:30 that evening Chancellor Lamont announced the suspension of the pound from the ERM.

This decision was not made within the context of the EC Monetary Committee, but the Committee did meet in emergency session that night in Brussels to acknowledge (or as they put it, "take notice") of what Britain had done. Following an all-night meeting, the Monetary Committee announced also that the lira would be de facto suspended, as well, and that the Spanish peseta would be devalued 5 percent.

This was, without question, a first-order crisis for the ERM—two currencies effectively dropped out and a third was devalued. But did the institution fall apart? In the days immediately following the crisis, the vitriol flowing between London, Bonn, and Frankfurt made it easy for journalists to conclude that it had—and to suspect that the damage might easily spill over to other aspects of the Community. Back and forth criticisms over the events of Black Wednesday got so nasty that the British Foreign Office at one point summoned the German ambassador for consultations—an unprecedented move between two EC member states.[69] These exchanges were motivated in part by real anger between the two states, in part by misunderstanding, and in part by the need to posture before domestic political factions that smelled blood in Major's climbdown. But they had the effect of making the ERM appear even more brittle to currency traders, who saw in the upcoming French referendum on Maastricht a golden opportunity to exploit what seemed to be the imminent fracturing of the EMS.

The Crisis: Phase 2

On Friday, September 18, traders drove the franc to within one centime above its D-mark floor. Tietmeyer that day made several public statements in support of the franc, but without obvious effect. Banque de France (BDF) currency market interventions (reported later to be on the order of $10 billion, some of which

---

[69] Cameron (1995, 30) describes the extraordinary exchanges that took place between Lamont, Kohl, Schlesinger, and the representative of the British Treasury, as each blamed the others.

was borrowed from the Bundesbank) didn't help much either.[70] That weekend all eyes were on the upcoming French referendum. The positive outcome—razor-close as it was—seemed to barely change currency traders' calculus. On Monday, September 21, the franc fell to one-half a centime above its D-mark floor despite continuing heavy intervention by central banks. That afternoon and the next morning, Schlesinger, Tietmeyer, and Waigel (all in Washington for a previously scheduled G-7 conference) each made vehement public statements in support of the franc.

According to Buchan and Dawkins of the *Financial Times*, these statements were part of a coordinated strategy worked out in Washington among the French—Sapin, Trichet, Jacques de Larosiere (then governor of the Banque de France)—and the Germans—Schlesinger and Tietmeyer from the Bundesbank, and Kohler and Waigel from the government.[71] While Sapin and Kohler flew back from Washington to implement their joint defense, Kohl and Mitterand met on Tuesday, September 22, in Europe to reinforce the French-German link and perceptions of their shared commitment to Maastricht. Despite these political signals and continued heavy central bank intervention, currency markets kept up the pressure on the franc and brought new pressure on other currencies as well—the peseta, escudo, krone, and punt in particular. By late Tuesday the entire ERM seemed on the brink of disaster.

A turning point came on Wednesday, September 23, one week after Black Wednesday. In conjunction with the strategy agreed on in Washington, the BDF announced early that morning a moderate increase in a short-term interest rate and then released a joint French-German statement that the franc and mark were fairly valued and would be supported by joint intervention.[72] The Bundesbank that day did two unusual things. It intervened intramarginally—that is, it bought currencies on a voluntary basis before they hit their floors—and it announced publicly that it was doing so at the time.[73] The BDF spent perhaps $17 billion on intervention in the week after Black Wednesday, a substantial portion of which it probably borrowed from the Bundesbank. The Bundesbank itself probably spent somewhere between $7 and $20 billion to support the franc that week, and (according to Schlesinger) a total of around $60 billion total during the month of September to support weak ERM currencies.[74] By the end of the trading day on Wednesday, the franc was up several centimes and other currencies as well were

[70] See Buchan and Dawkins 1992, 15.

[71] Ibid. See also *Financial Times*, 22 September 1992, 1; 23 September 1992, 2.

[72] *Financial Times*, 24 September 1992, 2.

[73] Intramarginal intervention, as I discussed earlier, has rarely been practiced within the EMS. According to Cameron (1995, 32), "it was the first time since the founding of the EMS that the Bank had revealed it was doing so at the time of the intervention."

[74] See Cameron 1995, 32–33; and the interesting article by Dawkins (1992, 2).

trading safely within their ranges. It appeared, at least for the moment, that the ERM had been saved.

What happened here can be explained through a few simple observations. The pound and the lira were each in an untenable position. Italy was uncompetitive; Britain was stuck with stifling interest rates in the midst of a recession, probably an overvalued currency, and a somewhat ambivalent commitment to EMU. In that context, what is striking about phase 1 is how hard states actually tried to hold to operational rules. Recriminations after the fact did not extend to breaking down the collective choice rules of the institution; these rules were followed, for the most part, in managing the crisis. The Bundesbank spent nearly as much money trying to defend the pound as it did the franc, but the franc was in a better position in terms of fundamentals and was thus probably easier to defend. It seems also that the Germans learned from the first phase of the crisis, at least about what did not work. And it is certain that the level of cooperation between France and Germany was higher than that between Britain and Germany.

This probably reflects long standing characteristics of both relationships, but it also follows in part from the nature and the sequencing of events. After Black Wednesday, political expectations about the future of the ERM changed tenor. The loss of the pound and the lira were unfortunate events that were damaging to the ERM. The possible loss of the franc in the next crisis phase was seen widely as a different kind of event, threatening certainly the existence of the EMS and possibly the future of Maastricht—and by implication the next stage of European integration—as well. Once the crisis took on this broader set of implications for nested institutions, the behavior of the central states in the drama changed. Germany and France, governments and central banks, spoke more or less with one voice in a way that had not happened in the first phase of the crisis. This was sufficient to calm the markets for a time. But the crisis was not yet over.

The Crisis: Phase 3

The next attack on the ERM came in mid-November, when currency traders began to pressure the Swedish krona—a currency which, although not formally within the ERM, had been pegged to the ECU since 1991.[75] The Swedish government, which had raised overnight interest rates to 500 percent during the September phase of the crisis, now appealed to the EC Monetary Committee for access to EC currency support funds. The Monetary Committee rejected

---

[75] This peg was an important part of the Swedish government's strategy for building support behind its application for EC membership. The speculative attack was fueled by poor results from a government bond issue that was needed for refinancing.

Stockholm's request, actually reinforcing the boundaries between formal members of the ERM and aspirants like Sweden (who as yet, presumably, had no legitimate claim on the resources of the system).[76] On November 19 the Swedish government raised interest rates again and tried—but failed—to pass an emergency package of spending cuts aimed at cutting public sector borrowing. Capital continued to flow out of krona and into D-mark, leaving the Central Bank with no real option other than to abandon the peg, which it did later that day.

Sweden's surrender was a significant signal to currency markets. Stockholm was seen as having great political will and substantial incentives (as an EC applicant) to maintain the peg. If it could be forced to devalue, what then of the weaker currencies that were within the system? Trading on Friday, November 20, pushed downward the punt, escudo, and peseta near to their ERM floors. Spain that night requested a meeting of the Monetary Committee.

After a long Sunday parley in Brussels, the Committee announced a 6 percent devaluation of both the peseta and the escudo.[77] This was essentially a proactive move taken before currency markets forced the hands of the Spanish and Portuguese governments. Realistic options were now more clear than they had been. The threat to the ERM would probably have been greater if either country had held out for its overvalued currency, now that devaluation was nearly sure to happen, by force or by choice. As it was, the decision to devalue was taken by consensus, within the Monetary Committee, according to the collective choice rules of the ERM. In effect, the ERM was being reconfigured gradually in a way that would lead to the necessary change in operational rules that would allow the institution to survive.

The obvious remaining target at the end of November was the punt, which hung on only through the Bank of Ireland's massive interest rate hikes.[78] The Danish krone also dropped close to its floor against the D-mark despite similar rate increases in Denmark. Early December brought new pressure against the franc, which three small interest rate hikes and large interventions did little to ease. Another round of coordinated French-German defense followed: Kohl and Mitterand held a summit, Sapin and Waigel issued common commitments to the ERM, and the central banks of the two countries engaged in joint interventions.[79] On December 10, Norway (another EC aspirant) abandoned its ECU peg. More importantly, the Bundesbank Council maintained its determined stance not to lower German interest rates unless and until monetary conditions within Germany changed. This pushed the franc perilously close to

---

[76] "Krona Flotation Followed EMS Rebuff to Sweden," *Financial Times,* 21–22 November 1992, 3.

[77] *Financial Times,* 23 November 1992, 1.

[78] Three-month punt rates went from 14.5 to 20 percent, and overnight rates were raised first to 30 and then to 100 percent.

[79] *Financial Times,* 5–6 December 1992, 1.

its D-mark floor, prompting another round of publicly announced, intramarginal intervention by the Bundesbank. But even this dramatic action, along with a public statement by Schlesinger that the franc–D-mark exchange rate was justified by "fundamentals," could not keep the franc out of the danger zone, and by the end of the week it was down to less than one centime above the D-mark floor.[80]

Christmas and New Year's provided some breathing space, but in the first few days of 1993 the franc fell right back to where it was before the holidays. This set off another round of intervention along with a joint statement by the central banks and finance ministries of Germany and France that they would work together in "close cooperation . . . to ensure the proper functioning of the ERM."[81] On January 5, 1993, the two governments staked their defense on the declaration that "the actual central rate of the two currencies is fully justified on the basis of their economic fundamentals."

The punt, however, could not stand similarly on fundamentals—and neither massive intervention nor blistering interest rate hikes could save it.[82] Even so, the Irish government (which had made the "hard punt" policy a center of its economic program) fought hard, raising overnight rates at the end of January to 100 percent. When this failed to boost the currency, Ireland too had run out of options. On Saturday, January 30, the Monetary Committee announced a punt devaluation of 10 percent.[83]

At the end of January 1993, one way to read the situation was to say that the ERM had collapsed. Indeed, with the exception of hard "core" currencies essentially linked to the D-mark, all other currencies (save the franc and the Danish krone) had been devalued.[84] But there was another way to read the situation, which was to say that the broad realignment needed to compensate for shocks to the system had been de facto completed.

It had not happened smoothly or in planned fashion. There was bitterness and even a sense of betrayal, at least publicly, on the part of leaders of some states who intimated that the Germans had taken advantage of their dominant power position within the system. But polemics aside, the Bundesbank had been

---

[80] *Financial Times*, 18 December 1992, 18.

[81] *Financial Times*, 6 January 1993, 1.

[82] Ireland had a low inflation rate and was running a current account surplus, but at the cost of high interest rates and unemployment touching 18 percent. The punt was hurt by the deterioration in Ireland's terms of trade with Britain (Ireland's biggest trading partner) as the pound lost 15 percent of its value against the punt between September 1992 and January 1993.

[83] Ireland's Minister of Finance tried to limit political damage by lashing out, much as Norman Lamont had done in September, at France and Germany but also, in this case, at Great Britain. See *Financial Times*, 1 February 1993, 1.

[84] The krone did come under speculative pressure in early February, but pressure eased after the Bundesbank cut rates on February 4.

remarkably consistent and had stuck to its declared orthodoxy all along. Months earlier, and before the crisis had begun, the Bundesbank made plain its economic arguments for an ERM revaluation and had offered to cut German interest rates in return—an unappreciated bid for compromise. And on February 4 following three phases of crisis which had essentially produced the realignment, the Bundesbank council moved to reduce German rates (the Lombard rate went down half a percent to 9 percent, and the discount rate went down a quarter of a percent to 8 percent).

The striking fact of February 1993 was that the revaluation of currencies, a necessary adaptation to the shock of German reunification, had been carried out and for the most part in accordance with the collective choice rules of the ERM. It had happened under pressure and at the cost of some tough rhetoric. But it could hardly have been otherwise given the political incentives (made worse by Maastricht) that had come to surround realignment. Arguably, the EMS entered 1993 bruised and battered but with its essential institutional elements still very much intact. The tough test of that would come in the next phase of the crisis several months later.

The Crisis: Phase 4

The fourth phase of the crisis began brewing in the spring of 1993. The successful defense of the franc along with some very good indicators of French economic performance had raised monetary self-confidence in Paris. When new Prime Minister Edouard Balladur took office at the end of March, French inflation was running at about 2 percent which was about half that in Germany at the time; and the French budget deficit (about Fr 410 billion, or $70 billion) was (despite its record size for France) still considerably smaller than that held by Bonn. But this was just part of the story. Some French numbers certainly looked good compared to German numbers at the moment, but France did not have the sustained low inflation track record that would provide market confidence in the long-term value of the franc. The Banque De France was not yet fully independent of political control, which had to add an additional discount factor to its credibility. Finally, France was living with record high unemployment, touching 11.5 percent in May, and expected to rise by perhaps another full point by the end of the year. Germany may not have looked quite the economic stalwart that it had in past years, but France was still far from that role.

Nonetheless, the new government in Paris capitalized on the perception of strength and reduced interest rates in hope of prodding the economy gently out of recession. Between February and June 1993, three-month money market rates in France fell from 12.3 percent to 7 percent, which was slightly less than comparable rates in Germany at that time. Late in June, the Banque De France moved to reduce its key intervention rate, which brought that rate below the Bundesbank discount rate for the first time in twenty-six years. This was a politically salient and risky move. It caught the attention of the currency markets, bringing a round of mild downward pressure on the franc. The Banque De France in early July gently reversed its course—after the Bundesbank cut its discount rate by half a percent, the Banque De France allowed itself only a quarter of a percent cut. Meanwhile, three-month money market rates in France edged up while Germany's were falling, so that they were within ten basis points of each other by the second week in July. Despite this, the franc continued to slip.[85]

France by the summer of 1993 had locked itself into a tough political bind surrounding ERM that made the franc appear vulnerable. What mattered to currency markets were not just fundamentals, but also expectations about the ability and willingness of the French government to raise interest rates to defend the franc. France's enviably low inflation rate had not come cheaply: the recession in the country had been deep and long, and the GNP was expected to shrink by a further 0.7 percent in 1993. French unemployment, already the highest among the G-7, looked set to reach 12.5 percent by the end of the year.[86] To raise interest rates under these conditions would seem, from a purely domestic politics point of view, nearly an act of suicide.

What was happening across the English channel tightened the political bind for France. In the short term, Britain's exit from the ERM looked like a viable strategy. British exports were booming—industrial production and retail sales were up nearly 4 percent on the year; and unemployment fell to 10.4 percent. The devaluation had not brought any noticeable inflationary pressures in Britain (at least not yet). Professional economists argued over whether the British "recovery" had been underway before Black Wednesday and they disagreed even about the short-term stimulative effects of devaluation; many also predicted that there would be an inflationary price to pay not long in the future.[87] But the French electorate was less interested in what had to seem like esoterica. What was happening in Britain made it terribly easy for opposition politicians in Paris to argue that making a low interest rate "dash for growth" was the best medicine for France's ills. As an *Economist* editorial put it in July, "each cheery new economic statistic from Britain provokes another beleaguered French politician to suggest the obvious: France should copy Britain and quit the ERM."[88]

---

[85] *Economist*, 10 July 1993, 76.

[86] *Economist*, 17 July 1993, 41.

[87] Ten-year bonds in Britain were at this point yielding eighty basis points more than French ten-year bonds, pointing to higher expectations of inflation over the longer term—although how much of this was a result of Britain's ERM exit, is difficult to say.

[88] *Economist*, 24 July 1993, 13.

Balladur, an unusually popular prime minister, was certainly less vulnerable to facile assault on the franc fort policy than a less popular leader might have been. But he was not immune. Attacks by prominent political figures, including his nominal ally Philippe Seguin (the leading anti-Maastricht figure in France), pushed Balladur into a political corner.[89] In a widely publicized interview of July 12, Balladur defiantly raised the stakes by declaring that if France wanted a change in the franc fort policy, it would have to change its prime minister to get it. This was more or less an invitation to currency traders to test Balladur's mettle, and that is precisely what they did.[90]

On July 14 the franc brushed aside new increases in French money market rates and fell back to one centime above its D-mark floor. The Bundesbank council convened the next day for its regular biweekly meeting, but the domestic indicators did not support a cut in interest rates. German inflation measured 4.2 percent in the twelve months prior to June, and the money supply was still growing much faster than Bundesbank targets. The council did not reduce rates, which left only one more scheduled meeting (on July 29) at which it would be possible to do so before the summer recess. On July 21, the German government announced that its closely monitored measure of money supply, M3, grew at a rate of 8.3 percent in the six months to June, considerably above the declared Bundesbank target of 4.5 to 6.5 percent. Just as hopes of an interest rate cut the next week were being dashed by these numbers, the Bundesbank raised some eyebrows by moving to reduce its fourteen-day repurchase rate slightly (from 7.28 percent to 7.15 percent). This confounded some expectations but did not prevent the franc from falling further that day to less than one centime above its floor.

French and German delegations met secretly the next day in Munich and agreed to several additional measures for a coordinated defense of the franc.[91] On July 23, the Banque De France raised overnight borrowing rates to 10 percent, and the two governments issued another joint statement in support of currency parities. Five days later, and just one day before the critical July 29 meeting of its governing council, the Bundesbank cut again its fourteen-day repurchase rate—and this time by twenty basis points, to 6.95 percent. Bundesbank officials would later claim that this was not a conscious policy choice but simply a result of sparse bank bidding for the available money—as a way of responding to criticisms that the Bundesbank had raised expectations unfairly and set itself up for

---

[89] Seguin in July called the franc fort policy a "social Munich" (*Economist*, 17 July 1993, 41).

[90] Currency traders reacted also to signs of Franco-German tension. In June, the French finance minister made an unusual public call for coordinated interest rate cuts between the two countries. Waigel reacted negatively, by canceling a planned French-German meeting on economic policy.

[91] Specifically, they agreed to increase the ceiling on bilateral swap credits to a reported 30 billion D-marks and to coordinate interest rate policy changes.

disaster. Intentions aside, that was pretty close to the effect. The repurchase rate reduction along with the consistent statements supporting the franc did raise widespread expectations that the next day's meeting would bring a significant cut in the much more important discount rate.

It did not happen. On July 29 the Bundesbank chose not to cut its key discount rate (then at 6.75 percent). It did cut the less important Lombard rate (which acts a ceiling for German money market rates) by more than fifty basis points, but the markets read this as sui generis. On the whole, the Bundesbank stuck to its policy to give priority to German monetary conditions (which hardly justified any interest rate cut at all) and to its primary commitment to control the money supply at home. The *Financial Times* later reported that Tietmeyer had suggested a modest cut in the discount rate principally for the sake of the ERM but that Schlesinger had overruled him. Schlesinger instead offered the Lombard rate-cut, along with a promise that the Bundesbank would allow money market rates to fall gradually. The latter move Schlesinger announced in an off-the-record briefing with a small group of German journalists, and it was not made public until the next day. This was a classic kind of understated policy move, coming just when the markets were looking for something much bigger, a "costly" signal of Bundesbank commitment to the ERM.

Surely, Schlesinger was in a bind of his own. To generate that kind of signal, he would have had to compromise on what he was trying foremost to protect—the Bundesbank's anti-inflationary credentials. But the halting moves of July 29 might have been worse politically than no move at all. On Friday, July 30, the franc collapsed in early European currency trading. Meanwhile, top French and German monetary officials convened a secret meeting at Bercy.[92] While they talked, the Banque De France exhausted its swap credit with the Bundesbank; by the end of the day the Banque De France had spent around 300 billion francs, leaving a net deficit on currency reserves of over 180 billion francs.

This was the final phase of the crisis and the most pivotal for the ERM. De la Loisiere immediately asked the Germans to offer a further cut on repurchase rates and, more importantly, to commit to unlimited intramarginal intervention to support the franc. The Germans denied both requests. By 11 A.M. the franc had hit its D-mark floor, setting off obligatory intervention by both central banks.

With the New York market set to open in just a few hours, the Germans proposed that there be a formal "lifting" of the obligation to intervene and that they

---

[92] Waigel, Schlesinger, Tietmeyer, and Gert Haller (state secretary of the Finance Ministry) represented Germany; Finance Minister Edmond Alphandery, de la Larosiere, Trichet, and Herve Hannoun (deputy governor of the BDF) represented France. De la Loisiere, not Alphandery, led the negotiations for the French side—recognizing the Germans' pique at Alphandery's public gaffe in June.

close official lunchtime fixing of currency values. This would essentially mean the de facto suspension of the ERM, at least until the monetary committee could meet and develop a broader strategy over the weekend. The Germans certainly hoped that this would force a revaluation decision at the Monetary Committee, and they were almost certainly trying to rescue both themselves and the Banque De France from spending enormous sums of money on interventions that could prove futile. But the French rejected this plan, arguing that it would be interpreted widely as a defeat specifically for Paris and its crucial franc fort policy. So intervention continued and actually accelerated after markets opened in the United States. *The Financial Times* estimated later that the scale of this intervention may have been as much as twice what the Bank of England spent in September, on the order of 32 billion pounds.

What is noteworthy here is that the Bundesbank did not, in fact, need French approval to suspend intervention, nor did it need any help from the monetary committee to force revaluation. The Bundesbank could have simply and unilaterally suspended its obligation to intervene, as it had explicitly reserved the right to do when Germany joined the ERM in 1979. In fact, the circumstances of 1993 matched nearly precisely the exit contingencies which the Bundesbank had specifically established in 1979. To invoke that escape clause would certainly have been an unprecedented move, but so were all the other possible options.

The ERM was not going to survive with its operational rules intact. That much was certain owing to both the nature of the external shock that had started the crisis and the faulty management decisions that had been made early in the crisis. What really was at issue now was the survival of collective choice and constitutional rules, the higher-level and more essential elements of the institution.

Had Germany gone its own way at this point and unilaterally "broken" the ERM, this would have been a clear violation of collective choice. Given the timing of events—particularly the proximity of the crisis to German reunification, the Maastricht Treaty, and other tensely contested EU policy issues (such as the recognition of post-Yugoslav republics—Germany's partners might very well have interpreted it also as a flagrant breaking of constitutional rules, (in other words, the broader set of EU institutions and norms surrounding the ERM). Given the stakes I think it plausible to suggest that this would have meant a grave political crisis for the EU as a whole that could readily have had substantial upward ripple effects through the entire structure of nested institutions.

As it was, the destiny of the ERM was to be determined that weekend in a multilateral framework, within the Monetary Committee in Brussels. The bargaining was hard, and it took all weekend to come to a decision. In the early morning of August 2, the result was clear: all currencies except the guilder and the D-mark would move to 15 percent bands. Figure 2.2B depicts this final phase of the crisis.

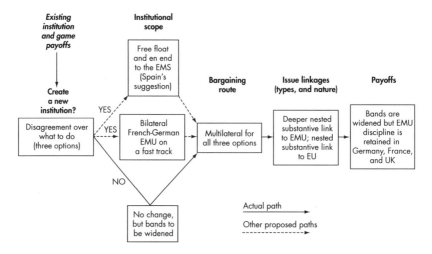

FIGURE 2.2B. Institutional changes in the EMS

What did this mean for the ERM? The general assessment at the time was that 15 percent bands were de facto equivalent to a free-float, and that the so-called agreement was a cosmetic cover to a collapse of the system. *The Economist,* for example, wrote that although "better than nothing" 15 percent bands "mock the intent of the ERM."[93] Expectations were widespread that each country would now go its own way, in a possible race for competitive devaluation. Quoting *The Economist* again, "RPR doubters and struggling French businessmen will lobby hard for a British-style dash for growth led by interest rate cuts."[94] Financial markets certainly shared that expectation: stocks and bonds all over Europe surged after August 2, reflecting widespread beliefs that interest rate cuts were on the way. In mid-August stock markets in London, Paris, Zurich, Britain, and Amsterdam hit all-time highs, and even the German market had a boom.[95] But the reality would turn out to be different.

The behavior of states in the wake of August 2 makes better sense when placed in the context of what we know about the positions of some states and the issues on the table at the fateful Monetary Committee meeting of the previous weekend. The French at this meeting called for Germany to leave the ERM, and let the D-mark float freely against all other currencies (which themselves would remain linked). This would shift the political onus of exit to the Germans

[93] *Economist,* 7 August 1993, 21.

[94] Ibid., 22.

[95] Pushing the German market up was the argument that other countries would cut rates, speeding economic recovery throughout Europe; that would in turn stimulate demand for German products, boost German exports, and rebound profits to German firms.

and lead to de facto devaluation of other currencies (since the D-mark would presumably float upwards). Jacques Delors also supported this plan. But it was confounded immediately when Holland announced that in a secret deal with Germany three days before, the two states had agreed that the guilder would remain tied tightly to the D-mark. When Belgium and Denmark said that they too wanted the same arrangement, the French plan was doomed, since it would have effectively left France at the head of an emasculated ERM with no other strong currencies.

The ERM realistically could have collapsed at this meeting in at least three additional ways. The first way would have been for the Monetary Committee to accept formally a solution that must have been in everyone's mind, but that Spain actually placed on the table: to dissolve the ERM entirely and move to a free float. According to *The Economist,* this "drastic step" was one that the "ministers only narrowly averted."[96] The system could have collapsed also through a failure to agree on any measures (either to save it or to bury it by mutual agreement). This too was possible: "the negotiations almost broke down entirely three times."[97] Finally, the system could have collapsed with a cosmetic agreement to disagree. If the Move in unison to wide bands had been followed by unilateral behavior such as low-interest rate dashes to growth and competitive devaluations, it would have signaled such an outcome.

It was according to this third scenario that most people interpreted the actual outcome at the time. And it naturally followed in this interpretation that there would be severe implications for the network of norms and institutions surrounding ERM. For example, as *The Economist* put it, "Franco-German relations are embittered, Europe's currencies are in actual or potential disarray; the notion of European economic, monetary, and political union looks, if not nonsensical, certainly illusory. . . . [This] has dealt a severe blow to three pillars . . . European Union, the Franco-German alliance, and the strong franc."[98] But as I have already suggested, that interpretation proved to be off the mark. The ERM did move to 15 percent bands, a considerable change in operational rules for the system. But this was not simply a cosmetic overlay for unilateral action. Nor did the series of crises seem to have more than a short-term impact on the larger network of EU institutions or the French-German relationship at its core.

Consider what member states did in the immediate aftermath of the crisis resolution. Confounding currency, bond, and equity markets across Europe, the French government proclaimed that it would not submit to short-term enticements and reduce interest rates rashly. This was not a low cost move, given

---

[96] *Economist,* 7 August 1993, 24.
[97] Ibid.
[98] Ibid., 21–22.

France's low inflation (which seemed to make interest rate cuts possible) and the continuing evidence of British success in reducing unemployment by rate cuts (which seemed to make it almost necessary, at least politically). Nevertheless, French Minister for European Affairs Alain Lamassoure announced in the wake of August 2 that it was now more important than ever for Paris to resist temptation. In his words, "with wider margins we have more liberty to make mistakes but that is not a reason to make them."[99]

Other governments also maintained commitment to the system. For example, Denmark (arguably now the weakest currency in terms of fundamentals) on August 3 actually raised one-month rates to 25 percent and overnight rates to 250 percent to defend the krone. Market outcomes say something about the way state actions were judged externally. On August 4, despite the new 15 percent bands, most currencies were not very far outside the old narrow bands—the franc sat only a little more than 1 percent below the old floor; the Belgian franc, Spanish peseta, and Portuguese escudo had actually risen against the D-mark. No currency in the system was more than 4 percent below its central rate. The signals were hardly those of a system that had just collapsed.

The Bundesbank's behavior also confounded expectations. Just as the French and others did not make full use of their newfound freedom to cut rates, the Germans did not make use of their similarly new license not to cut. On August 3 the Bundesbank cut its fourteen-day repurchase rate to 6.8 percent and the next day cut its twenty-eight-day repurchase rate to just below the 6.7 percent discount rate. Meanwhile, the Banque de France left its discount rate unchanged. Although the Bundesbank did not cut its discount rate from 6.75 percent in August it soon renewed its gradual but consistent interest rate reductions. The German discount rate dropped fifty basis points in September, and another fifty basis points in October.[100] In February 1994 the Bundesbank cut again, to bring the discount rate to 5.25 percent—which was 3.5 percent lower than it had been a year earlier.

No one can peer into the collective mind of the Bundesbank and say for certain to what extent these moves represent "political" interest rate cuts made for the sake of the EMS. But the data on Germany's domestic economy makes it look as if EMS considerations had to be playing a significant role. Germany was coming out of its recession: excluding the eastern Länder, GDP in the fourth quarter of 1993 had increased 2.6 percent (the best performance in the EU, save Britain). German inflation, meanwhile, was still third highest in the EU—consumer prices rose 3.4 percent in the year, with only Italy and Spain doing worse.

---

[99] *The Economist*, 7 August 1993, 22. Alphandery followed up with a public promise on August 17 that France would not consider reintroducing capital controls in any form (including taxes on foreign exchange holdings).

[100] Tietmayer took over as president from Schlesinger on October 1, 1993.

M3 money supply was up 8.9 percent in 1993, more than double the Bundesbank target. If the Bundesbank was focused solely on its domestic objectives, interest rate cuts under these circumstances would have been at the very least surprising.

By the middle of 1994 Germany's discount rate was at 4.5 percent, a five year low. And ERM currencies were almost all sitting within or close to their previous narrow band boundaries. It was not a long step from there to the revival of discussions about returning to narrow bands, or moving forward to EMU perhaps on a schedule only minimally modified from Maastricht. By the autumn of 1994 EU finance ministers were again talking explicitly about a single currency and were considering ways to loosen (at least in a de facto sense) the Maastricht convergence criteria.[101]

The conversation at the end of 1994 was about how, not whether, to move forward within the framework of the EMS. And while there still may be some wishful thinking taking place on specifics, the overall picture becomes progressively harder to dismiss as cosmetic overlay, particularly as Europe continues to move rapidly toward EMU. As of 1996 there was still much debate and disagreement among member states as to precisely how they ought to proceed, but the fact of the discussion—and its tone—looked much more like evidence of a resilient institution, than of one that has either collapsed or been abandoned.

Understanding the Outcome

Four general reasons might account for why states acted as they did in the wake of the crisis. The most prosaic is simply that central banks held rates up as part of their efforts to rebuild reserves. A second reason is that governments may have been trying to "punish" currency speculators who had made spectacular profits at their expense. Certainly many government officials would have enjoyed that, but it is unlikely that vengeance by itself would have been as strong a motive as the broader political incentives to cut rates. A third reason is that governments acted to save the "essential goods" the ERM provided to them. This makes greater sense, particularly as the passage of time has shown that the states' behavior was not just a matter of "parrots [who] stay sitting in their cages long after the door has been opened."[102] A final reason concerns the nesting of this good and the institutions connected with it, within the broader institutional framework of the EU. It is important to consider how the last two reasons played themselves out.

[101] See for example Gardner 1994, 14.

[102] This quote (which captures much of the contemporary analysis) is from Alison Cottrell (1993, 72), an economist for Midland Global Markets.

First we must take a step backward to emphasize several central features of the drama. The EMS provided to its members a set of valuable goods, at least some of which had characteristic features of a CPR. The combined actions of the German government and the Bundesbank after reunification led basically to an exploitation of the CPR. Opportunism (with or, more probably, without guile) seems to be the driving force behind German behavior here. There is nothing terribly surprising about that, since it seemed possible for the German government to get away with this defection. Kohl and those around him probably believed that they could do what they did in this case without damaging the EMS too badly; and they seem to have believed as well that Germany was on legitimate ground asking others in Europe to assist in paying some of the costs of reunification, if indirectly. The Bundesbank (though ironically an organ of the same "international actor") responded to the government's moves with interest rate policies designed to control inflation in Germany. Another way to put this, is to say that the Bundesbank stuck to its long-standing commitments and sanctioned the German government for its defection. The costs for sanctioning? Quite low in this case, since the Bundesbank was insulated politically and had at least some ambivalent sentiments about full EMU.

Yet the Bundesbank's most fundamental goals—to sustain Germany's hardcore monetary reputation and its anchor role in the EMS—were generally consistent with the goals of the other state actors in the system. There was a strongly shared interest to sustain the CPR in the face of the exogenous shock. The problem came in parceling out among member states the costs and burdens of what was happening in Germany. Here there were substantial differences among states. *But the system did not break down with Germany's defection, even though Germany was the largest and most important actor.* As "defections" go, this one seems to have had a very modest long-term impact on core elements of cooperation.

It becomes easier to understand why that is so if we explicitly drop the implicit notion that all defections are—in behavioral terms—the same. This is not true in Europe. Adding more texture to trigger strategy thinking opens up the issue of compliance in stories about decentralized cooperation. "Graduated sanctions" require lots of information at low cost about what other actors have done and why, as well as about mechanisms for "testing out" over time the quality and reliability of that information and its interpretation. These are useful elaborations on the classic collective action argument about privileged groups, which depend on the "visibility" of actions taken (or not taken) by important actors.[103] Seeing what those actions are, and understanding why they were taken, makes possible the "contingent self-commitment" that underlies voluntary organizations.[104]

[103] See Olson 1965.
[104] See Ostrom 1990, 99.

I believe that this mattered greatly for the maintenance of the EMS under challenge. Two critical beliefs underlie quasi-voluntary compliance: that the system will continue to deliver the goods and that others will contribute a fair share to that end. If someone seems not to be doing so, the relevant question in the EMS becomes, Why not? It is worth asking that question in an environment like the EU. A small number of actors who live together in a densely institutionalized space where monitoring is cheap and easy, communication equally so, and low-cost mechanisms for negotiation are available, may find it cost effective to differentiate among defections according to intention. Some violations are the result of "opportunism with guile"; others may represent disagreement over management decisions or the quality of existing rules. This seems particularly likely when external shocks plunge the system into uncharted territory offering unforeseen temptations to states with strong reputations for "following the rules."

Differentiating between these kinds of defections should matter greatly to member states in a voluntary organization. In this specific case, other states' interpretations of Germany's behavior were critical. The essential difference between my argument and the alternative argument, which portrays Germany as a hegemon and everyone else as simply a responder to its hegemony, is how member states interpret the intentions behind Germany's defection and how that modifies their expectations for the future. If other states expect Germany to be an exploitative hegemon, a system based on quasi-voluntary compliance should break down.[105] It breaks down because beliefs change: members no longer expect that the system to which they are contributing will deliver the collective goods they want, and they no longer presume that they can rely on others to contribute their fair share—certainly not Germany, but even other countries come to be seen as unreliable.

This didn't happen. Surely, the popular media (particularly in Britain) and some political elites raised the spectacular spectre of German exploitive hegemony, but this faded rapidly. In retrospect this looks more like tabloid pandering and domestic political posturing than mainstream or widely accepted views of events particularly among elites. If underlying beliefs had really changed, member states might have (indeed, they logically should have) withheld contributions to the system, as they easily could have done under the 15 percent bands. And it seems unlikely that there would have been a revival of serious discussions as early as 1994 about moving forward with some modified version of the Maastricht EMU scheme.

The question now needs to be pushed back one stage: Why is it that interpretations of German behavior and expectations about the future that could support a continued general compliance equilibrium were sustained? Several things made

---

[105] I am borrowing the phrase "exploitative hegemon" from David Spiro, professor of political science at the University of Arizona.

an important difference—some of which are captured in design principles for voluntary organizations.

K-Group Logic

K-group logic, which depends in part on two design principles (clearly defined boundaries and monitoring arrangements), is a piece of the explanation. EMS member states make up a relatively small group whose actions are highly visible one to another. A country like Sweden, linked de facto but not de jure to the EMS, was left to its own devices when its currency came under pressure; member states were not. The actions of both the German government and the Bundesbank were highly visible to their partners in the system, as were many of the motivating forces that lay behind those actions. Other governments knew and understood the unprecedented pressures Kohl faced with reunification. They later criticized him for faulty management decisions and for indulging in wishful thinking. But at the time that Germany was making its choices, leaders of other states recognized (at least implicitly) Kohl's dilemmas.

And while Bonn's original econometric predictions about the costs of reunification were commonly thought to be too optimistic, the real width of the discrepancy would turn out to surprise almost everyone, not just the Germans. Other EMS members saw that the Bundesbank and the German government had "split" and that their actions had combined to produce the problem. While not exactly an inadvertent defection, neither was it the strategic opportunistic move of a calculatingly guileful actor. Reunification was a unique historical shock that confronted Germany with a dire emergency and a strong temptation to pawn off some costs, and the crisis, took place in the context of real value disagreements over the quality and appropriateness of operational rules in the ERM. These are exactly the conditions of defection that voluntary organizations are supposed to be able to survive.

The History, Structure, and Legitimacy of Extant Institutions

Supporting this logic was a densely institutionalized environment in the EU carrying norms and "ways of doing things" that proved critical in the management of the crisis. Another design principle for voluntary organizations—congruence with "local conditions"—meant in this case that the EMS would have to be structured such that it could respond to the power and size realities and changing world-market conditions that impacted on the process of monetary cooperation. Plainly, the Bundesbank had to be able to get a lot of what it wanted, and it did get a lot, but by no means all. It did not get a "prophylactic realignment" at the outset of GEMU. It did not get an early realignment at the start of the crisis. It did not even get a realignment on Friday, July 30, when it was hemorrhaging money to save the franc solely in order to buy time for the weekend meeting of the Monetary Committee.

The rules of the EMS would necessarily have to change in ways that would keep the Bundesbank on board. That is not the same as Germany writing the rules and everyone else following along. Collective choice arrangements in the EMS allowed all member states affected by the operational rules to participate in modifying the rules—first through the Monetary Committee and ultimately in the Council of Ministers. Effective power to make decisions is not shared equally, of course, but if the system is not working correctly all participants have a voice in how to change it. Certainly France and Germany were the central figures in the debate that produced the "15 percent solution." But other countries were able to speak their preferences. They were also able to form coalitions that, for example, blocked de facto the original French proposal to let the D-mark float.

This is important because operational rules need to be changed over time as markets evolve. This is expected. The congruence of any real-world institution with "local conditions" is not a unique resolution to *the* problem. *The* problem changes. The EMS needs to learn, as it did from the experience of the snake and later from the perverse incentives in Maastricht, what kinds of operational rules might be workable and what kinds of rules might not be. What seems important in this process is that the learning be mainly of a collective sort. For legitimacy to be sustained over time, key actors would need to learn similar lessons about the sources of operational failures—in part to support assumptions about each other's intentions underlying the behavior they observe. Put aside the immediate rhetorical backlash against the Bundesbank and the "Anglo-Saxons" and the "speculators." With passing time it became more clear that member states shared a substantial degree of consensus on what went wrong (as well as what went right) in 1992–93.

The Bundesbank acted in ways that were consistent both with its mandate and its established historical track-record. It more or less successfully walked a very fine line between the domestic and international demands of its anti-inflationary, nonpoliticized credibility concerns, and the eminently political Europe-oriented demands of being the anchor currency in the ERM. Germany made progressive interest rate reductions—albeit more slowly than some others wanted—that did allow rates to fall, gradually, around Europe. The maintenance of momentum towards a low-inflation recovery throughout the EU in 1994 could be read as a piece of evidence vindicating the Bundesbank's approach.[106] The system as a whole got the broad realignment it needed. Stronger

---

[106] Of course, there were many other reasons for this recovery, and I do not claim that Bundesbank behavior was either necessary or sufficient for that to happen; only that it was a contributing factor.

currencies on fundamentals (like the franc) moved back toward realistic valuations. And core countries within the system resisted the very substantial political incentives to use the freedom of 15 percent bands to lower interest rates and make a short term dash for growth and jobs.

All around the system, what seemed remarkable was the high level of continued compliance with norms. Partly in consequence, the broader goal of EMU in Europe returned to the forefront of the political agenda with surprising speed. And while there is still disagreement over the details of what comes next, there is much less disagreement that something will in fact come next—that is, that EMU of some kind is imminent even if not precisely on the Maastricht timetable and/or the Maastricht terms.

The actions of Italy and Britain in the first phase of the crisis are the major exceptions to this point. Italy's September 1992 devaluation was worked out in a bilateral deal with the Germans; the British withdrawal later that month was unilateral. In neither case was the Monetary Committee or any other EC institution involved (although both moves were later "agreed to" or "taken notice of" by the Committee). There may have been extenuating circumstances and/or misunderstandings in the Italian case that would attenuate in the long run the impact of this breach.[107] That is less the case for Britain. Italy soon expressed its desire to rejoin the ERM as soon as conditions were appropriate, and did rejoin in December 1996. Britain took a very different tack, arguing that the ERM must change (in unspecified ways) before it could once again consider membership.

But if my interpretation in this chapter is valid, the shoe is at least partially on the other foot. It is Britain that must change more so than the ERM or the plans for EMU in order for that country to reenter the system. What would matter is other states' interpretation of Britain's motives and strategy that led to noncompliance. A future government might try to stress the effort and costs London incurred to try to bolster the pound within the ERM. But that has not yet happened as of January 1997.

I offered in this chapter an interpretation of events in the 1992–93 ERM crisis that contrasts with traditional interpretations driven by collective action theory or intergovernmental bargaining perspectives on European integration. I portray a cooperative outcome where an institution undergoes change successfully. I hope the interpretation is sufficiently compelling to demonstrate the potential of

---

[107] Norman et al., in their 11 December 1992 *Financial Times* exposé, focus on the difficult decisions facing Jean-Claude Trichet (director of the tresor and, at the time, also chair of the EC Monetary Committee) and his possible errors of judgment, although they point out that under the circumstances "Trichet's behavior accorded with the letter of the Community's arcane [sic] rulebook."

this kind of argument (and the broader agenda from which it is drawn) to open up modified lines of debate about international politics in Europe and particularly the importance of nesting.

Regime arguments in principle allow for a great deal of cooperative behavior on the basis of shared norms, principles, rules, and decision-making procedures. For this reason, it is beside the point to observe that nothing in this story is inconsistent with regime theory. A better question is to ask to what extent the kind and level of cooperative behavior seen in this chapter exceeds or is more elaborate than the standard expectations that we typically associate with regimes. It is to some degree a matter of judgment about the descriptive and analytical utility of concepts, and thus I don't claim to settle the matter but only to justify my position.

Regimes that are intricately nested one within another should support higher levels of cooperation than those that are not. The EU is certainly a set of nested regimes, but that is a minimum description. The "institutional environment" concept goes several steps further, to where technical/efficiency criteria and power considerations—even traded off and logrolled between sets of regimes in different issue-areas—are less important than are standards of legitimacy and norm-based procedures.

The EU is made up of many potential decision-making fora where there is almost continual contact between states at many different levels. Looking at how issues get tracked into decision-making channels would be one way to start differentiating nested regimes from institutional environments. How important are strategic games played out by state actors who try to channel crisis management decision making into that forum where their autonomous, parochial preferences are likely to be best served?

Nested regime dynamics show up most forcefully in the central importance of French-German bilateral negotiations and arrangements. Certainly these two states went extremely far with each other in making costly commitments and breaking precedents to retain monetary cooperation between them. That monetary link, nested deeply within the Franco-German political relationship, was in turn central to the future of Maastricht. Monetary union was the most carefully prepared and most completely laid out part of the treaty, in essence its heart and soul. And because the EC was at the same time looking impotent elsewhere (particularly in Yugoslavia) the burden of political symbolism falling on the ERM was great.

Destruction of ERM would have demolished the Maastricht plan for EMU. On technical criteria, not everyone thought that would be a bad thing. Many Britons, some Germans, and others were not enthusiastic for monetary union of any sort. And even some who in principle supported monetary union believed that the current system and scheme for moving forward was not the best way to bring it about. On that view, destroying ERM would give a golden opportunity to start all over and do it right.

Technical criteria aside, that point neglects the political hurdles that stand in the way. Institutional environments set standards of legitimacy and ways of doing things that are connected to the normative foundations of existing institutions. The notion of reconstructing French-German monetary links on a different institutional base runs against the basic logic of that environment even more than it neglects transaction costs and friction that exist in an environment of nested regimes. The possibility of a "mini-EMU" made up of a smaller core group of countries that excluded others runs against that logic as well. The EU is, in reality, already practicing "variable geometry" through opt-outs, dispensations, and the like. But this can only go so far. The primary limiting factor remains the network of existing institutions and what they establish as legitimate.

What happened in the 1992–93 crisis was institutional evolution of the kind envisioned by Douglass North—marginal change to adapt to changing conditions. And while core relationships were maintained and even strengthened in the process, that did not happen at the expense of the norms and standards of legitimacy that apply to the EU as a whole. France and Germany could have gone ahead and dropped the broader scope of European integration to save their bilateral ties. They still could do so. The range of discussions over forging a "hard core"—more precisely, over what that would mean—show that this kind of option is not outside the scope of cognitive possibilities. But if my argument here is correct, it is outside the scope of political possibilities set by the logic of nested institutions.

REFERENCES

Aggarwal, Vinod K., 1985. *Liberal Protectionism: The International Politics of Organized Textile Trade* (Berkeley: University of California Press).

Alesina, Alberto, and Vittorio Grilli, 1993. "On the Feasibility of a One-Speed or Multi-Speed European Monetary Union." *Economics and Politics* 5 (July).

Balladur, Edouard, 1987. "The EMS: Advance or Face Retreat." *Financial Times,* 17 June.

Balls, Edward, 1993. "The Delicate Art of Persuasion." *Financial Times,* 4 August.

Barber, Lionel, and Norman Peter, 1992. "Monetary Tragedy of Errors." *Financial Times,* 11 December.

Bates, Robert H., ed., 1988. *Toward a Political Economy of Development: A Rational Choice Perspective* (Berkeley: University of California Press).

Buchan, David, and William Dawkins, 1992. "How the French Fought to Save the Franc." *Financial Times,* 20 November.

Cameron, David, 1995. "Transnational Relations and the Development of the European Economic and Monetary Union." In Thomas Risse-Kapper, ed., *Bringing Transnational Relations Back In.* (Cambridge: Cambridge University Press).

Dawkins, William, 1992. "French Weaponry Secured Win in Battle for Franc." *Financial Times*, 3 November.

Eckstein, Harry, 1966. *Division and Cohesion in Democracy: A Study of Norway* (Princeton, N.J.: Princeton University Press).

Eichengreen, Barry, and Charles Wyplosz, 1986. "The Unstable EMS." *Brookings Papers on Economic Activity* 1.

Emminger, Otmar, 1986. *D-Mark, Dollar, Wahrungskrisen* (Stuttgart: Deutsche Verlags-Anstalt).

Frieden, Jeffery, 1993. "Economic Liberalization and the Politics of European Monetary Integration" (July), Manuscript.

Funabashi, Yoichi, 1989. *1944—Managing the Dollar: From the Plaza to the Louvre,* 2d ed. (Washington, D.C.: Institute for International Economics).

Gardner, David, 1994. "End of Recession Revives Single Currency Hopes." *Financial Times*, 12 September.

Garrett, Geoffrey, 1993. "The Politics of the Maastricht Treaty." *Economics and Politics* 5 (July).

Goodman, John B., 1992. *Monetary Sovereignty: The Politics of Central Banking in Western Europe.* (Ithaca, N.Y.: Cornell University Press).

Koeune, Jean-Claude, and Jaques van Ypersele, 1985. *The European Monetary System: Origins, Operation and Outlook* (London: St. James Press).

Levi, Margaret, 1988. *Of Rule and Revenue* (Berkeley: University of California Press).

Ludlow, Peter, 1982. *The Making of the European Monetary System: A Case Study of the Politics of the European Community* (Boston: Butterworth Scientific).

Marsh, David, and Peter Marsh, 1993. "Lessons of Europe's Currency Turmoil." *Financial Times*, 30 April.

Olson, Mancur, 1965. *The Logic of Collective Action* (Cambridge: Harvard Press).

Ostrom, Elinor, 1990: *Governing the Commons: The Evolution of Institutions for Collective Action* (New York: Cambridge University Press).

Sachs, Jeffrey, and Charles Wyplosz, 1986. "The Economic Consequences of President Mitterrand." *Economic Policy* 2 (April).

Shepsle, Kenneth A., 1989. "Studying Institutions: Some Lessons from the Rational Choice Approach." *Journal of Theoretical Politics* 1, no.2.

Story, Jonathan, 1988. "The Launching of the EMS: An Analysis of Change in Foreign Economic Policy." *Political Studies* 36.

Tsoukalis, Loukas, 1977. *The Politics and Economics of European Monetary Integration* (London: Allen and Unwin).

Weber, Steven, 1994. "Origins of the European Bank for Reconstruction and Development." *International Organization* 48 (Winter).

CHAPTER THREE

An Empty Nest? Reconciling European Security Institutions in the Bosnian Crisis

BEVERLY CRAWFORD

The end of the Cold War, the Soviet threat, and the Soviet Union itself left Europe with the task of constructing a new security order. The absence of a clear post–Cold War security doctrine, doubts about NATO's continued usefulness, isolationist mutterings in the United States, and various efforts to breathe life into dormant but potentially competing institutions led many observers to predict institutional chaos in Europe's security future, chaos that would set European nations against each other and draw the United States and Russia into European security conflicts.[1] These observers compared the present period to the shifting, ad hoc alliances and ineffective collective security arrangements that bred suspicion and fear in the interwar period. Others interpreted efforts to create regional security arrangements as a threat to the Atlantic Community and to consensus building at the international level.[2] Still other analysts have suggested that the post–Cold War institutional arrangements in European security are surprisingly robust and compatible with one another and with the United Nations, suggesting a new "division of labor" similar to Aggarwal's substantive linkage forms rather than a competitive struggle among institutions and their member states.[3]

I gratefully acknowledge the comments made by Vinod Aggarwal, Beth Kier, Lise Svenson, and Steven Weber. This paper could not have been completed without the diligent research assistance of Nick Biziouras.

[1] See Mearsheimer 1990 and 1994.
[2] For these arguments see Betts 1992.
[3] See Weber 1992, 360–95, and Aggarwal, chapter 1, this volume.

What are the dominant forces shaping the strength, nature, and scope of the post–Cold War European security regime? Is the emerging European security order characterized by cooperation among European nations within international institutions? Are those institutions compatible with one another and with global efforts to cooperate on security issues? Or is Europe developing an independent regional security regime that is increasingly distinct from the Atlantic community? Alternatively, are security regimes weakening in Europe in the aftermath of the Cold War, reflecting growing competition and discord among European states with regard to the requirements for security in Europe?

To provide partial answers to these questions, this paper examines the evolving Western response to the war in the former Yugoslavia. This war proved to be crucial in initiating both cooperation and discord in European security issues. It was the first war on European soil since 1945. When it began in 1991, it was hailed in European policy circles as the "hour of Europe," an occasion for the European Community (as it was known at the time) to bolster and hone its "common foreign and security policy" and act, through European institutions independently of the Atlantic community, to solve a regional conflict.[4] When regional institutions failed to resolve the crisis and the war widened to Bosnia, drawing in a wider array of multilateral institutions, many policymakers saw it as a test of "the willingness of Europeans and Americans to adjust their Cold War political and security institutions and missions to the changing geo-strategic circumstances in and around Europe."[5] Indeed, the case would determine the extent to which Europe would act independently in security issues, the extent to which unilateral or multilateral responses to security problems would be chosen, and the extent to which European security institutions would be "nested" with global institutions. As Aggarwal argues, this is the need to either create new institutions or modify existing ones.[6]

Students of international politics have argued that the study of a particular crisis can shed light on the conditions for international cooperation and the conditions that undermine it. Some positions taken to resolve a particular crisis lend themselves more easily to cooperation than others and can either provide building blocks for future cooperation or tear down those blocks and weaken the institutional basis for cooperation. Initial bargains to resolve particular substantive issues will create the conditions that constrain and direct future bargains or halt cooperation altogether.[7]

The end of the Cold War and the beginning of the war in Yugoslavia provided the initial impetus for a set of bargains among European states, Russia, and the United States, that would directly impact their odds of security cooperation. In

---

[4] See the *Economist*, 22 July 1995, 48.
[5] See *New York Times*, 2 December 1994, A4.
[6] See chapter 1, this volume.
[7] Sandoltz and Zysman 1989, 95–128.

this paper, I trace those bargains and their impact on the strength, nature, scope, and compatibility of security institutions in Europe. Indeed, as this drama unfolds, we shall see that states could choose to act unilaterally or within multilateral institutions, that the institutions themselves had distinct and sometimes conflicting objectives, and that their members, not surprisingly, used various institutions as both shields and weapons in their political battles with one another. I divide the case into two bargaining rounds: the set of decisions that led to the recognition of Croatia in 1991 and bargains struck to end the conflict in Bosnia that began in April 1992.

The argument can be stated succinctly: When the war began, European Community members decided to attempt a resolution to this regional conflict alone, without the involvement of global institutions or the United States. European institutions, however, were unprepared to act decisively to mediate a diplomatic solution. In particular, the norms guiding multilateral responses were conflicting and weak. In that environment and driven by domestic political forces, Germany took the unilateral step of recognizing Croatia as a sovereign state.

The recognition of Croatia had three important effects. First, it provided a warning to the international community of the dangers of acting unilaterally; at every subsequent decision point, states made compromise decisions within international institutions to preserve their security and foreign policy cooperation in order to prevent each other from intervening on opposing sides in the conflict. What Germany saw as a substantive link between the right for self-determination and international recognition, other countries saw as a tactical move that was based solely on power calculations.

Secondly, the recognition of Croatia and the failure of EC efforts to provide a diplomatic solution to the conflict widened international involvement and brought in the United States and the United Nations and expanded the effort to coordinate activities. Ironically then, Germany's unilateral move in the first round of the conflict led to the strengthening of incentives for multilateral cooperation and the coordination of European institutions with NATO and the UN. That is, it led to more intense cooperation (perhaps even institutional cooperation) as well as an institutional division of labor. Regional institutions, however, were not nested within global organizations. (See table 1.1, chapter 1, this volume.)

Third, the recognition of Croatia by the international community led to the recognition of Bosnia as an independent state and to a widening of the war; this further limited the ability of international institutions to take sides in what was defined by the recognition of Bosnia as a "civil war." This limited the international community's goals to: (a) working toward a diplomatic solution that would uphold the value of tolerance in the form of preserving a multiethnic community in Bosnia, (b) attempting to moderate the fighting and end it through diplomacy, and (c) protecting human rights and providing humanitarian aid.

In pursuit of these three goals, the overwhelming norm that guided their effort was the preservation of multilateralism and not the preservation of Bosnia. And for the United States, the goal was to strengthen NATO. When pursuit of the three-pronged substantive solution to the Bosnia crisis threatened to undermine multilateralism or when goals conflicted with each other, the great powers always chose a strategy that would preserve their cooperation over a strategy that would effectively halt the bloodshed and protect human rights.

The policies constructed to press liberal values upon the belligerents and bring about a diplomatic resolution to the war were also weak and conflicting. Efforts to implement those policies failed as long as western states were unwilling to use military force to force the belligerents to the bargaining table, keep them apart, and make aid available. The policies necessary to implement one goal undermined others and weakened the effort as a whole. The belligerents tried to undermine multilateralism. As multilateral efforts failed, domestic pressures to pursue alternative policies exacerbated the problems of implementation. These pressures, particularly in the United States, again raised incentives to reach a negotiated solution in a multilateral framework, lest domestic forces undermine international cooperation.

Despite the fact that states chose to act within multilateral institutions rather than unilaterally or bilaterally, and despite the fact that institutions were largely able to coordinate their efforts, the weakness of the "meta-regime"—the norms guiding multilateral activities—made institutional nesting less important in this case than in other cases. Although a strong commitment to multilateral cooperation helped to end the war and left a set of institutions well positioned to coordinate their activities in the future, it is not yet clear whether these institutions are guided by coherent norms. In the terms of Aggarwal's framework, an institutional division of labor was evident in this case, but the meta-regime was weak. Indeed, with only a commitment to multilateralism, the participants could not agree on a nested security architecture. In the end, the best they could do was to develop a division of labor. If the actors do not have a cognitive consensus on a common definition of the European security problem or one that will allow them to agree on an appropriate institutional hierarchy, an empty institutional nesting structure will be constructed.

Round I: The Beginning of the War

In April 1990 the ultranationalist Croatian Democratic Union (HDZ) won Croatia's first democratic elections since 1945.[8] Croatia's new HDZ president,

---

[8] See Crawford 1996, 485–521.

Franjo Tudjman, immediately refused minority rights to the 600,000 strong Serb population, and the first constitution that he implemented violated the principles on minority rights established by the Conference on Security and Cooperation in Europe (CSCE).[9] When Tudjman refused to disassociate Croatia from the fascist Ustashe regime, local Serbs demanded that Serb-dominated territory be taken out of Croatia. On June 25, 1991, Croatia and Slovenia declared independence from Yugoslavia. The Yugoslav National Army (JNA) was called out to prevent the secession of these two states, but both states resisted, and fighting broke out.[10]

What follows is a stylized description of the rationale behind the four choices available to the European Community, the United States, and the United Nations when hostilities broke out. Each was expected to have different implications for the future direction and strength of EC foreign policy cooperation, and each would presumably have a different impact on the odds of peace in Yugoslavia.

Two procedural outcomes were available. At one extreme, the EC could have decided *not* to act jointly at all; it could simply have done nothing, and the United Nations was the likely body to mediate the conflict. Indeed, the EC had never acted independently to resolve a regional military conflict outside its borders. At the other extreme, the EC could take an active, independent role in regional conflict resolution. The crisis presented an important opportunity to strengthen policy coordination of the European Political Cooperation (EPC, now renamed the Common Foreign and Security Policy, on CFSP) and to engage in an independent European conflict resolution effort. A cooperative response to the crisis was a logical extension of the general commitment to coordinate and unify policy in preparation for the signing of the upcoming Maastricht Treaty, which would carve out an institutionalized realm for European foreign and security policy cooperation.

Two substantive alternatives for a common policy presented themselves. The first was a joint effort to preserve Yugoslavia. The rationale was both legal and political: to maintain the territorial integrity of an established state and to preserve the status quo of the international order in the aftermath of communism's collapse. Post-communist states were actively participating in reshaping European political and security institutions, and their disintegration threatened to weaken and discredit those institutions. Particularly since these states were moving toward democracy, self-determination via fragmentation would mean a loss of control by new democratizing governments and could potentially raise the specter of nationalist rivalries in Europe again.

---

[9] See Plestina 1992 and Hayden 1992, 31–62.
[10] See Glenny 1992.

The alternative was an EC policy designed to speed the disintegration of Yugoslavia by jointly recognizing republics demanding independence and to then help negotiate a peace settlement. The supporting argument was that the right of self-determination had historically implied the creation of local and responsive government as a counter to imperial domination. It was a right enshrined in the UN decolonization practices and implied in the UN Charter.[11] This option would effectively ignore the requirement for self-determination on the part of minorities in seceding states.

Given the EC's weight in the diplomatic community, choosing this option would transform the war into an international one between states, as opposed to an internal conflict between factions within an established and legally recognized state, thus widening the conflict resolution effort to include not only the EC but the United Nations and the United States. If Croatia and Slovenia were granted recognition, and if the JNA continued to fight on Croatian soil, Yugoslavia would then be identified as the aggressor. The international community could then impose sanctions and use other means to deter aggression. The test would then be how European institutions would coordinate their activities with one another and with the United Nations.

With regard to procedural options, the EC chose to act jointly; its members were eager to build an independent foreign policy and security capability in Europe after the Cold War; with regard to substantive options, there was a broad consensus on preserving Yugoslavia. Domestic concerns in European states also influenced this choice: many separatist movements in EC member states had called upon the principle of self-determination to justify claims for varying degrees of autonomy, and therefore granting recognition on the basis of self-determination was a sensitive issue within the EC. Catalonia had asserted its independence within Europe, and France and Belgium were facing similar problems with regions that had pressed for more independence. Further, it was widely believed that recognizing the right of self-determination without securing the protection of minority rights was imprudent and unjustifiable. And the granting of collective rights and autonomy to any minority group ran counter to the dominant liberal principle protecting individual rights enshrined in EC law.[12] In essence, there was a cognitive consensus within the epistemic community in the Western powers about the soundness of the policy.

In early 1991, therefore, the EC promised association and possible membership to a *united* Yugoslavia, hoping that this "carrot" would help the presidents of the six Yugoslav republics reach a peaceful agreement. On the day before Croatia

[11] The role of the United Nations in decolonization was based on the principle of national self-determination. See Claude 1971, 481–82 and Pomerance 1982.

[12] These two reasons for agreement on the first option were given by four senior EC officials interviewed for this project by the author in Brussels on 17–19 May 1993.

and Slovenia declared independence, the EC offered Yugoslavia a five-year, 807 million ECU loan. And when fighting broke out, it took the position that a looser Yugoslav federation should be negotiated among the six republics and insisted that Croatia and Slovenia suspend further steps toward independence. It threatened to cut $1 billion in aid to Yugoslavia until peace was restored.[13]

The Community also took active steps to mediate the military conflict when it began. The foreign ministers of Italy, Luxembourg, and the Netherlands negotiated the "Brioni Accord" with Serbia, stipulating the withdrawal of all Yugoslav troops from Slovenia—effectively ending the war there—but left open the question of Croatian independence because Serbia would not agree. EC ministers were able to negotiate an agreement between Slovenia and Croatia to suspend their independence declarations for three months if the JNA would withdraw its troops.

On July 3, CSCE officials requested that the EC send an observer mission to Zagreb to monitor the agreement and monitor a hoped-for cease-fire agreement. This was at the request of the Soviet Union, which preferred that the CSCE take a back seat to the EC with regard to this crisis, fearing that CSCE involvement would serve as a precedent for interference in the Baltics.[14] EC foreign ministers took up the challenge and agreed to establish a monitoring mission.[15] The European Monitoring Mission (EMM), a "first" in European Political Cooperation, was born, suggesting that the crisis was indeed helping to forge new levels of policy coordination and institutionalization and helping to create new practices in support of dispute resolution in Europe. In order to compel the warring parties to accept binding mediation on the part of the EC, EC members agreed that they would jointly suspend arms sales and economic aid to Yugoslavia.[16] Later, the UN joined the arms embargo, which would become a bone of contention when the war spread to Bosnia one year later.

But Germany was already urging the EPC to change course. Hans Dietrich Genscher, Germany's Foreign Minister, declared that continued cooperation with Yugoslavia should be dependent on the cessation of the threat and use of force. He argued that "Serbian aggression" (identified by Germany as the cause of the conflict for the first time) could not be tolerated.[17] At a July 5 EC foreign ministers meeting, Genscher argued that the EC should declare "that the peoples of Yugoslavia [should] decide their fate themselves," and that the Community should consider joint recognition of both Croatia and Slovenia.[18]

---

[13] Cited in Krieger 1994, 30, see also Cviic 1993, 74.
[14] See *Der Spiegel*, 8 July 1991, 128.
[15] *Declaration on Yugoslavia*, 82d EPC Ministerial Meeting, the Hague, 10 July 1991.
[16] *Frankfurter Allgemeine Zeitung*, 10 July 1991, 5.
[17] See *Washington Post*, 2 July 1991, A16.
[18] "Genscher will einheitliche EG-Politik," *Frankfurter Allgemeine Zeitung*, 6 July 1991, 6.

Genscher's views thus initiated a fierce debate over the meaning of self-determination and on the consequences of translating that principle into a policy of diplomatic recognition of those regions in Europe who declared a desire to become independent states. For Germany, the concept of self-determination had acquired a specific meaning in the domestic context. The idea of self-determination had long been an important principle in German policy toward the German Democratic Republic (GDR). The principle of self-determination constituted the core of the West German "national tradition" in foreign policy, that is the core of what can be termed its foreign policy political culture.[19] It was also a key element of a policy that urged other Western states to accept that principle with regard to East Germany. The rhetoric of self-determination had been the core of the Christian Democriatic Union (CDU)'s winning strategy in the 1990 elections. To the extent that Germany had an independent foreign policy after World War II and before unification, it was the pursuit of the German national interest in self-determination for the people of the GDR.[20] Indeed, it can be argued that self-determination had become a "norm" in German foreign policy as part of a dominant world view.[21] With regard to the crisis in Yugoslavia, the rhetoric used to justify Germany's position suggests that politicians easily and consciously linked the recent East German victory for self-determination and unification with the aspirations of the Croatian and Slovenian people for independence from Yugoslavia. Volker Ruehe, then the CDU's General Secretary, later to become Germany's Defense Minister, argued that it was not defensible to apply a different yardstick to Yugoslavia "when we achieved the unity and freedom of our country through the right of self-determination."[22] Social Democratic Party (SPD) spokesmen argued that this right was the basis of all international law. Thus, Germany must support recognition as the best policy to implement this principle.[23]

It is logical to ask why the principle of "self-determination" in domestic German rhetoric was focused only on Croatians and Slovenians and not on the Serb population living in Croatia. One-third of the Serb population lived outside the territory of Serbia, and as the narrative suggests, those in Croatia were subject to human rights violations.[24] French and British diplomats were

[19] On the importance of these traditions in general see Eichenberg and Dalton 1993, 514.

[20] For details on the various incarnations of this policy see Haftendorn 1983, Hanrieder 1989, and Paterson 1992.

[21] On the role of norms and how they set standards for behavior and provide a way to organize action, see Katzenstein 1991, 3–4.

[22] *Washington Post*, 2 July 1991, A16.

[23] *Der Spiegel*, 8 July 1991, 128–29.

[24] Part of the explanation for the absence of minority rights for Serbs under the 1990 Croatian constitution lay in the provisions of the 1974 Yugoslav constitution that were carried over to the constitution of Croatia. That Yugoslav constitution recognized nations and nationalities; nations were

keenly aware of the vulnerability of Serbs living outside the Republic of Serbia. Indeed, an important justification for the creation of Yugoslavia as a state in 1918 had been the principle of self-determination: the right of all Serbs, as well as Croats and Slovenes to live in a single state. For Serbs, the alternative had been to create a "Greater Serbia" which would have left Croatia under imperial domination. Thus, in 1918, Croatian political elites agreed to join Yugoslavia. France and Britain had supported the creation of Yugoslavia for various geopolitical reasons; part of the support had been an acceptance of the Serbian claim to the right of self-determination. Now again, officials in the French and British foreign ministries believed that to realize this principle, the preservation of Yugoslavia was preferable to the alternative, the creation of a "Greater Serbia."[25]

Germany, on the other hand, had not been a party to the creation of either the first or the second Yugoslavia; unlike the case of France and Britain, there was no tradition in German foreign policy of acceptance for Serb self-determination. Nor had there been an assessment of the best means by which this principle could be implemented.[26]

Genscher also believed that a common policy on recognition would internationalize the dispute, allowing it to be taken up in the United Nations. With this option, the focus of mediation and conflict resolution would move from the European Community to the United Nations and bring in the United States and NATO. Pursuit of this alternative would thus indicate continued commitment to Atlanticism and a preference for international as opposed to independent regional practices of mediation and conflict resolution. The diplomatic recognition of Croatia and Slovenia would represent continuity in the pursuit transatlantic political and security cooperation and recognize the constraints of international law on external intervention.

Other EC members, however, balked at this position, claiming that recognition would lead to "more war and bloodshed."[27] A compromise was reached:

---

groups that had their own republics: Serbia, Croatia, and Slovenia. Nationalities were minorities (Hungarians and Albanians) that did not have their own republic in Yugoslavia. Nationalities received human rights protection under the Yugoslav constitution, but nations did not. Thus Serbs living outside of Serbia or Croatians living outside of Croatia could not invoke constitutional minority rights guarantees.

[25] In addition, Tito's Yugoslavia had been an important ally against Hitler, and Yugoslavia had played an important role in Cold War rhetoric. For details on French and British policy in the Balkans see Nere 1975, Lamborn 1991, Bartlett 1989. The best source on British policy toward the Balkans is Seeton-Watson 1967 and the best source on early French policy is Keiger 1983. The most important general source is Jelavich 1983. On French and British policies in the postwar period, see Pavlowitch 1989.

[26] See Axt 1994, 358.

[27] See *Frankluper Allgement Zeitung*, 10 July 1991, 5.

the EC would support a loose Yugoslav confederation if the JNA pulled back, however, it would recognize Croatia and Slovenia if the JNA continued to fight. In order to compel the warring parties to accept binding mediation, EC members jointly suspended arms sales and economic aid to Yugoslavia. In late July Kohl invited Tudjman to a meeting in Germany—the first European leader to do so—but he cautioned him not to count on recognition soon because Germany was bound to the common EC policy.[28]

In Croatia, however, the bloodshed continued, and Tudjman walked out on high-level peace talks on July 22. Because the JNA refused to leave Croatia, Genscher pressed the EPC to make good on its threat of diplomatic recognition.[29] In preparation for an August 6 ministerial meeting with Yugoslav representatives, Genscher argued that representatives from Slovenia and Croatia should also be invited. Other EPC members refused, claiming that as long as EC policy was the preservation of Yugoslav integrity, only Yugoslav representatives should come to the meeting. Losing the argument, Genscher demanded that the EC place economic sanctions on Serbia and that recognition for Croatia and Slovenia be placed on the meeting's agenda.[30]

The meeting, however, was a great disappointment. EC members moved neither closer to the German position, nor closer to their goal of preserving Yugoslavia. The issue of recognition was not broached, but EC aid to Yugoslavia was frozen. The EPC had earlier requested that the Western European Union (WEU) provide potential military options to back up the EC's mediation efforts. But at the meeting, the WEU reported that it lacked a mandate to send troops outside the NATO area. A cease-fire agreement was reached, but with no enforcement, it would be broken in less than two weeks.

Clearly the EC was losing in its effort to preserve a united Yugoslavia. Another blow fell after the August 19 Soviet coup, when most republics of the USSR declared their independence. As EC members quickly extended recognition to them, the rationale for *not* recognizing Croatia and Slovenia weakened.[31] Furthermore, it was during this period that public officials began to talk about "divisible" peace in Europe. NATO's official policy statements paid lip service to Europe's geographic unity and interdependence, but expressed reservations about intervention in post-communist conflicts. The war in Yugoslavia was not expected to widen,[32] and when it became clear that core national interests of EC members were not threatened, its salience was reduced.

[28] See *Los Angeles Times* 27 July 1991, A3.

[29] See *New York Times* 29 July 1991, A3.

[30] See *Frankluper Allgement Zeitung*, 30 July 1991, 2; and 6 August 1991, 1.

[31] For a discussion of the war and negotiations see *The Times* (London), 7 September 1991.

[32] See *NATO Press Service*, press communiques M-1 (91) 42, 6 June 1991; M-2 (91) 60, 21 August 1991; and S-1 (91) 86, 8 November 1991.

In September the EC sponsored another European "first": a European peace conference at the Hague. But Croatia and Slovenia declared secession from Yugoslavia on the very day the conference began, and on the second day, Macedonia voted for independence.[33] Then, for the first time, the EC asked the WEU to serve directly as its military arm, and requested that it develop options to strengthen the EC's cease-fire monitoring capability. But the WEU was stymied by internal disagreements and failed to do so.[34] And in the midst of the conference, Kohl raised the possibility of Germany's unilateral diplomatic recognition of Croatia and Slovenia in a widely publicized visit to the United States.[35]

But on October 1, Serbia and Montenegro excluded the other republics from federal leadership, and EC officials admitted that these two republics could no longer be regarded as the legitimate successor to Yugoslavia.[36] Nonetheless, the EC continued in its effort to find a peaceful resolution to the conflict. The EPC declared that "the principles of the CSCE with regard to borders, minority rights, and political pluralism" guided its approach, and any outcome that violated those principles was unacceptable. It would not accept a unilateral change of borders.[37] On November 8 it imposed economic sanctions on all of the Yugoslav republics, including Croatia, further deepening German resolve to grant recognition. Nonetheless, Germany adhered to the sanctions.

On December 2, the EC lifted the November 8 sanctions on Croatia and Slovenia, thus tacitly although not officially declaring Yugoslavia the aggressor, and Genscher announced that Italy, Austria, and possibly Poland were ready to recognize Croatia and Slovenia.[38] A few days later, Swedish Foreign Minister Ugglas called for recognition, but warned that Sweden would remain in step with the EC.[39] Genscher's problem was that Germany's clear supporters looked embarrassingly like the World War II coalition that had backed fascist Croatia. Kohl countered that the prorecognition group has gone beyond what they called "the 1941 coalition" to include Belgium and Denmark. On December 8, he announced that Germany would recognize the two republics, and that Sweden, Italy, Austria, and Hungary were likely to follow.[40]

This announcement was a miscalculation, because it indicated to British and French officials that Germany was moving outside the EC policy framework. On December 13, France and Britain attempted to block Germany's move by intro-

---

[33] See *The Christian Science Monitor*, 4 September 1991, 1; *New York Times*, 2 September 1991, 3; *New York Times*, 8 September 1991, 9; and *The Economist*, 28 September 1991, 55.

[34] See Salmon 1992, 251–52.

[35] Helmut Kohl, Tanner Lecture at the University of California at Berkeley, 13 September 1991.

[36] Krieger 1994, 33.

[37] EPC, *Declaration on Yugoslavia*, 18 and 28 October 1991.

[38] See *Frankfurter Allgemeine Zeitung*, 3 December 1991, 4.

[39] See *Frankfurter Allgemeine Zeitung*, 5 December 1991, 6.

[40] See *Reuters*, 16 December 1991.

ducing a UN Security Council resolution warning that no country should disturb the political balance in Yugoslavia by taking unilateral action. The United States was conspicuously absent from the debate on this resolution, but it had earlier issued an official statement that recognition should only be part of a larger peace settlement.[41]

This threat only served to harden Genscher's position, and on December 15, he announced that Germany would recognize the two republics before Christmas. Hoping that this counterthreat would force EC agreement on the German position, Kohl said that he would wait until after a meeting of EC foreign ministers the following day before actually making the announcement.

And at first, Kohl's counterthreat appeared to pay off. The UN Security Council dropped its resolution against Germany,[42] and at a December 16 European Political Cooperation (EPC) meeting called to discuss the diplomatic crisis, only two issues were on the agenda: the timing of recognition, and the conditionality requirements.[43] Germany argued for recognition before Christmas, but Lord Carrington claimed that this would "torpedo" the peace process. After long debate Genscher agreed to a compromise: if a set of specific human rights conditions were fulfilled, EC recognition would take place on January 15, 1992. These conditions would follow those set out by the CSCE: protection of minorities, recognition of CSCE principles, and the recognition of the borders and the territorial sovereignty of neighbors.

The issue of conditionality was the Achilles heel of the compromise. The EC stipulated that minorities be granted autonomy with respect to local government, local law enforcement, the judiciary, and education as conditions for recognition.[44] Petitions for recognition would have to be submitted by December 23 to the arbitration commission of the peace conference to meet the January 15 deadline. That commission would then determine whether the conditions had been met.[45]

Officials in both Croatia and Germany anticipated problems with these requirements. Tudjman had refused to protect minority rights, and it was clear that Germany would ignore the Badinter Commission's recommendations if they were negative. Indeed, Germany had already decided that Croatia had fulfilled the requirements for recognition *before* it had submitted its petition to the

---

[41] See *New York Times*, 8 December 1991.

[42] See *New York Times*, 16 December 1991, 1.

[43] Interviews of EC officials by the author, 18–19 May 1993.

[44] Conference pour la Paix en Yugoslavie, Avis no. 5, Paris, 11 January 1992.

[45] The transcript of the declaration at the end of this meeting specifically stated that "the application of those republics which affirm [the above preconditions, principles, and procedures] will be presented by the chair of the conference on Yugoslavia to the Hague commission for approval before the date of execution [January 15]." See also *Frankfurter Allgemeine Zeitung*, 18 December 1991.

EC. On December 13, after having found a human rights lawyer to approve the Croatian law on minorities, the German government independently announced that the governments of Slovenia and Croatia had fulfilled all the conditions for recognition.[46] Other EC members were shocked, but the EC was in a weak legal position with regard to Germany's announcement. The December 16 agreement did not make clear what steps the EC would take if the conditions for recognition were not met. Macedonia was also expected to submit an application, but the same conditions would not apply: recognition would only be considered if Macedonia changed its name and renounced any claims on Greek territory.[47] Genscher believed that states practiced a double standard with regard to conditionality requirements for diplomatic recognition, and that conditionality must not hinder recognition in this case.[48] This was a failed substantive linkage because the target saw it as a tactical link and, as Aggarwal illustrates in the introduction, the solution would soon prove to be temporary and capable of dealing only with the externalities of the problem. (See table 1.2.)

Indeed, on December 17 Genscher announced that the diplomatic recognition of Croatia and Slovenia was now "automatic." He declared that should the arbitration commission decide that Croatia did not meet the criteria, Germany would proceed with recognition nonetheless. Kohl announced that Germany would recognize any Yugoslav republic that undertook by December 23 to adopt the conditions set out by the EC.[49] "Adopting" conditions became tantamount to "fulfilling" them.

Then, in a move that astonished everyone, Germany formally and unilaterally recognized Slovenia and Croatia on December 23 before the Badinter Commission met to assess the fulfillment of conditionality requirements. This preemptive move was triggered by Genscher's fear that the EC would refuse to extend recognition, claiming that its conditions had not been fulfilled. Indeed, on January 11, 1992, the Badinter Commission declared that the Croatian constitution did not meet the conditions of the EC's "Declaration on Yugoslavia."[50] But with Germany's preemptive move, the EC had little leverage if it adhered to its conditionality requirements. Thus, the Badinter Commission simply requested that Tudjman give his personal assurance that language would be added to the Croatian constitution conforming to EC requirements. Tudjman complied,[51] and the EC granted recognition to Croatia and Slovenia on January 15, 1992. "Acceptance" did indeed mean "fulfillment" of the conditions in this case, and the conditionality requirement was conveniently swept under the table.

---

[46] See *Frankluper Allgement Zeitung*, 16 December 1991, 2 and 6h.

[47] See *Frankluper Allgement Zeitung*, 18 December 1991, 2.

[48] Interview with author, Bonn, 26 May 1993.

[49] See *Frankluper Allgement Zeitung*, 18 December 1991, 3.

[50] Conference pour la Paix en Yougoslavie, Avis no. 5, Paris, 11 January 1992.

[51] Letter from Franjo Tudjman to H. E. Robert Badinter, Zagreb, 15 January 1992.

AN ANALYSIS OF ROUND I

In the round of negotiations that led to the recognition of Croatia, the EC had begun with the desire to strengthen its own regional foreign policy and security institutions by intervening diplomatically in this crisis (See figure 3.1A). All EC members strongly believed that a multilateral approach to the crisis was preferable to unilateral or bilateral approaches; only a multilateral approach could succeed in preventing different countries from taking sides with one or the other of the warring parties.[52] But European negotiators quickly found that the regional security institution, the WEU, was not prepared to enforce diplomatic agreements, and partly as a result of this institutional weakness, efforts to mediate the crisis failed. And while the aims of the peace conference were attacked by the warring parties themselves, with Europeans helpless to stop them, Germany's insistence on EC recognition of Croatia with no concessions to Serbs living there weakened the process from the inside. As long as the Western powers disagreed among themselves, there was little chance that they could pressure either Slobodán Milosovic the Yugoslav President, or Tudjman to end the conflict.

Had the conflict in Yugoslavia threatened members of the EU militarily, the gains from cooperation within EU institutions would have rapidly increased, and the costs of defection from joint decisions would have increased as well. NATO policy on threats to its members were very clear; its policies on out-of-area conflicts were not clear at all. When the issue was downgraded to a foreign policy problem as the new concept of "divisible peace" gained popularity, the costs of not acting in concert decreased, and central decisionmakers had the luxury of acting in accord with the preferences of domestic political elites.

The first round ended with Germany's unilateral decision to recognize Croatia, with the EC's hasty decision to follow in order to preserve European unity, and with the entrance of the United States and the United Nations into the conflict to help moderate the ferocity of the war and pursue a diplomatic settlement (See figure 3.1B).

Many observers have argued that structural factors reflecting international power relationships and manifested in political conflict account for this outcome: Germany was expanding its relative power position in an international system that was moving toward multipolarity, and it calculated net gains from unilateral action. This argument is most common in journalistic accounts: a more powerful Germany in a multipolar world was attempting to recreate its World War II alliance with an independent Croatia and impose a "divide and conquer" strategy in the Balkans to protect its interests and enhance its relative

---

[52] See chapter 1, this volume, and Ruggie 1992.

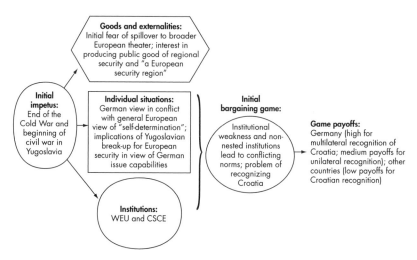

FIGURE 3.IA. Debating possible recognition of Croatia

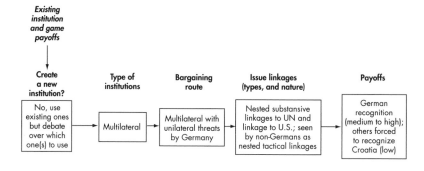

FIGURE 3.IB. Forcing the recognition of Croatia

power in the region.[53] In Aggarwal's framework this approach suggests that the solution was a purely tactical link and thus was highly likely to be unstable and short-lived because of its usage as a "stick." France and Britain, for their part, were attempting to rein in Germany—according to the structural argument— and used their positions on the UN Security Council to sanction Germany. Institutions were used as a thin veil to cover these changing power relationships, and Germany's unilateral move as a manifestation of its growing relative power suggests that international structure is the most important determinant of outcomes.

[53] See Rondholz 1992, 829–38 and Axt 1992, 351.

The structural argument, however, lacks empirical support. Recall that throughout this episode, Germany adhered to EC decisions and to an EC embargo that included Croatia.[54] And during this same time period, Germany sustained its commitment to multilateralism in other issue-areas. At virtually the same time that Germany unilaterally recognized Croatia, it was an important force in pushing Europe toward monetary union, helping to create enduring restrictions on its own economic independence.[55] And at the height of this diplomatic crisis, Germany joined with France to create Europe's only internationally integrated military unit.[56] As we shall see, Germany cooperated fully in multilateral institutions in ensuing negotiations over the fate of the former Yugoslavia. For example, when the war in Bosnia escalated in 1994 and Croatia sent troops there, Germany pressured Tudjman to pull back.[57]

A more convincing explanation for this outcome can be found in the weak and conflicting norms of international institutions, qualities that lead them to fail as guides to action. As European officials debated the wisdom of recognizing Croatia as a sovereign state in 1991, and as they discussed the relationship of diplomatic recognition to the prospects of peace, conflicting CSCE norms of self-determination, the inviolability of borders, and conditionality requirements for diplomatic recognition of states seeking independence provided confusing guidelines. Domestic politics in Germany played a role in undermining normative consensus on both self-determination and the conditions for diplomatic recognition, but domestic politics could define Germany's position in this case because international norms were in conflict and thus proved to be a weak basis for multilateral decisions. In terms of Aggarwal's framework, since European security was seen as a public good that displayed jointness and could be amenable to exclusion, it became a two-person prisoners' dilemma game where defection was the dominant strategy in every round.

The Helsinki Final Act provided conflicting guidelines for action on demands for self-determination. While Principle 2 of Basket 1 of the Helsinki Final Act provided for the inviolability of borders, Principle 8 upheld the right of self-determination.[58] A particular commitment to self-determination in the context of the Cold War had grown in German domestic politics, and that commitment conflicted with French and British understanding of that principle.

International norms governing diplomatic recognition were also weak. As Yugoslavia and the USSR fragmented and new states claimed independence, other considerations such as political stability, whether a state would change its name,

---

[54] See *Foreign Affairs* 70 (1992): 226.
[55] See Sandholtz 1993, 31–35.
[56] See *Los Angeles Times*, 19 November 1991, 1.
[57] See *Radio Free Europe/Radio Liberty Daily Report*, 7 February 1994.
[58] See Osmanczyck 1985, 333–54.

its possession of nuclear weapons, and its military power were often more important than human rights considerations in determining whether diplomatic recognition would be granted.[59] Indeed, Western countries recognized the four nuclear republics of the former the Soviet Union; U.S. officials declared they had received sufficient promises from them that they would democratize and maintain strict control over nuclear weapons.[60] What the EC demanded of Croatia in return for recognition was more than a promise—it was full implementation of human rights practices. This principle of conditional recognition based on human rights considerations was only selectively targeted and enforced.

Finally, although there was strong agreement that decisions should be reached in multilateral fora, there was disagreement among European states over which institutions should take the lead and how they could act in concert. CSCE was prevented from playing a prominent role by the Soviet Union. The Soviets had balked at the idea of CSCE involvement, shifting responsibility to the EC. As a result, the most prominent institution was the EPC, which had indeed grown in strength under German leadership. But when this episode unfolded, it required no binding commitment to its agreements, had no powers of enforcement, and had no military capability. Sanctions against defection did not exist. Germany had license to threaten unilateral action, increasing others' fears of its defection; France and Britain acted on those fears, attempting to sanction Germany for its preferences, in turn increasing Germany's fears that others would defect from a joint policy of recognition.

Furthermore, German officials believed that a common policy on recognition would internationalize the dispute, allowing it to be taken up in the United Nations. With this option, the focus of mediation and conflict resolution would move from the European Community to the United Nations and bring in the United States and NATO. Pursuit of this alternative would thus indicate continued commitment to Atlanticism and a preference for international as opposed to independent regional practices of mediation and conflict resolution. Genscher believed that this alternative would not necessarily represent a failure of European efforts but instead indicate continuity in the pursuit of transatlantic political and security cooperation and recognize the constraints of international law on external intervention.

The outbreak of war in the former Yugoslavia, followed closely on the heels of the Cold War's end and coincided with the demise of the Soviet Union. Together, these events provided the initial impetus to stimulate multilateral regional efforts to provide for European security under new international conditions. The

[59] See Rich 1993, 36–65.
[60] See *Frankluper Allgement Zeitung*, 27 December 1991, 1.

major players in this initial round of bargaining over how to manage this crisis were the members of the European Community, particularly Britain, France, and Germany. These actors' central concern was to strengthen the regional European security regime by responding to this crisis; there was no effort to create new institutions, because existing institutions created during the Cold War were searching for a new mission; this crisis potentially provided one.

What emerged almost immediately in negotiations within the EC was a difference in beliefs and ideas over the most appropriate intervention to halt the conflict. Germany's domestic political culture shaped the beliefs of its political elite and international negotiators; self-determination for Croatia was substantively linked to the promotion of liberal values and freedom from totalitarianism. British and French historical experience dictated an alternative view of self-determination that linked respect for minority rights to the promotion of liberal values. The meta-regime in this issue-area was weak: international institutions had conflicting norms regarding self-determination and thus provided a weak guide to multilateral action. Thus Genscher was forced to play a "two-level game" by both pressing for an international agreement that would satisfy domestic political elites and urging international agreement on Germany's terms by citing domestic pressure. In addition, Germany did not want to pursue an exclusive regional solution to the Yugoslav conflict, but wanted to bring in the United States and the United Nations as key actors. Germany threatened unilateral action in order to force its partners to agree to a multilateral response on its terms. Further, there is circumstantial evidence that Genscher attempted quid-pro-quo bargaining: concessions in other issue-areas if EC partners would agree to a joint recognition policy. *The Economist* reported that John Major had given his word that, in return for German support of the British position on a number of issues at Maastricht, he would support the German position on Croatia.[61] The pursuit of tactical linkage as a bargaining strategy failed, however, and Germany acted unilaterally.

As we shall see, Germany's unilateral act had important consequences for the next bargaining round and for future attempts to reach multilateral agreements and nest institutions in response to the Bosnian crisis. The recognition of Croatia foreclosed choice and led to the multilateral recognition of Bosnia. But it did not lead to a consensus on the normative issue of self-determination. It was not clear—though recognition supported it—that Croatia and Bosnia as independent states had the right under international law to force large Serb minorities to submit to a policy of secession from Yugoslavia. It was construed by Serb populations as a belligerent intervention in an unresolved civil war in Yugoslavia.[62]

[61] *The Economist*, 18 January 1992, 49.
[62] See Kenney 1995.

Furthermore, Germany's unilateral act posed a warning against the dangers of unilateralism on the part of the Western powers and perhaps even on the part of Russia in the Balkans, and it thereby had the effect of actually strengthening the resolve on the part of all actors to act within multilateral institutions. Finally, the recognition of Croatia brought in the United States, the United Nations, and Russia as central actors in the bargaining process and led to further requirements to coordinate an institutional response.

ROUND II: THE WAR IN BOSNIA

10,000 people had perished in the war in Croatia by December 1991, when Cyrus Vance, on behalf of the United Nations, successfully negotiated a cease-fire agreement between Croatia and the JNA. Croatian Serbs had captured one-third of Croatian territory—the Krajina region and Western Slavonia—and had established a proto-state in these regions. In January, the UN Security Council voted to dispatch fifty UN observers to the Krajina region held by Croatian Serbs and, eventually, to send UN troops there to replace JNA troops. Krajina Serbs accepted the plan in February, and Germany pressured Croatia into acceptance.[63] Croatia's acceptance meant that, for the time being, Croatia would not fight to win back territory. Subsequent events however, suggest that the Great Powers had sent a signal to Croatia to bide its time; which it did; and at the appropriate moment, it seized the Krajina with virtually no international opposition. The deployment of a UN peacekeeping force in Croatia to separate the Krajina Serbs from Croatian forces was relatively unproblematic; the UN Protection Force (UNPROFOR) was sent to keep a peace that had been negotiated between the belligerents. The truce held until May 1995, when Croatians began to retake land in the Krajina.

But while the bloodshed had stopped in Croatia, the war in Bosnia was only just beginning. On February 29, 1992, Muslim voters in Bosnia overwhelmingly supported independence in a republicwide referendum; Bosnian Serbs boycotted the election and, with their overwhelming superiority of weapons, promised to destroy the state of Bosnia-Herzegovina. One month later, Bosnia was ravaged by war. On April 6, 1992, the EC and the United States recognized Bosnia as an independent state; by May, the UN General Assembly voted to accept Bosnia into the UN. It also denied Yugoslavia's UN seat to the "new" Yugoslavia (Serbia and Montenegro) and, following the EC's lead, imposed trade sanctions on Yugoslavia.

The diplomatic recognition of Bosnia closed off an important alternative for the international community: that of intervention on behalf of one or the other of the

---

[63] See *The Economist*, 15 February 1992, 50.

warring parties. Given the population distribution in Bosnia (Serbs, Croats, and Muslims), recognition also put the West in the position of supporting a government whose claim to legitimacy was certainly in question. The war within Bosnia was now considered a "civil war" under international law as long as Yugoslavia did not intervene on behalf of the Bosnian Serbs. Under international law, which provided normative guidelines to the central western actors in this case, aggressors are more difficult to identify in a civil war, and international intervention is illegal.

Therefore, with the recognition of Bosnia, only two paths of response were open to the international community. The first was to do nothing; the outcome of war would determine Bosnia's fate, and with the arms embargo on Bosnia, it would likely be carved up between Croatia and Serbia. Alternatively, the international community could again try to help negotiate a diplomatic resolution to the Bosnian conflict. This second path was the one chosen. It was chosen for three reasons. First, international institutions were looking to hone their skills in a new conflict; this time more institutions were involved and each one wanted to prove itself. And without multilateral intervention of some kind, states would be tempted to take opposing sides in the dispute, raising the odds of political tensions in Europe. Germany supported Croatia, Russia supported "rump" Yugoslavia, and the United States supported the Bosnian Muslims. The specter of 1914—when the Balkan tinderbox ignited war among European powers—haunted the decision-making process. It was not that there was a danger of wider war resulting from opposing alliances, but rather the danger of heightened political tension—clearly suggested by Germany's partisan response to the initial crisis. That tension, it was believed, would undermine multilateral institutions which were under intense scrutiny in the post–Cold War period. It would also undermine the effort to bring Russia and Eastern Europe into the West, and Russia was too weak to pursue an alternative policy on its own.

The second reason for choosing a diplomatic path in the crisis was that the collapse of communism shaped the goals of the major powers. That collapse meant that the values of the West had "won" the Cold War, that these values of peaceful conflict resolution, tolerance, equality, and dignity of the individual were under attack in the Yugoslav war. Defense of these values thus guided other aspects of the western response. They guided the Russian response as well, since Russian leaders desperately wanted to become part of the West.

Thus, because absence of a multilateral response might encourage unilateral action on opposing sides, and because core Western values were under attack, incentives were high for all Western powers and Russia to actively encourage a diplomatic solution that would end the war and preserve Bosnia as a single, multiethnic state.

The third reason for the pursuit of a diplomatic rather than a military settlement of the conflict was that the central aims of the major powers were to moderate the ferocity of the fighting,[64] primarily through an arms embargo on Bosnia, and to provide humanitarian aid to the victims of the war through UNPROFOR, using airlifts and no fly zones.

A central obstacle to successful multilateral strategies to meet these goals became gradually apparent. To the extent that successive diplomatic solutions presented by the major powers failed to meet with the approval of the belligerents, opportunities opened for domestic actors in the West and Russia to shape the outcome. Those pressures were contradictory and threatened multilateral cooperation. Domestic pressures in both the United States and Britain to lift the arms embargo on Bosnia undermined the effort to moderate the fighting. Domestic pressure in Russia to lift the sanctions on Yugoslavia, countered by pressure on the part of Germany to tighten those sanctions, interfered with new diplomatic efforts.

These conflicting preferences were not lost on the warring parties, and they used the conflicts among the major powers to gain advantage on the battlefield. The Muslims, perhaps knowing that they could not win unless they persuaded the West to support them militarily, provoked Serb offensives against civilian areas. The Serbs, knowing that the Russians did not approve of NATO airstrikes without its consent, constantly goaded NATO into air attacks.[65]

What follows is a brief account of the pursuit of the three central goals: diplomacy, halting the bloodshed, and humanitarian relief. In each case I will consider the interaction of (1) bargaining among the major powers, (2) bargaining between the major powers and the belligerents, (3) events on the battlefield, and (4) domestic pressures.

DIPLOMACY

Before the war in Bosnia began, an EC-sponsored conference in Lisbon was held to discuss alternative solutions to the impending crisis. The plan proposed a structure for the Bosnian state similar to the one eventually cemented in the Dayton Agreement: ethnic divisions within a unitary state with a weak federal structure. This initial proposal, endorsed by the Bosnian Serbs, was rejected by the Bosnian government. In the next three years, three successive plans formulated by Western diplomats were presented to the belligerents. Negotiations in each round—both among the major powers to shape the plan and between western and Russian officials and the warring parties—had important consequences for the stability of the region, for the strength and credibility of international institu-

---

[64] See Glenny 1995, 62.
[65] Glenny 1995, 62.

tions, and for the ability of these institutions to coordinate their activities. In other words, the bargaining routes for institutional formation were a function of the type of good, the actors' individual situations, and the existing institutional frameworks.

The Vance-Owen Plan

Until the war began in Bosnia, the United States had taken no diplomatic initiatives, at the request of France and Britain, who both sought a European solution to this regional crisis. The Lisbon Conference represented that attempt, but its failure drew in additional actors. In late May 1992, U.S. Secretary of State James Baker complained that the EC was doing nothing about the escalating crisis in Bosnia and was simply waiting for the United Nations to act. His comments prodded the EC to impose sanctions against Yugoslavia at the end of May without waiting for the United Nations to do the same. Supporting Serbia, Russia was hesitant to impose UN sanctions.[66] Nonetheless EC pressure forced Russia's hand, and the Security Council voted for sanctions on May 30.

The independent imposition of EC sanctions indicated growing tensions over the coordination of an institutional response to the crisis. British officials approved of a UN peacekeeping mission, but opposed a UN sponsored diplomatic effort, arguing that it would undermine Lord Carrington's EC initiative. CSCE officials attempted to find a role for that institution in this new crisis; they wished to be seen as a regional organization under UN auspices, with the power to coordinate peacekeeping operations.[67]

The United Nations, however, eclipsed the CSCE, which moved into the background (only to resurface much later with the Dayton Accords). The extent of this eclipse is evident in the December 1994 meeting of the CSCE to discuss issues of security and conflict resolution. What was remarkable about the meeting was that Bosnia was not discussed and that Russia vetoed any mention of Serbian aggression in CSCE debate.[68]

In August 1992, the EC and the United Nations held a joint conference in London on the crisis in the former Yugoslavia. Tudjman, Milosevic, and local Serb and Croat leaders in Bosnia attended. A new international peace conference to be held in Geneva was launched at that meeting led by Lord Owen of Britain and Cyrus Vance of the United States. Attempts to mediate the crisis began again, this time in an international rather than a European forum.

Given the large population of Serbs in Bosnia and their overwhelming superiority in weapons, any peace plan that could be negotiated would mean that the

---

[66] *The Economist*, 30 May 1992, 49.
[67] Statements from the CSCE Summit in Helsinki, 9–10 July 1992.
[68] See *This Week in Germany*, 9 December 1994, 1.

Bosnian government must cede a large part of its sovereignty to stop the war. The West saw quite soon that its goal of maintaining a viable multiethnic state must be abandoned and, in October 1992, the Vance-Owen plan was unveiled, which proposed to divide Bosnia into ten geographic units within a single Bosnian state, granting the Serbs and Croats autonomy within Bosnia. The plan conceded a major point to the Bosnian Serbs: it prevented Croats and Muslims from remilitarizing areas the Serbs would cede under the plan. UNPROFOR would move in to protect those area.

According to David Owen, all major European countries and Russia supported the plan, and the Bosnian Serb leadership was on the verge of signing it. The major obstacle was the United States. The new Clinton administration had just come into office and hesitated to lend its support. Warren Christopher defended Clinton's hesitation, arguing that the plan appeared to ratify Serb gains. But Owen contends that Clinton disapproved of the plan because it was formulated in European institutions and in the United Nations and did not bear the stamp of U.S. leadership and thus could not gain domestic support.[69] As soon as Clinton's refusal to support the plan became public, both the Bosnian Muslims and the Bosnian Serbs soundly rejected it as well. The Muslims believed that the United Nations was too weak to protect Muslim and Croat civilians in Serb dominated areas from Bosnian Serb militias; indeed the U.S. State Department undermined Muslim support for the plan by telling Bosnia's President Izetbegovic that the United States would support him if he demanded changes.[70] Finally, the Bosnian Serbs did not want to sustain the "fiction" of Bosnia as an independent state and felt forced to give up too much of the wrong territory.

Domestic Pressures

The failure of the Vance-Owen plan to gain approval led to contradictory domestic pressures in the West and Russia that threatened to unravel the multilateral decision-making process. In the United States and Britain, public opinion called for Western intervention on behalf of the Bosnian Muslims. In April 1993, 61 percent of the British public supported armed intervention against the Bosnian Serbs, and John Smith, the British labor leader, called for the bombing of Bosnian Serb positions. In the United States, public opinion overwhelmingly supported a lifting of the arms embargo. Clinton's National Security advisor, Tony Lake, called for the West to intervene on behalf of the Bosnian Muslims. The new German Foreign Minister Klaus Kinkel called for the EU to break off diplomatic relations with Yugoslavia.

[69] See Owen 1996.
[70] See Glenny 1995, 63.

Internal pressures were also at work in Russia, opposing a lifting of the embargo on Bosnia, and supporting a lifting of the arms embargo on Serbia. Yeltsin feared that Russian acquiescence in a lifting of the arms embargo on Bosnia would alienate voters who might swing toward the hard core nationalists.[71] He was also apparently pressured by economic forces to lift the embargo on Serbia; *Moscow News* reported that Russian participation in sanctions against Yugoslavia and Iraq cost $30 billion per year in lost contracts.[72] Indeed, by March 1994, the Russian Duma's Lower house had voted 280 to 2 to lift the embargo on Serbia.[73] In the face of the Bosnian Serb rejection of the Vance-Owen plan, these domestic pressures increased tensions among the great powers over future strategy. As Aggarwal argues, the stability of the domestic coalitions is an important factor in the determination of a country's individual situation, thus affecting both the negotiating strategy and the payoff structure of the game. Supported by Germany, the United States called for tougher sanctions against Yugoslavia in an effort to pressure Milosevic to push the Bosnian Serbs to comply. Russia had wanted to pursue the opposite strategy: to dangle the carrot of easing the sanctions in order to get Milosevic to put more pressure on the Bosnian Serbs.

These tensions were felt in international negotiating fora. Throughout 1993, Germany tried to convince other Europeans in the CFSP to lift the arms embargo against Bosnia. At a June dinner with EC leaders, Chancellor Kohl read a letter from Clinton in support of lifting the embargo and urged others that this was the only moral course of action. Mitterand, however, argued that the embargo should be lifted only if the safe areas were abandoned since a lifting of the embargo would endanger French peacekeepers, thus raising domestic opposition. Germany backed down, and the EC agreed to shore up the safe havens.

Clinton, too, recognized the danger to multilateralism of increasing tensions over embargo strategy. Indeed, Clinton did not want to make any moves in Bosnia that might undermine stability in Russia.[74] He therefore did not push the demand for a lifting of the arms embargo in international fora.

A pattern began to emerge that would be repeated: bargains struck among the great powers for a diplomatic solution were resisted by the belligerents; failure to negotiate an acceptable plan to end the war led to domestic calls in Russia and in the West for opposing strategies; domestic pressures for contradictory policies threatened to undermine a unified multilateral diplomatic resolution to the war. Because a unified bargaining stance and multilateral solidarity were the highest priorities among great power decisionmakers, they scurried to reach a

[71] See *Christian Science Monitor*, 12 September 1994, 6.
[72] See *Moscow News*, 21 October 1994, 5.
[73] *Europe: Magazine of the European Community*, no. 337, June 1994, 19.
[74] See *The Economist*, 10 April 1994, 57.

common position that would also be acceptable to the belligerents. This was necessary to avoid further domestic pressure. In the absence of a substantive linkage, all solutions were bound to be somewhat unstable. The result, as we shall see, was a plan that further undermined the goal of multiethnic tolerance and weakened a future for Bosnia as a unitary state.

The Muslim-Croat Federation and the Contact Group Plan

In March 1994, the United States persuaded the Bosnian Muslims and Croats to form a Muslim-Croat Federation with the signing of the Washington Accords. To induce the Croats to sign the accords, the United States promised that Tudjman could regain parts of his territory, largely inhabited by Serbs and lost to the Croatian Serbs in the war. The United States also helped Croatia build up its army by sending advisers and by permitting weaponry to flow into Croatia.[75] Muslims were allowed to purchase weaponry. The Washington accords halted the fighting between Bosnian Muslims and Bosnian Croats and provided for an eventual confederation with Croatia, thus de facto undermining the legitimacy of a separate Bosnian state.

This new federation also opened the door for a new diplomatic effort. In May 1994, the foreign ministers of Greece, Belgium, Germany, the EU, France, Russia, the UK, and the United States met in Geneva. They created what was called the "Contact Group" (composed of representatives from the United States, France, Britain, Germany, and Russia) to begin substantive negotiations again with the warring parties. At the meeting in which the Contact Group was created, the foreign ministers reaffirmed their support for Bosnia as a single state with internationally recognized borders despite internal divisions between Muslims, Serbs, and Croats; they instructed the Contact Group to begin substantive negotiations immediately and to do all that it could to ensure a political solution.[76]

The Contact Group proposed a plan that would turn Bosnia into two parts: a 49 percent Bosnian Serb and 51 percent Muslim-Croat federation. This would require that the Bosnian Serbs surrender one-third of their territory and give up plans to create a union with Serbia. The plan's success depended heavily on Milosevic to weaken his support for the Bosnian Serbs and thus pressure them into acceptance by closing its border to Bosnia—thereby halting the flow of arms and other supplies—and permitting UN monitors along border areas in exchange for the easing of sanctions. The Contact Group also urged Serbia to recognize Bosnia as an independent state and, under the urging of the United States, proposed that NATO troops enforce the cease-fire.

---

[75] See Mearsheimer and Van Evera 1995, 18.
[76] See *This Week in Germany,* 13 May 1994, 1.

External cooperation to pressure the warring parties to agree to the plan was remarkable. Russia joined American and British diplomats to urge Radovan Karadzic, the president of the self-proclaimed Serbian Republic of Bosnia, to accept the plan, and they declared that they would take a stronger stand against the Serbs if they latter did not cooperate. Both German Foreign Minister Klaus Kinkel and Russian Foreign Minister Kozyrev agreed to jointly use their influence with participants in the conflict to promote a cease-fire and accept the plan.[77] Kozyrev objected only to the transfer of command over Bosnian operations from the United Nations to NATO.[78]

Russia's pressure on Serbia seemed to pay off; Milosevic, ordered the border between Serbia and Bosnia closed on August 5, and two months later, the United Nations eased sanctions against Yugoslavia. The Belgrade airport was reopened; sporting and cultural links were resumed. Nonetheless, the oil and trade embargo would remain in effect until Serbia recognized Bosnia as a unitary state.[79] Milosevic agreed to recognize Bosnia as a state but not as a government in return for the lifting of the sanctions. Russia suggested a two hundred-day suspension of the sanctions in exchange for recognition, but the four non-Russian Contact Group members feared that Russia would use its veto in the Security Council to ensure that the sanctions would not be reimposed and leverage over Milosevic would be lost.[80]

Nonetheless, despite Russia's cooperation and signs that Serbia would pressure the Bosnian Serbs into acceptance, they resisted the plan. Although the Muslim-Croat Federation accepted the agreement in principle, Bosnian Serbs demanded changes in the plan that the Muslims refused to adopt. A Bosnian Serb referendum rejected the Contact Group plan in August, and the Bosnian Serb army attacked UN positions, surrounded Sarajevo, blocked relief convoys, and attacked Bihac.

The international community, however, was unable to jointly respond to these attacks with concerted and coordinated military force. The Clinton Administration threatened to lift the arms embargo on Bosnia if the Serbs did not accept the plan by October 15, 1994. Again this unilateral threat heightened tensions both within the Atlantic alliance and with Russia. A lifting of the arms embargo would place French and British ground troops at risk, and both France and Britain declared that if the arms embargo were lifted, they would be forced to withdraw their troops.[81] France, with 4,500 of the 23,000 UN troops had the largest troop presence there, while Britain had 3,300.

---

[77] See *This Week in Germany*, 26 November 1994, 2.
[78] See *New York Times*, 29 July 1994, A3.
[79] See *The Economist*, 8 October 1994, 54.
[80] See *The Economist*, 27 May 1995, 43.
[81] See *New York Times*, 2 July 1994, 3.

Yeltsin still feared that if Russia cooperated with a lifting the of arms embargo on Bosnia, the move would play into the hands of radical nationalists who supported the embargo because it aided the Bosnian Serbs. Indeed, a lifting of the arms embargo would most likely have intensified the war and would certainly have heightened tensions between Russia and the United States and, thus, undermined the multilateral goals in Bosnia (the moderation of the ferocity of the fighting, and the diplomatic effort).

As a result of pressure from France, Britain, and Russia, Clinton backed down, and the October 15 deadline passed without the United States lifting the arms embargo and without Bosnian Serb acceptance of the Contact Group plan. Clinton did say, however, that the United States would no longer enforce the arms embargo on Bosnia, and announced a deadline of April 15, 1995, for the total withdrawal of U.S. participation in the embargo.[82] That deadline, too, came and went; the consequences for multilateralism were judged to be too dangerous. In closed-door negotiations, Clinton argued that if NATO's role in Bosnia were not enhanced, he would continue to press for a lifting of the arms embargo on Bosnia.

The West was thus unable to break the negotiating deadlock. Similar to the situation in the first negotiating round, international negotiators could not enforce agreements. As long as the warring parties preferred the possibility of battlefield victory to the certainty of a compromise at the negotiating table, their incentive to reach a negotiated settlement would be low. Leverage on the part of the great powers would heighten that incentive, but the great powers could not provide the coordination needed to exert the necessary influence. Clearly defeated, the Contact Group declared its plan a "basis for negotiations" only.

The American Plan and the Dayton Agreement

This deadlock in international negotiations between the Western powers and Russia on the one side and the belligerents on the other, again opened a window of opportunity for domestic political actors in their bid to dominate the agenda. In July 1995, the United States Congress attempted to put pressure on the Clinton Administration to lift the arms embargo on Bosnia. Senator Bob Dole and Democrat Joe Lieberman sponsored a resolution to end the arms embargo that passed in the Senate, 69 to 29, exceeding the two-thirds majority that would be needed to override a promised presidential veto.[83]

These domestic calls for the lifting of the arms embargo threatened multilateral efforts to find a diplomatic solution to the war. A diplomatic solution meant

---

[82] *Facts on File,* 17 November 1994, 849.
[83] See *The Economist* 29 July 1995, 16.

that the West must maintain neutrality vis-à-vis the belligerents. Indeed, although official resolutions from all international institutions condemned the Bosnian Serb practice of "ethnic cleansing," they were careful to omit the word "aggression." Domestic pressure to point out an "aggressor" threatened to unravel the multilateral bargaining process and thus raised the incentive on the part of the Clinton Administration to take a more assertive role in conflict resolution to save multilateralism in Bosnia. Indeed, the impending 1996 presidential elections had an impact on this decision as well. Once again the domestic coalitional structure of the actors was altering the payoff structure of the game.

In the summer of 1995, the United States initiated an alternative to the failing Contact Group plan. This alternative would prove to be the skeleton of the final peace accord initialed the following November. The American plan built upon the Contact Group proposal in that it maintained the 49 to 51 percent split between the Bosnian Serb and Muslim-Croat territories. But the Serbs would keep the Muslim enclaves of Zepa and Srebrenica, which they overran in July 1995, and the Brcko corridor connecting the two parts of their territory would be widened. Muslims would gain territory around Sarajevo.

The plan stipulated that Croatia and Bosnia recognize each other's prewar frontiers, and international sanctions on Serbia would be lifted when it recognized Bosnia as an independent state. Bosnia would remain a recognized state, but areas with a Serbian majority population would be free to confederate with Serbia. The Muslim-Croat federation would be permitted under the plan to confederate with Croatia. In practice, then, Bosnia would de facto cease to exist as an independent entity, even though it would continue to exist de jure.

To press for agreement, the United States used a series of "sticks" to prod each of the belligerents. To pressure the Bosnian Serbs into agreement, the United States stated that it would support a lifting of the arms embargo on the Bosnian government, a withdrawal of UNPROFOR, and a launching of NATO air strikes against the Bosnian Serb positions if they refused to accept the plan and continued their attacks. To pressure the Bosnian Muslims, who initially opposed the plan because it gave Zepa and Srebrenica to the Bosnian Serbs, U.S. officials persuaded Croatia to limit its assistance to the Bosnian government. A withdrawal of assistance would weaken them to the point at which they would be unable to reject the plan. U.S. diplomats encouraged Tudjman and Izetbegovic to agree on a joint military campaign against the Bosnian Serbs in territory adjacent to Croatia, but also encouraged Croatia to abandon plans to help the Muslims in central Bosnia.

All the major powers seemed enthusiastic about the plan, although they disapproved of the threat of air strikes.[84] Attitudes changed, however, after a mortar attack in Sarajevo at the end of August 1995 killed thirty-seven civilians. Assuming

---

[84] See *The Economist*, 19 August 1995, 41–42.

that the attack was launched by Bosnian Serbs, NATO began serious aerial bombardment of Bosnian Serb positions; this was the biggest military assault in NATO's entire history. At the same time, with encouragement from the United States, a joint Muslim-Croat offensive captured much of northwest Bosnia, and on October 12, a cease-fire was reached. The belligerents went to the negotiating table in Dayton, Ohio, on November 1, and a peace accord was initialled by the presidents of Bosnia, Croatia, and Serbia on November 21.

As noted above, the Dayton agreement was built on the original American plan. Sarajevo would be the capital of an independent Bosnian state; the presidency, like that of Tito's Yugoslavia, would rotate among Bosnian Serbs, Croats, and Muslims, and the central government would be a weak one. Western Slavonia and Krajina would become part of Croatia. Zepa and Srebrenica would remain in Bosnian Serb hands.

A vague, institutional division of labor seemed to emerge in Dayton: the OSCE—long inactive in this crisis—was given the task of supervising the 1996 Bosnian elections, monitoring human rights activity, and promoting arms control, while the EU was responsible for creating a plan for the economic reconstruction of Bosnia. Although the United Nations stepped into the background, the United Nations High Commission on Refugees (UNHCR) was assigned the task of heading humanitarian efforts. The "empty" part of this nesting arrangement was the office of the high representative, who was appointed by the Paris Peace Conference and confirmed by the UN Security Council but would not represent the UN. The representative would float among institutions, without an institutional base, and would have little clout.

Unlike the agreements reached in the first round of negotiations, the major powers agreed to cooperate to enforce the accord with joint military power. To the rapid reaction force, NATO added IFOR, the joint implementation force. IFOR troops were instructed to employ standard NATO rules of engagement, meaning that they could act to preempt an attack if they knew that one was imminent. The plan stipulated that IFOR could retaliate heavily against the first sign of resistance.

The need for this level of enforcement capability and for the dominance of NATO over the military operation had been achieved through a painful series of negotiation failures caused by the lack of enforcement capabilities. Recall, for example, that in the first bargaining round, the WEU did not have the willingness or the ability to enforce cease-fire agreements. As we shall see below, the entrance of the UN and of NATO forces into the conflict led to coordination problems that further reduced the West's enforcement capability, its ability to moderate the ferocity of the fighting, and its ability to deliver humanitarian aid. The Dayton Accord promised to rectify these failures.

PEACEKEEPING AND PEACEMAKING

As noted above, this goal was perhaps the most difficult one to realize, since no international institution was prepared to take on this task, and because the intensity of the war was directly related to success or failure at the negotiating table. For example, in May 1992, the UN Security Council decided to extend UNPROFOR's mandate to Bosnia, over the objections of Marrack Goulding, then head of peacekeeping operations. Goulding believed that the situation in Bosnia was not "ripe" for peacekeeping; the peacekeepers could not possibly begin their operation under a mandate on which the various belligerents disagreed.[85]

With each diplomatic failure, the fighting intensified, and the intensification required the West to formulate a new plan to moderate it. After the Vance-Owen Plan was rejected, France and Britain lobbied the United States to support the creation of "safe havens" for Bosnian civilians. UN troops, however, could not protect the safe havens alone and would need protection themselves.

By June 1993, the UN Security Council approved a "joint action program" establishing six "safe areas" at Sarajevo, Srebrenica, Zepa, Tuzla, Goradze, and Bihac. But the resolution left unclear whether NATO would use air strikes to retaliate against attacks on those areas or whether it would be the UN troops that would retaliate. Clarity on this issue and the prominence of NATO's role would only be achieved after the attack on the Sarajevo market in February 1994.

On February 5, 1994, and attack on an open market in Sarajevo left over sixty civilians dead. Assuming that the attack was launched by Bosnian Serbs, the sixteen members of NATO issued an ultimatum demanding the withdrawal of Serbian artillery to at least twenty kilometers from the center by February 21. The UN Command reported that the mortar fired into the market could easily have been fired from a Bosnian army position, but NATO ignored the report. If the Bosnian Serbs did not withdraw, NATO threatened to attack their military positions. The credibility of this threat was demonstrated when NATO jets shot down four light Bosnian Serb planes over Banja Luka for violating the flight ban.

NATO's action had broad support among the Western powers, but it was the support of Russia that was crucial to the maintenance of multilateral solidarity. Indeed, although Russia opposed the idea of a NATO command in Bosnia, Russian officials requested that the Serbs respect the NATO ultimatum. Further, Yeltsin agreed to send Russian peacekeepers to Bosnia as part of the UN peacekeeping operation.[86]

---

[85] See Rieff 1994, 1.

[86] *Europe: Magazine of the European Community*, no. 337, June 1994, 19.

Nonetheless, there were institutional tensions over who had the authority to launch air strikes. Until July 1995, there existed a "dual key" arrangement that required both UN officials and military commanders to approve air strikes. Disagreement over the rules of engagement, however, made that arrangement ineffective. When Bosnian Serbs attacked Bihac in November 1994, NATO announced that it could not attack Bosnian Serb positions because the UN refused authorization to attack. For their part, UN officials believed that an attack would amount to a declaration of war.[87] Each NATO airstrike had provoked the Bosnian Serbs to take UN peacekeepers as hostages and had increased pressure on the United Nations to pull back. On May 7, a major shelling from Bosnian Serb positions into Sarajevo led Rupert Smith, UNPROFOR's commander, to order air strikes. At first, his orders were countermanded by officials at UN headquarters in Zagreb, who argued that Croatian Serbs would retaliate with attacks in Croatia and those attacks would endanger UN troops. Nonetheless, on May 25, NATO conducted air strikes against Bosnian Serb positions near Sarajevo.[88] Confusion increased with the growing tension between the UN and NATO commands.

The problem was inherent in the UN mandate. As the secretary-general reported, "even though the use of force is authorized under Chapter VII of the Charter, the United Nations remains neutral and impartial between the warring parties, without a mandate to stop the aggressor (if one can be identified) or impose a cessation of hostilities. Nor is this peace-keeping as practiced hitherto, because the hostilities continue and there is often no agreement between the warring parties on which a peace-keeping mandate can be based."[89] NATO, on the other hand, did not suffer under similar constraints.

The only way to resolve the tension, if NATO were to continue to launch air strikes, was to provide NATO commanders with more autonomy. In July 1995, NATO commanders won permission to summon air strikes without the approval of UN officials. Rising institutional tensions and rivalry had opened the political space for this solution, and when Russia finally agreed, NATO came to take the lead in military engagement. Increasing autonomy was accompanied by task expansion: plans were launched for the creation of a "Rapid Reaction Force" of 4,000 troops to assist in a possible UN withdrawal and NATO commanders increased their own authority over military action. On July 23, 1995, the first units of the Rapid Reaction Force were deployed from central Bosnia to Mount Igman, after Serb artillery had killed two French peacekeepers. Nonetheless, NATO remained constrained, and the force had orders to fire only when the Serbs attacked UN personnel and vehicles.

[87] See *New York Times*, 9 November 1994, A1.
[88] See *The Economist*, May 27, 1994, 43.
[89] UN Document A/50/608/1995/1, 3 January 1995.

A number of events combined to place NATO in a position of institutional prominence: the WEU's earlier failure to enforce cease-fires, the United Nations failure to protect "safe havens," NATO's successful show of force and the demonstration of its ability to coordinate military activity, France's participation in NATO's military activity, and finally, Russia's agreement to NATO intervention. NATO, therefore, was assigned the task of peacekeeping after the signing of the Dayton Accords. The army of 60,000 (called Joint Endeavor and deployed to enforce the accords), was to carve Bosnia into three zones, managed by the United States, France, and Britain, all under the same U.S. commander. A joint committee of NATO ambassadors and Russian ambassadors was designated to handle conflicts and approve any significant changes in the peacekeeping operation.

HUMANITARIAN GOALS

In April 1992, the UN Security Council created the United Nations Protection Force (UNPROFOR) to protect humanitarian relief efforts and ensure the safety and security of the Sarajevo airport.[90] On June 8, the Security Council expanded the UNPROFOR mission to include the task of reopening the Sarajevo airport for relief supplies, and the Bosnian Serbs allowed UN peacekeepers to take control of the airport.[91] On August 13, the Security Council approved the use of "all means necessary" to supply humanitarian aid to Bosnia, but cautioned that this not be interpreted as an attack on the Bosnian Serbs.[92]

In October 1992, the Security Council had established a ban on military flights in the airspace of Bosnia and Herzegovina, in order to ensure the safe delivery of humanitarian assistance.[93] Still opposing NATO air strikes and the lifting of the arms embargo, Russia called for full implementation of UN sanctions, UN border patrols between Serbia and Bosnia, and a war crimes tribunal. In May 1993, a war crimes tribunal was established.

The tribunal issued its first indictment at the end of 1994, charging twenty-two Serbs with murder and rape at a notorious prisoner of war camp at Omarska.[94] On April 24, Richard Goldstone, chief prosecutor for the tribunal, named Radovan Karadzic as a suspected war criminal.[95] On July 25, 1995,

---

[90] Resolution 749 (1992), adopted by the Security Council at its 3066th meeting on 7 April 1992.
[91] Rieff 1994, 2.
[92] Resolution 771 (1992), adopted by the Security Council at its 3106th meeting on 13 August 1992.
[93] Resolution 781 (1992), adopted by the Security Council at its 3122nd meeting on 9 October 1992.
[94] See *The Economist*, 7 January 1995, 52.
[95] See *The Economist*, 29 April 1994, 15.

Karadzic and Ratko Mladic were indicted by the International Criminal Tribunal for Former Yugoslavia for war crimes, grave breaches of the Geneva Convention, and genocide (killing or causing serious bodily or mental harm to members of a group).[96] A Croatian General, Tihomir Blaskic, was also charged with war crimes. The Dayton Accords stipulated that those indicted by the international tribunal could not hold elected office, but the accords did not require that the Bosnian government turn over those indicted to the tribunal.

While the war crimes tribunal was busy indicting war criminals, Franjo Tudjman in Croatia was preparing for the largest single "ethnic cleansing" of the war. He began by threatening not to renew the UN mandate that was to expire on March 31, 1995. In response, Klaus Kinkel traveled to Croatia to exert pressure on him to do so. The pressure seemed to work, and the mandate was renewed. Nonetheless, in March, Croatian troops launched a major offensive in the Krajina region. Angry Croatian Serbs shelled Zagreb in retaliation. By the summer of 1995 with the blessing of the United States, Croatia had retaken the Krajina, causing 150,000 Serbs to flee from their homes to northern Bosnia and Serbia.[97]

And in Bosnia, as well, the humanitarian situation had deteriorated greatly. Humanitarian aid slowed to a trickle as the Bosnian Serbs reclaimed heavy weapons around Sarajevo. On May 25, 1995, the Bosnian Serbs took UN troops hostage, and UNPROFOR claimed that it needed the "strategic consent" of the Bosnian Serbs to carry out its job. NATO began to pull back after losing an F-16 fighter plane.[98]

Finally, safe areas were becoming increasingly unsafe, and the UN was barely able to deliver food to them. Srebrenica and Zepa fell to the Bosnian Serbs, while 450 UN peacekeepers there stood helplessly by. They asked NATO to halt the air strikes, claiming that the strikes encouraged the Bosnian Serbs to take dozens of UN hostages. Nearly 30,000 women and children and old men were forced out of Srebrenica and another 10,000 out of Zepa. According to the United Nations human rights investigator Tadeusz Mazowiecki, Bosnian troops captured around Srebrenica were subjected to "barbaric acts on an enormous scale."[99]

By August 1995, UNHCR reported that more people had been uprooted in Bosnia than anywhere else in the former Yugoslavia, both absolutely and as a share of the population. Of the prewar population of 4.4 million, 1.3 million were displaced within Bosnia. Another 500,000 sought shelter in Serbia and

---

[96] See *The Economist*, 29 July 1995, 38.

[97] See *The Economist*, 12 August 1995, 42.

[98] See *The Economist*, 24 June 1995, 46.

[99] See *The Economist*, 29 July 1995, 38. Mazowiecki resigned his post as human rights investigator on 27 July 1995.

Croatia, and over 500,000 moved outside the former Yugoslavia. Before the war, there were 600,000 Serbs in Croatia of a total population of 4.8 million. With the Croatian offensive in the Krajina, 150,000 were left. Before that, perhaps 200,000 had already left Croatia.[100]

Sadly, the goal of bringing humanitarian relief throughout the four years of war in Bosnia was largely a failure. Nonetheless, UNHCR had increasingly shown itself to be highly efficient during this period; the UN had provided food and shelter to over one million refugees, while, at the same time, providing shelter and supplies for refugees in Rwanda and elsewhere. UNHCR was thus given the task of providing for refugees in the Dayton Accords.

The new post-Dayton task was overwhelming. The accord suggested that refugees would be able to return to their homes. This would presumably mean that people would live as they did before the war started, which was unlikely. Even after the accords were initiated, people were being forced from their homes, and the United Nations was powerless to stop further "ethnic cleansing." UNHCR would clearly exacerbate tensions if it tried to implement this vaguely worded part of the plan.

ANALYSIS OF ROUND TWO

In the second round of negotiations leading to the Dayton Agreement, the EC, the United States, and Russia began with a strong incentive to reach multilateral agreement and avoid unilateralism. (see figure 3.2A.) Indeed, this procedural norm—rather than any particular substantive norm—provided the basis for cooperation. Cognitive considerations, combined with a change in international structure led to a commitment to multilateralism. Collective memory raised the specter of 1914, although none of the actors feared a wider war—indeed, the first round of bargaining had led to the conclusion that this war would not spread beyond the borders of the former Yugoslavia. Nonetheless there was heightened fear that tensions would erupt in an unsettled post–Cold War environment. That fear strengthened the procedural norm of multilateralism.

It was this commitment to multilateralism, combined with the participation of new actors—the United States, the United Nations, and Russia, that set the stage for the second round of negotiations. After a brief struggle over whether the EC would continue to solve the crisis alone and what roles the EC, the OSCE, and the UN would play, the principal actors chose the UN as the institution with the widest membership as the sponsor of negotiations. Tensions among the actors over appropriate strategy led to domestic pressures for alternative policies. Those

---

[100] See *The Economist*, 19 August 1995, 42.

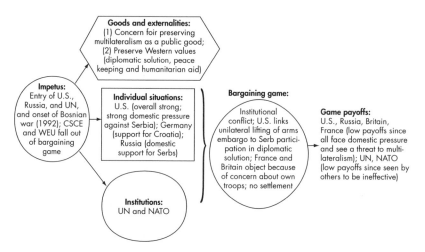

FIGURE 3.2A.   Coping with the Bosnian war

pressures combined with collective fears of chaos in post–Cold War Europe, led to an increased commitment to multilateralism. Indeed preserving multilateral agreement among the European powers and the United States, as well as preserving NATO, was preferred over a workable solution for Bosnia. The drive to resolve institutional conflicts between the UN and NATO and the assumption of leadership on the part of the United States led to NATO's dominance as the military enforcer of the accord and a retreat of the United Nations to the background. By the time the agreement was initialed in Dayton, NATO had been strengthened beyond anyone's wildest hopes or fears. (see figure 3.2B.) International institutions had engaged in a workable, if not always fully harmonious division of labor. Not only had Russia been cooperative but the Bosnian crisis had led France and Britain to a major foreign policy and defence coalition; France moved discreetly closer to NATO, allowing French troops to serve under NATO command. The French move toward NATO allowed the British to relax their opposition to the development of a European defense through the WEU. French officials also indicated that they were keen to maintain an American presence.

Furthermore, in the midst of the Bosnian crisis, European leaders began to deliberate how they might prevent future "Bosnias" from erupting. In 1993 the French Prime Minister Edouard Balladur called for the establishment of a stability pact, that is, a conference of European nations to mediate, sign bilateral treaties between potential belligerents, and make aid dependent on compliance. At the EU Copenhagen Summit in June of that year, the idea was broadly ac-

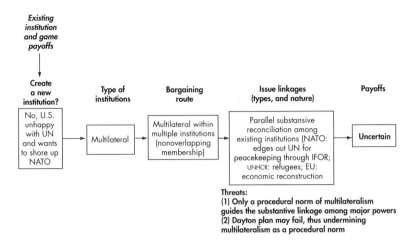

FIGURE 3.2B. Development of the Dayton agreement

cepted. No new institution would be created, and the CSCE, NATO, and the WEU would coordinate implementation.[101]

Realist approaches to international negotiation would not have predicted this outcome. At the outset two major players, France and Russia, were outside of and opposed to an expansion of NATO's military tasks. Even member states at the end of the Cold War were uncertain about NATO's utility in the post–Cold War world. As the first round of negotiations demonstrated, institutional norms were weak and conflicting in the rapidly transforming post–Cold War world. Under these conditions, none of the institutions that mattered so much in this case *should* have mattered. And because the old institutions were built within the Cold War framework, high incentives existed for them to disappear.

International structure, however, did matter. A weakened Russia, anxious to be part of the West had no choice but to join in the multilateral framework. France, though it preferred a European solution to the crisis, was not strong enough to push the process in a different direction. The United States, as the strongest power, exerted leadership in its effort to bolster NATO, and the strategy worked.

Central to a complete explanation of this outcome, however, is the meta-regime: the procedural norm of preserving multilateralism at every stage of negotiations in the second round. Commitment to this norm reduced the opportunity for domestic forces in the western states and in Russia to play a significant

---

[101] See *The Economist*, 17 July 1993, 50.

role in shaping the outcome. This contrasts sharply with the outcome of the first bargaining round, in which conflicting institutional norms provided a weak guide to joint policy, and a weak commitment to multilateralism permitted Germany's defection. When institutional guides are weak, domestic forces are likely to be more important in accounting for the final outcome.

Nonetheless, other more substantive norms may come into conflict as the Dayton Accord is implemented. IFOR, for example, can serve as a buffer for the warring parties, but there have been intense disagreements over how much force should be used to implement the plan and over the rules of engagement. Chapter 6 of the UN Charter provides for the "pacific settlement" of disputes—lightly armed peacekeeping—while chapter 7 provides for a more robust response to "acts of aggression" and other threats. Reports of disagreements over which chapter should dominate are already surfacing. And a consensual agreement on "aggression" will be hard to reach.

The agreement on the future of Bosnia also embodies a conflict that can severely weaken the accord. The preservation of Bosnia as a unitary state is intended to uphold the western value of multiethnic tolerance. On the other hand, Bosnia is partitioned into three ethnic regions, two of which have powerful patrons. The partition reflects the practical and only feasible method of settlement. But the combination is unstable and even deadly. The weak central governments and rotating presidency are throwbacks to Titoist "ethnofederalism." Ethnofederalism was an important cause of Yugoslavia's demise and of the outbreak of war.[102] A weak federal system may lead to internal chaos, while the ethnic regions, supported by Croatia and Serbia, may make a new military bid for Muslim territory.

This conflict is echoed in the plans for the refugees. As noted above, the plan suggests that refugees will return to their homes, again mirroring the values of preserving a multiethnic state. But actually implementing that value has already exacerbated tensions and threatened an unraveling of the peace.

To conclude, the procedural norm of multilateralism, set down in previous institutional arrangements and reinforced by fears arising in the wake of Germany's defection from cooperation, has been a dominant force in shaping the West's and Russia's response to the war in Yugoslavia. How the great powers responded to that war—the institutions in which decisions were made and the decisions themselves—will shape the future of the post–Cold War security order. The outlines of that order are now clear: Europe failed to develop an independent regional security regime in this crisis, and regional security institutions will coordinate their activities with increasingly compatible global institutions. The analysis of this

---

[102] See Crawford 1996 and Crawford and Lipschutz 1997.

episode suggests a successful case of institutional cooperation, coordination, and division of labor, perhaps even nesting. Earlier conflicting norms seem to have been eclipsed by the overwhelming commitment to multilateralism.

But all of this institutional cooperation has come at the expense of Bosnia. If the bloodshed begins again, then institutional cooperation and NATO's new life will have been purchased at the expense of peace. While the future of European security will have been enhanced by what leaders learned in these two rounds of negotiations over the breakup of Yugoslavia, and while they may have eventually learned to nest their institutions, for Bosnia that nest may be empty.

Considered as a test of the neorealist hypothesis, the Yugoslav and the Bosnian wars illustrate the inability of neorealist claims to deal with the institutional formation in the post–Cold War situation. Despite the end of the Cold War, the neorealists were proved wrong in their assumption about the emergence of a hegemon and the resultant provision of the public good (i.e., European security) through issue linkage. Neither did hegemons link the security issue to other issues in order to enforce participation in the formation of institutions and compliance with the new rules. Despite the potential for a reordering of the power structure of the European security arrangements, nesting was not achieved.

Similarly, the institutional framework did not appear to be as thick as the neoliberal institutionalist explanation would lead me to export. Despite the valued roles of NATO, WEU, and the OSCE and their ability to provide the public good, security, their members continued disputing the link between one arena and another, that is, they disputed the linking of European institutionalized security arrangements to the need to deal effectively and quickly with the Bosnian and the Yugoslav security crises. Contrary to some neoliberal institutionalist claims, the members of the existing institutions were willing to free ride without the fear of undermining the existing institutions.

In terms of cognitive considerations, the Bosnia crisis demonstrates more than ever before the powerful effect that ideas have in the formation of the beliefs of those who make foreign policy as well as in the creation of a multilateral institutional structure. Yet, it should be noted that the cognitive approach stresses the role of ideas in determining action more in an ideological fashion than in terms of learning. The procedural norm of multilateralism, which had formed the basis of previous European security institutional arrangements as well as the assumption underlying postwar German foreign and security policy, became the most important force in the shaping of the West's and Russia's respective responses to the disintegration of Yugoslavia and the Bosnian conflict. Throughout 1991–96 the European policymakers and their American counterparts worked to arrive at a solution that would be based upon a multilateral intervention, both militarily and diplomatically. Multilateralism in this case was not chosen because of its information and coordination advantages and was only partly a result of the changes in the international structure in the post–Cold War era but because it reflected the beliefs of the makers of foreign policy. Much as the U.S. policymakers saw the maintenance of a united, multiethnic Bosnia to be an end in and of itself, so too was multilateralism seen by European policymakers to be an end rather than a means.

REFERENCES

Barlett, Christopher, 1989. *British Foreign Policy in the Twentieth Century* (Basingstoke, United Kingdom: Macmillan).

Betts, Richard, 1992. "Systems of Peace or Causes of War? Collective Security, Arms Control, and the New Europe." *International Security* 17 (Summer).

Claude, Inis, Jr., 1971. *Swords into Ploughshares* (New York: Random House).

Crawford, Beverly, 1996. "Explaining Defection from Cooperation: Germany's Unilateral Recognition of Croatia." *World Politics* 46 (July).

———, forthcoming 1998. *The Political Economy of Cultural Conflict* (Berkeley International and Area Studies Press).

———, ed., 1992. *The Future of European Security* (Berkeley: International and Area Studies Press).

Crawford, Beverly, and Ronnie Lipschutz, 1997. "Discourses of War: Security and the Case of Yugoslavia." In Michael Williams and Keith Krause, eds., *Critical Security Studies* (Minneapolis: University of Minnesota Press).

Cviic, Christopher, 1993. "Who's to Blame for the War in the Ex-Yugoslavia." *World Affairs* 156 (Fall).

Eichenberg, Richard, and Russell Dalton, 1993. "Europeans and the European Community: The Dynamics of Public Support for European Integration." *International Organization* 47 (Autumn).

Glenny, Misha, 1992. *The Fall of Yugoslavia: The Third Balkan War* (London: Penguin).

———, 1995. "Yugoslavia: The Great Fall." *New York Review of Books*, 23 March 1995.

Haftedorn, Helga, 1993. *Sichereit und Entspannung: Zur Aussenpolitik der Bundesrepublik Deutschland, 1955–1982* (Baden-Baden: Nomos Verlag).

Handrierer, Wolfram, 1989. *Germany, America, Europe* (New Haven: Yale University Press).

Hayden, Robert, 1992. "Constitutional Nationalism in the Former Yugoslav Republics." *Slavic Review* 51 (Winter).

Jelavich, Barbara, 1983. *History of the Balkans: Twentieth Century* (London: Cambridge University Press).

Katzenstein, Peter, 1991. "Coping with Terrorism: Norms and Internal Security in Germany and Japan." Paper presented at the American Political Science Association Conference, Washington, D.C.

Kenney, George, 1995. "Derecognition: Exiting Bosnia." *Policy Brief*, no. 5 (San Diego: University of California Institute for Global Conflict and Cooperation).

Krieger, Wolfgang, 1994. "Toward a Gaullist Germany?" *World Policy Journal* 11 (Spring).

Lamborn, Alan, 1991. *The Price of Power: Risk and Foreign Policy in Britain, France and Germany* (London: Unwin Hyman).

Mearsheimer, John, 1990. "Back to the Future: Instability in Europe after the Cold War." *International Security* 15 (Summer).

———, 1994. "False Promises of International Institutions." *International Security* 19 (Winter).

Mearsheimer, John, and Steven van Evera, 1995. "When Peace Means War." *New Republic*, 18 December.

Nere, Jacques, 1975. *The Foreign Policy of France from 1914 to 1945* (London: Routledge and Kegan Paul).

Osmanczyck, Edmund, ed., 1985. *Encyclopedia of the United Nations and International Agreements* (Philadelphia: Taylor and Francis).

Paterson, William, 1992. "Gulliver Unbound: The Changing Context of Foreign Policy." in Gordon Smith, William Paterson, Peter Merkl and Stephen Padgett, eds., *Developments in German Politics* (Durham: Duke University Press).

Pavlowitch, Stevan, 1988. *Yugoslavia and its Problems: 1918–1988* (London: Hurst).

Plestina, Dijana, 1992. *Politics, Economics and War: Problems of Transition in Croatia*, working paper 5.15 (Berkeley: Center for German and European Studies).

Pomerance, Michla, 1982. *Self-Determination in Law and Practice: The New Doctrine in the United Nations* (The Hague: Martinus Nijhoff).

Rich, Roland, 1993. "Recognition of States: The Collapse of Yugoslavia and the Soviet Union." *European Journal of International Law* 4, no. 1.

Rieff, David, 1994. "The Illusions of Peacekeeping." *World Policy Journal* 6, no. 3.

Salmon, Trevor, 1992. "Testing Times for European Political Cooperation: The Gulf and Yugoslavia, 1990–1992." *International Affairs* 68, no. 2.

Sandoltz, Wayne, 1993. "Choosing Union: Monetary Politics and Maastricht." *International Organization* 47, no. 1.

Sandoltz, Wayne, and John Zysman, 1989. "Recasting the European Bargain." *World Politics* 42 (October).

Seton-Watson, Hugh, 1967. *Eastern Europe between the Wars* (New York: Harper and Row).

Smith, Gordon, William Paterson, Peter Merkl and Stephen Padgett, eds., 1992 *Developments in German Politics* (Durham, N.C.: Duke University Press).

Rondholz, Eberhard, 1992. "Deutsche Erblasten im jugoslawischen Buergerkrieg" (The Burden of German History in the Yugoslav Wars). *Blaetter fuer Deutsche und Internationale Politik* 37 (July).

Weber, Steven, 1992. "Does NATO Have a Future?" In Beverly Crawford, ed., *The Future of European Security* (Berkeley: International and Area Studies Press).

CHAPTER FOUR

The Failure of the Nest-Best Solution: EC-EFTA Institutional Relationships and the European Economic Area

CÉDRIC DUPONT

In the late 1980s, after decades of parallel development, the twelve member states of the European Communities (EC) and the seven members of the European Free Trade Association (EFTA) attempted to build common institutions to address the double challenge of competitive world markets and new realities in Central and Eastern Europe.[1] They came up with a grand idea: the European Economic Area (EEA) project, which was to lead to a broad regional accord encompassing the two existing subregional institutions. The initial mandate of the EEA was to preserve subregional institutional diversity while minimizing the costs of it. For EFTA countries, this mostly meant sticking to their vision of "natural" economic integration while enjoying access to the EC Single Market at a very acceptable price. For the EC, the EEA was the best way to prevent the crowding-out of their club. They would extend some of the group privileges to EFTA members but without jeopardizing the individual benefits to existing

For comments I thank Vinod Aggarwal, Jerry Cohen, Jonah Levy, and Steven Weber as well as two anonymous reviewers for Cornell University Press.

[1] For the sake of convenience, I shall throughout the paper use the European Community (EC) as a generic title for the integration process from the Treaty of Rome to the current status. Although historical accuracy would force me to distinguish between the European Communities (EC), the European Economic Community (EEC), the European Community (EC), and the European Union (EU), I will not do so here.

members. Furthermore, the hope was that the new institution would help stem the pressure from Central and Eastern European countries.

The project materialized in 1992 when member countries of EC and EFTA signed an agreement to create a vast market of over 370 million consumers in which goods, capital, services, and persons would move freely. The agreement also provided member countries with a set of cooperative schemes in domains such as research and development, education, consumer policy, social policy, and the environment. But EFTA countries had to pay a high price for gaining privileged access to the Single Market. The EC took full control of decision making, imposed its agenda on EFTA countries, and even forced EFTA to build up some supranational structures. This price proved to be too high and quickly transformed the EEA into an obsolescent framework. In December 1992, Switzerland dropped out of the treaty after the government's defeat in the domestic ratification campaign. Six months later, Austria, Finland, Norway, and Sweden started bargaining over the terms of their entry into the EC, and the first three ultimately joined. At the same time, the EEA failed to attract the attention of Central and Eastern European countries and thus failed to stem the rush to the EC house. In short, then, the EEA was an overpriced product that quickly vanished.

This episode is puzzling: Why did the EC overprice the EEA product? There is no doubt that the EC was a regional hegemon and that EFTA was in a position of *demandeur*. There was thus a natural temptation for the hegemon to sell partial access to its limited inclusive club at a very high price and to definitely impose its conception of integration and sovereignty in Europe. But the EEA was also supposed to help produce a common pool resources (CPR) good—pan-regional stability.[2] And the EC needed some help from EFTA countries for this undertaking: First, the EC wanted to avoid having to accept new members coming from EFTA and thereby sending the message that it was enlarging. Second, it wanted to use the new joint institutional structure—not the EC—as an anchor for emerging economies and countries in Central and Eastern Europe. To secure the help of EFTA countries, the EC had to design a new institution that was not too asymmetric in terms of political authority. Why did it fail to do so? Unidimensional explanations are of little help. There was no change in the nature of the good to be produced. There was no cognitive change among EC decisionmakers on the usefulness of the EEA. There was no major power change between the actors involved in the case. So how can we explain the chosen path of action? To answer this question, this chapter relies on the notion of "institutional bargaining games" to account for the dynamics of institutional creation

---

[2] On common pool resources, see Ostrom 1990.

and decay between EC and EFTA countries from the mid-1980s to the mid-1990s.[3]

To address the effects of major contextual changes, EC and EFTA countries responded with the creation of a new institution—the EEA. The crux of the problem was that this new institution had to be reconciled with existing ones— EC and EFTA. The nature and type of the institutional linkage were especially problematic. Even though there were grounds for a substantive nested linkage of the existing institutions inside the new one, the process faced a major obstacle. The salience of the EC was high, and EC members were not ready to have it endangered by a nested position inside the EEA. They were ready to risk conflict with EFTA members rather than to yield on this point. From this perspective, the situation was potentially explosive, and EFTA countries provided the spark that ignited it. Under severe domestic constraints, several EFTA governments asked the EC for a large role in the future institution. These demands fueled EC fears that the Community would lose some control over its destiny. In particular, the European Parliament and southern member states opposed granting any significant concessions to EFTA members and forced the EC commission to follow a tough bargaining attitude. Imposing a high price for EFTA's access to the Single Market took precedence over getting EFTA's support for the provision of pan-regional stability, a CPR good. This strategy backfired because it pushed most EFTA countries to ask for immediate entry into the EC and directed all the pressure from Central and Eastern European countries onto the EC alone.

The first section of this chapter covers the road toward the EEA from the Luxembourg process through the Single European Act and its effects. Shocks during this period mostly affected EFTA countries who feared losing private goods from their privileged relationship with the EC. Given the EC's lack of interest in changing the existing bargaining game, and given that EFTA countries lacked the power to force change, no major institutional change occurred during that period. The second section of this chapter highlights how change materialized. The evolution in Central and Eastern Europe created new negative externalities in Western Europe and created the need for some joint action among Western European countries in order to preserve pan-regional stability and prosperity. To address this new challenge, the EC suddenly became more interested in a new partnership with EFTA countries, opening the way to the process of designing a new institution, the EEA. I examine how a cocktail of severe domestic constraints in EFTA countries, the high salience of the EC club, and sharply asymmetric power pushed the parties down the wrong road toward an overpriced EEA. The third and last section focuses on the movement away from

[3] See Vinod Aggarwal, chapter 1, this volume, for a description of the analytical framework linked with the notion of "institutional bargaining games."

the EEA toward EC membership for most EFTA countries. Membership provided these countries with better private goods than the EEA at roughly the same price. They thus had no reason to stick to the EEA. I conclude the article with some general lessons from the case on institutional change and nesting in processes of regional integration.

Toward the EEA: 1984–89

Ever since the splitting of Western European trade arrangements in the late 1950s, which was due to the failure of the Maudling Plan to establish a Wide Free Trade Area, relationships between EFTA countries and EC countries have remained a key issue in the evolution of Western European regional integration. Both political and economic concerns have shaped the marital life of this awkward couple and led to a range of unilateral, bilateral, and multilateral actions from both sides. I do not review here the historical evolution of these arrangements; instead I start in the early eighties after the full implementation of the series of free trade agreements that followed the entry of the United Kingdom, Denmark, and Ireland into the EC.[4] I describe the state of the situation at that time and consider it as being the "initial bargaining situation." I then turn to an examination of how the situation was affected by new developments on world markets and inside the EC.

The Initial Bargaining Situation

After the free trade agreements of 1972, which gradually led to the final removal of trade barriers on December 31, 1983, the relationships between EFTA and EC did not undergo major changes: EFTA countries expressed their willingness to develop closer economic coordination to avoid the potential drawbacks of divergent economic policies, but this had no effect. The EC was facing major internal and external challenges—enlargement to include Greece, the furthering of special economic ties with former French colonies, and domestic economic recession in the wake of oil crises—factors that made relations with the EFTA a secondary priority.

Western Europe was characterized by a clear separation between the EFTA and EC, each abiding by different regulatory arrangements. They developed links between each other but maintained their autonomy. Both were nested

---

[4] The free trade agreements were concluded between each EFTA member and the EC, along the lines of a kind of hub and spoke pattern as characterized by Baldwin 1994. For studies on the path to these agreements, see in particular Bachmann 1970 and Binswanger 1972.

under the GATT framework which regulated trade activities at the global level. Significant differences existed both at the meta-regime and at the regime level. The EC opted for economic and political integration, whereas the EFTA aimed for regional free trade. The EC regime was strong, with supranational bodies to enforce and monitor the regulations, whereas the EFTA was weak and exclusively intergovernmental. Both were rather liberal in nature, although the EC tended to be more restrictive with outsiders. Finally, the scope of the EC regime was broad, with a large agenda of trade liberalization, trade facilitation, and economic cooperation for goods and services, whereas the EFTA was limited to the trade of industrial goods. In sum, regulation of national actions was much stronger and broader for EC members than for EFTA members who often engaged in ad hoc measures to cope with rising externalities. As an illustration, each EFTA country negotiated separately its free trade agreement in 1972, even though there was a common pattern in all the bilateral agreements. "Bounded unilateral course of action" also characterized the failed attempt by Austria, Sweden, and Switzerland to negotiate association agreements with the EC in the period 1961–63. This mixture of coherent international regulations and fragmented national controls increased transaction costs and thus lessened the economic potential of regional trade despite growing interdependence among societies. Even though there were these shortcomings, there was no strong willingness among the members of the two groups to promote a game change. Externalities were not perceived as being major difficulties and political costs of changing course were prohibitively high.

Status Quo Plus: The Luxembourg Process

In the beginning of the eighties, the dual structure of trade arrangements in Western Europe became more of a problem for the various parties, which began to think of the possibility of changing the rules of the game. World competition, especially from newly industrialized countries in Asia, became increasingly costly to most Western European economies. This fostered a need for both domestic economic reforms and collective action at the regional level. This was not, however, joint collective action between the EC and EFTA. EC countries were concerned about the stagnation of intra-EC trade due to the fragmentation of the large EC market. As a consequence, they focused their efforts on ways to stimulate the internal dynamics, whereas EFTA members were much more interested in joint action. This was not surprising given the increasing dependence of EFTA countries on EC markets. This dependence was the direct consequence of the realization of free trade for industrial goods and of the severing of access to alternative markets.[5] With respect to trade flows, between 1972

---

[5] See Pedersen 1994, 28.

and 1986, intra-EFTA imports fell as a percentage of total EFTA imports from 15.9 to 13.3 percent, while EFTA's imports from the EC increased from 59.4 to 61.1 percent.[6] EFTA countries feared a loss of individual benefits from their relationships with EC countries and wanted to implement some institutional change to prevent an erosion of their privileges.

With the EC mostly focusing on its own deepening, change remained quite limited. The major development—the launching of the so-called Luxembourg process—remained primarily a cosmetic change with some symbolic value.[7] Meeting on April 9, 1984, to discuss the prospects of future joint cooperation, EC and EFTA ministers emphasized their willingness to deepen bilateral ties and, ultimately, to create a "dynamic European economic space." This rather vague label encompassed a broad agenda: (1) members from both organizations were obliged to increase their efforts regarding harmonization of standards, to remove nontariff barriers, to simplify border facilities, and to eliminate unfair practices; (2) cooperation was also to concern the fields of research and development; (3) there was to be coordination of employment policies; and (4) exchange of information on economic and trade difficulties was promoted. To monitor and supervise the follow-up of this program, EC and EFTA countries established a High Level Contact Group which began working on the removal of technical barriers to trade.

The First Major Shock: The Single European Act

Shortly after the launching of the Luxembourg process with EFTA, the EC adopted the Single European Act in December 1985, a program that aimed at transforming the European Community into a vast frontier-free economic and social area which would tend toward a political union with even closer cooperation on foreign policy and security.[8]

In terms of Aggarwal's framework, the internal market was the first strong shock to the existing institutional bargaining game between EFTA and the EC. (See figure 4.1A.) The development of the Single Market program immediately created fear among EFTA countries of being left out of economic integration in Western Europe. While this fear existed prior to the Single Act, it took a new dimension with the advent of the single market, especially when the first concrete

[6] *EFTA Trade,* 1986.

[7] Some authors see the "European prise de conscience" to be the real impetus toward a new relationship between the EC and EFTA (Pedersen 1994, 29–31; Laursen 1990). I consider it to be much more the continuation of an incremental process, as illustrated by the wording of the Luxembourg declaration—"consolidate and strengthen cooperation" through "flexible cooperation."

[8] See for instance Moravcsik 1991 and Cameron 1992 for an analytical account of the road toward the agreement on the internal market.

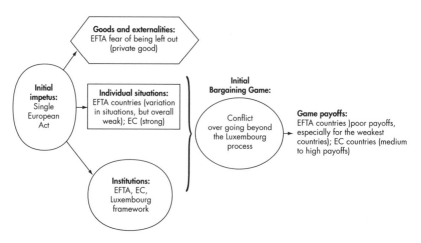

FIGURE 4.1A. The effects of the Single European Act

implications of the program began to appear in 1987–88. The best indicator of EFTA's fear of a "fortress Europe" can be found in foreign direct investment (FDI) flows. In 1985, 28 percent of EFTA's outward FDI went to the EC; in 1988 this figure was about two thirds.[9] Sweden and Switzerland were the most sensitive, but Finland and Norway also underwent significant changes. This increasing outward flow of investment was gradually eroding the productive base of EFTA countries. EFTA did not specialize in the fastest growing industries and had almost no interaction with the high-technology sector. Specialization in low-technology products or intermediate-technology products made EFTA countries especially vulnerable to fierce competition from the Third World. Privileged access to the EC market was thus extremely important. In addition to market access, cooperation with EC countries in R&D was crucial to develop new industries.[10]

Despite official EC denials that the Single Act would lead to "a fortress Europe" and commitments that it would be a partner and act to "strengthen the multilateral system," it was not clear to EFTA countries and firms how the EC could avoid restricting its markets somewhat. The EC Council of Ministers, because it was directly linked to the preservation of domestic interests, raised doubts about the Community's ability to meet the openness requirement. The increased power of the European Parliament in foreign relations was of little

[9] The major leap occurred in 1988 after the awareness that the Single Market would became a reality. FDI flows from the EFTA to the EC amounted to 2,086 million ECUs in 1985, 2,400 in 1986, 4,591 in 1987, and 10,904 in 1988 (Pedersen 1994, 31).

[10] Nell 1990, 351–52.

comfort because Parliament members might use market access as a tactical tool to promote political and social rights in outsider countries.[11]

In sum, the Single European Act threatened to disrupt EFTA countries' private access to the EC club. Concerned with this potential blow to their existing payoffs, they were willing to implement some change in the institutional game with the EC countries. But the room to maneuver was quite limited—both because of the lack of interest by their EC partners as well as stringent domestic brakes against supranational action. EC countries were concerned about crowding-out effects in their club and thus were not interested in selling access to it. At the same time, EFTA countries did not have much to spend on access anyway due to domestic political opposition to large European initiatives. As we will see in the next section, this resulted in the EFTA's attempt to make the best out of the existing institutional setting, while waiting for better times.

Responding to the Single European Act: Multiple Functional Cooperation

Reactions to and ways of remedying the potential negative externalities of the Single European Act differed according to national abilities to sustain the shock, domestic political constraints, systemic imperatives and the actors' perceptions of the nature of the problem. Figure 4.1B depicts the various paths taken by EFTA and EC countries during the years 1986–89. First and foremost, the parties *did not engage in building a new international institution* but continued to use the existing ones, that is the EC, the EFTA, and the Luxembourg framework between the two organizations. The EC favored the status quo—functional cooperation through the Luxembourg framework together with the continuation of some bilateral accords with single EFTA countries—which led to two bargaining routes, a multilateral one and a bilateral one. The EC's attitude stemmed from cognitive and domestic coalitional imperatives. There was a strong agreement among EC countries that priority should go to the full realization of the internal market and not to relationships with neighboring countries, including EFTA countries.[12] Widening would have hurt deepening and would have stopped the new impetus given by the Single European Act program. For the EFTA countries, on the other hand, the use of existing institutions was the only position commonly held. Members of the EFTA were converging on the need for something between adhesion and the status quo. This "muddling through" could hardly disguise

[11] On the new role of the Parliament vis-à-vis the external world, see, for instance, Corbett 1989.

[12] See for instance the declarations of Commissioner De Clercq during the Joint EC-EFTA ministerial meeting at Interlaken on May 20, 1987 (*Agence Europe*, 20 May 1987). De Clercq mentioned three guiding principles: (1) priority should be given to internal EC integration; (2) EC's autonomous power of decision should be preserved and (3) there should be a fair balance between benefits and obligations in any deal with nonmembers.

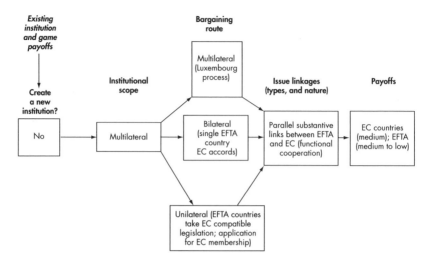

FIGURE 4.1B.   Responding to the Single European Act: Multiple functional
cooperation

individual differences. At the multilateral level, members diverged on the question of strengthening EFTA in order to improve their bargaining position with
respect to the EC, and also on whether a new institutional arrangement should
be a short-term or long-term venture. They also diverged on the respective
weight of multilateral and bilateral bargaining routes. The Scandinavian countries preferred a multilateral bargaining route through the Luxembourg process
and EFTA, whereas Switzerland sought a more balanced approach between bilateral and multilateral solutions.[13] Austria wished to pursue the unilateral option of seeking EC membership.

Different domestic political constraints and divergent economic interests
stemming from different economic specialization and domestic regimes explain
the variation in preferences and strategies. If all EFTA countries were largely dependent upon EC markets—much more dependent than the EC countries were
upon EFTA markets—different aspects of the EC internal market appeared to
be important to different EFTA countries. Austria was the most dependent upon
EC markets, and the presence of Austrian companies abroad had traditionally
been low, thus making export capacity all the more important for it.[14] Industry
was predominantly small scale, with a very low level of outward foreign direct

[13] These positions were revealed in the respective reports on European integration released by the
different governments in 1987 and 1988. See Hamilton 1991 for an analysis of the reports of the
Scandinavian governments, and Sciarini 1992 for Switzerland.

[14] Pedersen 1994, 79–85; Luif 1990, 189–93.

investment. In addition, the domestic market was highly segmented by domestic firms capturing high rents. Under these conditions, reforms were to achieve a higher level of competition through the removal of border procedures and through mutual recognition of diplomas and establishment rights.

These reforms could hardly be undertaken without an external push given the corporatist structure that protected the existing situation. Consensus politics would make the necessary redistribution of income, or rents, from existing firms to new entrants or new consumers almost impossible. As a consequence, political elites became increasingly interested in the option of joining the EC in order to push for the necessary reforms. In June 1988, the influential report of a working group on European integration of senior civil servants came to the conclusion that the multilateral approach through EFTA had hardly shown any concrete results.[15] The consensus—that the only way to get out of the economic difficulties was through full participation in the Single Market program—was not limited to political elites but also reached the broader society. Labor wanted to get rid of rent-seeking firms that jeopardized job creation. They saw an opening into the domestic market as the only way to do so. On the side of industry, deregulation had a strong appeal.[16] In sum, both domestic economic characteristics and domestic political feasibility pushed Austria toward the unilateral strategy of asking for EC membership.[17] Economic necessity was more heavily weighted by the Austrian government than the concern with neutrality. In other words, expected payoffs from EC membership largely outweighed existing payoffs outside the EC.

In contrast to Austria, the other EFTA countries thought that they could remedy the externalities of the Single European Act (SEA) without full participation in the internal market, let alone membership in the EC. In the Scandinavian countries, some industry studies came to the conclusion that large gains would come from the first stage of integration—reduced trade costs and increased intra-industry trade. The reason is that in these small, open economies, the dominance of domestic firms is weaker than in a country like Austria, and imports are more important.[18] Sweden, particularly, was looking for improvements in the goods sector, and equal access to public procurement markets for high-tech firms would seem to be one of the economically more important areas. For the Finnish government, compatibility of technical standards and norms was one of

[15] See Wieser and Kitzmantel 1990, 436.

[16] Ibid., 444.

[17] In Austria membership became a top priority at the beginning of 1988. The government no longer considered the EFTA an adequate substitute to full integration to the EC internal market, mainly because it could not offer sufficient participation in decision making. See Dupont, Sciarini, and Lutterbeck 1997.

[18] For detailed results of these studies, see Haaland 1990, 398.

their prime objectives.[19] In Norway, large natural resources, in energy in particular, prevented any sense of economic urgency.[20] And Iceland was primarily interested in having access for its fisheries products. For Switzerland, a well-developed banking and insurance sector was a key concern. The high level of internationalization of the Swiss economy, and the relatively wide array of exports markets, lessened the sense of economic urgency raised by the Single Act.[21]

In addition to these economic considerations, domestic politics and international systemic constraints ruled out the EC membership option. Neutrality was still a prevailing and domestically popular principle. The decisions on foreign policy and security issues inside the EC would endanger this deeply rooted principle. The Swiss people were also concerned about a possible erosion of their political system, which was based on direct democracy and federalism. In Norway, European integration was still a highly divisive topic, and no government had dared to venture too far into it. Finally, in Iceland, any move toward supranationalism was perceived to be prohibitively costly by the government.

THE EEA EXPERIENCE: 1989–91

In the late eighties, new developments in Central and Eastern Europe created new externalities that endangered the future consumption of the newly established CPR good for EC and EFTA countries—pan-regional stability in Europe.[22] In addition, these new developments created a fear of crowding-out effects in the EC club, especially among southern EC members. The shock needed to be responded to, and the EC turned to EFTA partners to implement a major institutional change—the creation of the EEA (see Figure 4.2A).

The Second Major and Decisive Shock: Changes in Central and Eastern Europe

Negative externalities from the development of the EC internal market program had clearly created a desire for a new institutional arrangement on the

---

[19] See Antola 1990.

[20] See Saeter 1990.

[21] This did not mean, however, that Swiss firms were not adapting to the Single Market program. See Brauchlin 1989 for a description of changes in the strategies of Swiss firms. For a contrasting perspective on Austrian and Swiss responses to the Single European Act, see Dupont, Sciarini and Lutterbeck 1997.

[22] During the Cold War, pan-regional stability was a by-product of bipolarity in Europe between NATO and Soviet Union. For EC and EFTA countries, this was either an inclusive club good (for members of NATO) or a public good which they could enjoy for free. The end of the Cold War transformed the nature of the good by adding a collective dimension to it (that is, by making it into a CPR). EC and EFTA could no longer rely exclusively on other arenas or actors to ensure the provision of pan-regional stability.

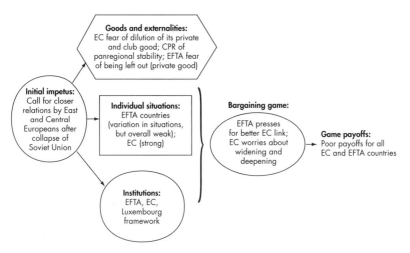

FIGURE 4.2A.   The effects of changes in Central and Eastern Europe on EFTA and EC relations

part of EFTA countries. However, the EC was not in a rush to promote change simply because externalities did not affect it. This situation changed in the late eighties in the wake of the economic and political reform processes in Central and Eastern Europe. These developments began to affect the EC payoffs in the existing game.

The priority of deepening was affected by economic and political pressure coming from the East. Economically, there were emerging demands for new trade arrangements, and the EC could hardly resist them without jeopardizing ongoing political reforms. The best cases were Poland and Hungary where political rights were expanded in 1988, leading to the entry of democrats in their Parliaments in 1989. As a consequence, the Community began to conclude special agreements with these countries. In November 1988, Hungary was the first member of the Council of Mutual Economic Assistance (CMEA) to get such an agreement. It included a schedule for the abolition of specific quantitative restrictions on Hungarian exports to the EC. Czechoslovakia signed a less wide-ranging agreement on industrial goods in March 1989. In September 1989, Poland signed an agreement similar to the Hungarian one.[23] These agreements themselves did not endanger the pace of the Community's deepening process; but there was clearly a fear that new demands would come from other countries and a concern that more far-reaching demands would emerge. This would be costly both politically and economically. In sum, the new shock endangered the future consumption of the EC club good by its current members and, at the

[23] See Nicolaïdis 1993 for more details on these accords.

same time, created the need for the provision of a new European CPR good, pan-regional stability. Members of the EC and EFTA did not have to worry about it in a bipolar Europe but the unraveling of the Communist pole forced them to address this issue. Keeping in mind the continuing concern of EFTA countries with their individual access to the EC club good, the shock radically transformed the strategic interaction between EFTA and EC by creating a mix of goods. Most significantly, there were not only goods characterized by the possibility of exclusion—club or private goods—but also a CPR good which required a new institutional structure. EC hegemony would not be sufficient to ensure the provision of this good, not the least because private benefits of EC members risked being jeopardized by a unilateral provision of the new collective good. Thus both sides had a strong interest in doing something to alter the existing situation, and they did not wait long to act.

The first step of the EEA process was taken in early 1989 by the President of the EC Commission, Jacques Delors. In a decisive speech to the European Parliament on January 17, Delors emphasized the need for a new partnership with the EFTA countries. He envisioned this new approach as a "more structured partnership with common decision-making and administrative solutions in order to increase the efficiency of our action."[24] EFTA countries reacted to the commonality of interests and values highlighted by Delors and responded positively to the proposal during a ministerial meeting in Oslo on March 15. They explained that enlarged cooperation under the Luxembourg process had not lived up to their expectations and hopes. They endorsed the necessity of exploring together with EC countries the "ways and means to achieve a more structured partnership with common decision-making and administrative institutions in order to make cooperation more effective."[25]

Delors's initiative and the positive response by EFTA countries led to a new dialogue between the two sides, initiated by a joint ministerial meeting in Brussels on March 20, 1989. Ministers noted the major progress achieved since the Luxembourg Declaration, and they confirmed their willingness to extend and deepen their cooperation. They asked for a comprehensive examination of the "possible scope and content of an expanded and more structured partnership between the Community and EFTA countries."[26] The parties concluded exploratory discussions in October and agreed to move on with the opening of formal negotiations.[27] Exploratory talks between January and March 1990 stiffened the parties' resolve to immediately open final negotiations.

---

[24] *Agence Europe,* 26 January 1989.

[25] *EFTA Bulletin,* no. 2, 1989, 6.

[26] *Agence Europe,* 20–21 March 1989.

[27] They defined the objectives of these negotiations to be (1) the achievement of the free movements of goods, services, capital and persons on the basis of the relevant *acquis communautaire* to be

Debating the Institutional Options: 1989–90

Institutional choices and linkages were key considerations and points of contention—both in the fact-finding and exploratory phases. Figure 4.2B illustrates
the alternative choices that were evaluated (dashed lines) and the path actually
favored by the parties (solid lines). To address the externalities of the new situation, both parties decided to engage in the creation of a new institution rather
than simply using existing arrangements. The reason behind this choice
stemmed from the nature of the goods at stake, from the individual situations of
actors, and from past performance of existing institutions.

The Luxembourg process between EFTA and the EC had clearly shown its
limits. Nine multilateral agreements had been signed, but they were limited
mostly to administrative procedures.[28] Functional cooperation was inadequate
to meet the new challenges and thus had lost its appeal to both sides. Another
existing option was an extended use of the EC. The Community itself opposed
such an option, at least for the near future. Priority had clearly been given to the
completion of the internal market before any widening to include new members. The EC feared crowding-out effects, and therefore wanted to build a new

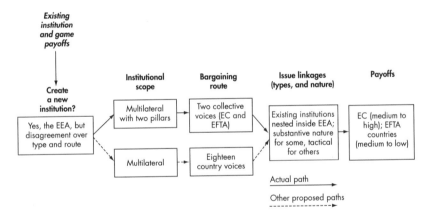

FIGURE 4.2B.   Designing the EEA

---

identified jointly; (2) the strengthening and broadening of cooperation in areas such as research and
development, environment, education, working conditions and social welfare; and (3) the reduction
of economic and social disparities between regions—the so-called principle of social and economic
cohesion. The resulting framework was to "respect in full the decision-making autonomy of the parties." *Agence Europe*, 23 December 1989; *EFTA Bulletin*, no. 4, 1989 and no. 1, 1990.

[28] Three were related to administrative measures facilitating border controls or information on
these; one covered export restrictions; one dealt with rules of origin; three concerned exchange of
information to increase transparency in governments' procedures; and the last one pertained to education (Nell 1990, 347).

institution that would help it preserve pan-regional stability without jeopardiz-ing the distribution of private goods to the existing members. In addition, most EFTA countries also ruled out an extended use of the EC. Austria was the only country in favor of adhesion out of economic urgency and decision-making au-tonomy. In that country, there was a strong consensus among elites in favor of joining the Community. The two largest parties, the Socialist and the Populist, favored adhesion and were united in a strong coalition government with 157 out of 183 seats in Parliament. If the Austrian government preferred to join the EC, it considered the creation of a new institution to be a second-best solution. Aus-tria chose to support this solution at least until the opening of negotiations over membership because it was the quickest road to Brussels.

In the other EFTA countries, concern with neutrality and sensitive domestic political constituents continued to rule out the EC membership option. Hostil-ity was greater in Norway, Switzerland, and Iceland but also quite strong in Sweden and Finland. In Norway, the Conservative Party broke the ice on pos-sible adhesion, but its coalition partners in the government, the Christian Peo-ple's Party, and especially the Center Party were opposed to such a move.[29] As a consequence, the biggest disagreement was over European affairs, ruling out possible adhesion.[30] In Switzerland, the four largest parties—radicals, conserv-atives, socialists, and agrarians—supported the government's "third way," that is, the search for a new partnership with the EC that would go beyond current bilateralism without endangering Swiss interests. Fears for Swiss national iden-tity, aversion to European red tape, and determination to preserve agriculture and direct democracy spurred the emergence of a minority coalition opposed to any change in the Swiss attitude toward Europe. This minority did not hold much weight inside Parliament, but had a strong following among the German-speaking population, especially in the small rural cantons. In Iceland, opposi-tion to adhesion was the only common denominator inside the coalition gov-ernment. While the Social Democrats favored closer ties with the EC and favored the creation of a new institution, the People's Alliance and the Progres-sive party were more reluctant about pursuing the EEA process. In Sweden, the minority Social-Democratic government was in a stable position with regard to

[29] Among the parties represented in Parliament, the Socialist Left held 17 seats, Labor 63, the Christian People's party 14, the Center party 11, the Conservatives 37, the Progress party 22, and one seat was occupied by a nonaffiliated member (Valen 1990, 278).

[30] The Center party which represented the primary sector was fiercely anti-EC and viewed the EEA process with suspicion. The Christian People's party represented the Lutheran bourgeoisie, who feared the prospects of a European Political Union but also the hegemony of the Catholic Church in Western Europe. On the contrary, the Conservatives were overwhelmingly in favor of closer ties with Europe either through some association formula or through full membership.

European affairs.[31] This was due to the existence of a compromise between the major parties regarding European integration. Sweden would make all efforts to improve its situation, short of EC adhesion. Finland was in a similar situation with the largest parties in Parliament favoring a deepening of links with the EC.[32]

EC adhesion was also economically suboptimal for these EFTA countries, despite the increasing pressure of increasing flows of foreign direct investments by both multinational and smaller firms in countries like Sweden and Switzerland. Rushing to the EC was not the first option because preserving the competitiveness of EFTA economies would require compatibility between European integration and world competitiveness.[33]

A third option, available only to the Nordic countries, was to use the existing pan-Nordic cooperative institutions, including the Nordic Council, the Council of Ministers, and the Joint Investment Bank. Although these institutions helped establish a Scandinavian identity, they could not serve as effective instruments to address the externalities created by the SEA.[34]

The high degree of salience that the EC had for its members deeply influenced the choice of pursuing a multilateral institution with two pillars, a bilateral bargaining route, and an asymmetric tactical nested linkage between the new and the existing institutions. This salience, however, was not sufficient to explain the institutional path chosen by the actors.

In terms of the type of new institution, the choice was not between unilateral, bilateral, or multilateral types, but among various multilateral types. Clearly, the EEA would encompass the eighteen members of the two existing institutions and would thus be multilateral in terms of membership. In terms of decision-making procedures, however, the EC did not want to have its own prerogatives diluted inside the new institution. At a meeting in Consendonck, Netherlands, in April 1988, the EC Commission stated that until the end of 1992, priority had to be given to deepening rather than widening. Any new development with EFTA had to respect this commitment or would otherwise meet the opposition of institutional actors,

[31] Social Democrats held 156 seats out of 349, but benefited from the passive support of the Communists who held 21 seats, thus preventing the formation of any blocking group. The other parties represented in the Riksdag were: Conservative (66 seats), Center party (42), People's party (44), and Greens (20) (Wörlund 1989, 82).

[32] The 1987 legislative elections had given 56 seats to the Social Democrats, 53 to the Conservatives, 13 to the Swedish People's party, and 9 to the Rural party. These four parties formed the government. Other parties included the Center party with 40 seats, Leftist Union with 20 seats, the Greens with 4 seats, and the Christian Union with 5 seats (Berglund 1991, 337).

[33] See interview of Georg Reisch, secretary-general of the EFTA, in *West-Ost Journal*, nos. 5, 3/4, June 1989.

[34] See Church 1990, 412–13.

such as the Parliament[35] or domestic constituencies, particularly in southern EC countries.[36] Whereas a truly multilateral framework would not meet this commitment, the Commission proposed an institutional structure with two pillars—the EC and EFTA. The salience of the EC cannot explain, however, why the Commission requested a strengthening of EFTA structures to ensure the feasibility of this option. Here efficiency and control were the main motives. The difficulties of the Luxembourg process beyond the stage of sectoral adjustments had highlighted the limits of EFTA as an effective partner. Intergovernmentalism and the systematic use of consensus in decision making made the organization ill adapted to a more ambitious European integration. In other words, EFTA's organizational principle had to be transformed to economize transaction costs.[37] In addition, with several individual EFTA members eager to strike an easy deal with the EC, a strengthening of the EFTA collective was a better device for the EC to control the more demanding countries like Switzerland.

On the EFTA side, several members welcomed the idea of reinforcing EFTA structures, because they considered the existing ones to be ill adapted to the new challenges. In the Nordic countries, decision makers shared the belief that the multilateral EFTA strategy did not make any sense if there was not a parallel course between all EFTA countries.[38] Without better coordination, the unilateral adaptation strategy was a better path from the perspective of engaging bilateral accession talks when the Community was ready to consider them. Strengthening EFTA could take many forms but one of the most often mentioned was the possible creation of a customs union.[39] For other countries (in particular, Iceland and Switzerland), the two-pillar track caused trouble similar to proposed adhesion to the EC. A strengthening of EFTA would lead to a transfer of power to a supranational body, a highly unpopular move among domestic constituents. Given that the economic benefits of such a construction would be far less than joining the EC, these two countries tended to consider the two-pillar option as part of a worst case scenario. Decision makers continued to believe that a third way between adhesion and a unilateral course of action was

[35] The Parliament had acquired greater power with the adoption of the Single European Act, in particular, the power to reject association agreements with external countries.
[36] These countries wanted the EC to ensure a balance between deregulation and economic and social cohesion. In other words, benefits of the internal market could only go to countries which would be willing to pay for it—cash payments for regional funds and implementation of the common agricultural policy, in particular. Given that these aspects were not covered by EC-EFTA agreements, southern EC countries did not see big opportunities for increased trade with EFTA countries, contrary to West Germany and other heavily industrial EC countries.
[37] In particular, substantial reduction in ex-post-transaction costs could be realized with a changed organizational structure. See Williamson 1985, 15–18.
[38] See Saeter 1990, 126.
[39] See Church 1990, 417.

both possible and would provide an effective means to address the externalities stemming from the deepening of EC integration. In Switzerland, they relied on the economic expertise of some academics to justify their position.[40] But this expertise did not distinguish between two-pillars multilateral and common multilateral decision-making, primarily because the academics focused on the economic application of a new agreement rather than on its likelihood.

Continuing division inside EFTA precluded a clear settlement of the choice of the type of new institution.[41] Although the EC option took precedence in October 1989 when EFTA countries accepted the *acquis communautaire* as the basis for the future agreement, under the pressure of the hardliners, EFTA continued to call for "a genuine joint decision-making mechanism in substance and form" and insisted on an equal footing with the EC in all matters and on the right to take initiatives.[42] At most, the Commission offered to accept an osmotic relationship between separate EFTA and Community pillars throughout the decision-shaping phase. Still some EFTA members, especially Switzerland, continued to think that there was some chance that the EC would change course on the issue during the negotiations. This misplaced hope had serious consequences in the negotiation process.

Actors finalized their choice during the exploratory phase that took place in the spring of 1990. In keeping with the two-pillar structure, negotiations were to follow a mostly bilateral road. Issues would be addressed in five negotiating groups: (1) free movement of goods; (2) free movement of capital and services; (3) free movement of persons; (4) horizontal and flanking policies; and (5) institutional questions. Each of these groups would proceed independently but would depend on directives from a leading group, the Joint EC-EFTA High Level Negotiating Group (hereafter HLNG). This supervisory committee was constituted on one side with the EC chief negotiator speaking on behalf of the Commission for the member states and on the other side with the chief negotiators of all EFTA countries speaking with the voice of one *primus inter pares*—the EFTA chief negotiator. The fragmentary nature of EFTA's voice created difficulties but did not threaten the bilateral nature of talks because EFTA members with special interests in some issues would be encouraged to seek compromise directly and

---

[40] The most influential report was the so-called Hauser report, Hauser 1991.

[41] Dissension between Nordic countries and Switzerland reached a climax during the EFTA summit in Kristiansand on 12–15 June 1989. Switzerland rejected the principle of majority voting inside the EFTA Council (*Agence Europe*, 15–16 June 1989), and as a result, Norway proposed that the Nordic countries inside EFTA go on without the other EFTA members (*Dagens Industri*, 5 July 1989).

[42] The *acquis communautaire* is the official term for applicable EC law, both primary (stemming from the Rome Treaty, and other such treaties) and secondary (regulations, directives, and decisions adopted since the Rome Treaty). The *acquis* also covers the relevant case law for the European Court of Justice (ECJ). *European Report*, 1 November 1989.

separately with the EC. The choice of the bargaining route was influenced by the Community's willingness to see the two-pillar construction quickly implemented. Negotiations would thus serve as a test case for a strengthened EFTA. The EC was particularly keen to have the EFTA countries speak with one voice, both for efficiency concerns and to help overcome the resistance of laggard countries. Indeed, the commission wanted to avoid having to consider individual demands from each EFTA country based on domestic imperatives and constraints. Forcing them to speak together shifted the onus of reconciling divergent domestic demands to EFTA, where opposition from individual countries could be overcome.

Regarding linkages, the key consideration in creating EEA was to encompass the two existing institutions in a larger framework. Delors hinted at this in a speech on January 17, 1989: "To make myself better understood, I will go as far as to say that we dream of a European village, governed by détente, in which economic and cultural activities could develop in mutual confidence. However if I were to draw this village today, I would see in it a house called 'European Community' of which we would be the only architects and careful custodians of the keys, ever prepared to open up our doors to enter into dialogue with our neighbor."[43] In this vision, EFTA members would belong to a second circle, the village called EEA, that was more flexible and less demanding than the EC. As the closest neighbors surrounding the Community's house, they would have privileged relationships and would be a test case for future relationships with Central and Eastern European countries. In terms of the analytical framework we are using in this book, there was clearly an attempt at nesting in the conception of the EEA. Both the EC and EFTA would belong to the same village. But the salience of the EC precluded a full nesting of the EC into the EEA. As a consequence, the EC pushed for a kind of partial nesting which would have different hierarchical implications for the two existing institutions. Some of the prerogatives and policy domains of the EC would remain outside the nest, whereas EFTA would be fully in it. Moreover, EFTA would be the nest-keeper in charge of welcoming Central and Eastern European countries willing to anchor themselves to Western European countries. As such, it could help the EC and share the costs of supporting these countries.

There were both *substantive* and *tactical* reasons to proceed with a partially nested design. Substantively, nesting was believed to be the only feasible route to cope both with deepening and widening issues in European integration. It allowed for a variable geometry approach that would nicely fit the different economic and political conditions of Western European states. Substantive nesting addressed systemic and domestic imperatives while responding to trends in transactions. From an economic point of view, there was a clear interest in coming up with concentric

---

[43] *Agence Europe*, 19 January 1989.

circles. Enhanced performance required a careful hierarchical ordering with different integration speeds embedded in a common framework.[44] Politically, Delors restated at a meeting of the General Affairs Council that the strengthening of cooperation with the EFTA could also be the basis for discussions with the countries of Eastern Europe.[45] There was now a larger acceptance inside the Community that the EEA was more than a simple matter of integration with the neighboring EFTA, as revealed by an editorial of *Agence Europe:* "The real problem of a Europe that claims to be a political entity with its own voice in the world [is that it] should not be concerned with how many members it has but with *the coherence of the fundamental choices and the nature of the links* that bind them."[46] From this viewpoint, the EEA was considered by the EC as the best possible link between the EFTA and the EC, as an osmotic process that could succeed.

But these sound motivations could not hide more tactical purposes. From the EC's perspective, the EEA offered a tactical response to systemic developments in Europe and on a global level. The EC was under increasing pressure from the United States and Japan to open up its borders and to avoid choosing the option of a "fortress Europe." The new relationship with EFTA combined the wish to gradually open the internal market to outsiders and the desire to prevent a disorganized flow of new applications for EC membership. The new structure could also be used to welcome East and Central European countries through association treaties.[47] In addition, at the global level, the EC could use the EEA to increase its influence on international regimes and world commercial negotiations.

Tactical reasons also guided the behavior of EFTA countries, especially Norway, Sweden, and Austria. In the latter country, the government publicly stated that the EEA was the shortest way to adhesion, and would be pursued until adhesion became a reality. In Norway, the EEA provided a way to avoid a premature domestic debate on EC membership that was considered to be the ultimate goal of the government. In Sweden, the changing systemic environment was gradually eroding the neutrality constraint, but the EEA was still the best option for improving the economic performance of the country. It was the best way to satisfy those domestic constituents concerned with economic necessity and those concerned with political security.

The Devil Is in the Details: Formal Negotiations 1990–92

After more than a year of sporadic preparatory work, formal negotiations on the creation of the EEA opened in June 1990. The initial situation was one of

---

[44] See Baldwin 1994 for an economic argument endorsing concentric structural arrangements.
[45] *Dagens Naeringsliv,* 18 October 1989.
[46] *Agence Europe,* 4 October 1989.
[47] See the interview of Horst Krenzler, the EC chief negotiator, in *EFTA-Bulletin,* no. 4, 1990, 20.

deep disagreement on some key institutional features, with severe domestic or institutional constraints pressing on both sides. This left little room for integrative bargaining in order to design an institution that had to take care directly or indirectly of the mix of goods—club goods, private goods, and CPR goods—discussed in the previous section. In such a context, there was no place for strategic mistakes. Yet EFTA could not have had a worse start, and this sent the whole process into a spiral of conflicts which, in the end, turned out to be a blow both to EFTA and EC countries.[48]

During preparatory work, the EC had made it clear that the *acquis communautaire* would be the substantive basis of the new institution and that it could not tolerate any erosion of its prerogatives. Yet EFTA countries thought that they could change the EC's position on these issues and thought that the best way to get some concessions, even small ones, would be to ask for much more than they could realistically expect to get. They thus started with very high initial requests. During the first formal meeting of the HLNG on July 24–25, they submitted a list of desired permanent exemptions from the *acquis communautaire*. They expressed the hope that they would be allowed to participate in the different committees that assisted the European Commission in the implementation of Community legislation for the areas to be covered by an EEA Treaty. They also requested the creation of a common supervisory organ to monitor the implementation of the legislation, a departure from the Community's desire for a system with two supervising pillars.[49] EFTA justified most of these demands on domestic political grounds. This initial strategy stunned the EC Commission and jeopardized much of EFTA's credibility. Reacting to this first HLNG meeting, the EC Commission expressed serious concern over the numerous list of exemptions that the EFTA countries had requested, especially over the permanent ones. From the Community's viewpoint, exemptions from the *acquis* should be limited to a country's fundamental, not political, interest and could not lead to a de facto suspension of any one of the four freedoms.

The initial divergence was so large that the process got stuck in an early stalemate, which could be likened to a dialogue of the deaf, until late in October. After such a bad start, EFTA countries had to make some concessions to try to relaunch the process. They agreed to explore the two-pillar principle for the surveillance mechanism but called for the creation of a common body to link the two pillars.[50] The EC Council restated its strong willingness to continue negotia-

---

[48] Elsewhere I have carefully analyzed this process of negotiations with formal game-theoretic tools. See, for instance, Dupont 1994.

[49] *Agence Europe*, 26 July 1990.

[50] In addition EFTA countries wanted complete freedom in choosing their own supervisory body. As a consequence, the new position differed only slightly from previous offers. With such a high degree of freedom, the EFTA could choose not to create its own pillar, and this would result in the common body that it had initially wanted.

tions, and recognized the "great political importance of having an agreement both on institutional and substantive matters."[51] The EC's explicit mention of institutional aspects was a nod of recognition to their political importance in most EFTA countries. On the following day, the ministers of these countries welcomed this positive signal with an official recognition of the need to reduce the number of exemptions from the *acquis* to a minimum.[52]

The prospects for a quick and smooth bridging of differences remained dim, however. This, coupled with a rapidly changing systemic environment, pushed the Swedish government to announce its intention to submit an EC application form to the Parliament on October 26, 1990.[53] The other EFTA members globally interpreted Sweden's decision as unfortunate. Switzerland thought that this action sent the wrong message when the negotiating parties were in a battle of wills.[54] In Finland and Norway some officials considered it an unfortunate break in EFTA solidarity and feared that Sweden intended to pave the way to demanding Nordic adhesion to the EC, a move that neither Norway nor Finland was ready to endorse at that time.[55]

Internally divided and externally pressured, EFTA countries could not avoid making additional concessions simply to keep the boat afloat. In preparation for the fourth HLNG meeting on November 21–22, they dropped their request for permanent exemptions and reduced the number of transitional ones.[56] The offer brought some relief and a new atmosphere of cooperation. Problems were still present, however, as revealed by the Joint Ministerial Meeting in Brussels on December 19, 1990, considered to be a "mid-term review." Both the EC and EFTA were quick to emphasize that improvement or compromise had taken place in several areas, but at the same time admitted that large stumbling blocks remained.[57] The intrinsic limits of the EEA framework had already appeared,

---

[51] General Affairs Council, 22 October 1990, 8.

[52] *EFTA Bulletin*, no. 1, 1991, 20.

[53] Press release from the Swedish government, 26 October 1990.

[54] See interview with the EFTA Chief Negotiator, the Swiss Franz Blankart, in *Neue Zürcher Zeitung*, 26 November 1990. In its message to the Parliament for the ratification of the EEA Treaty, the Federal Council considered Sweden's move important because it had two significant effects: first, a clear majority of countries now favored market access over institutional changes, and second, the Community was vindicated in its refusal to build an ambitious institutional framework.

[55] See declarations in *Agence Europe*, 8 December 1990.

[56] This offer was contingent on three conditions: (1) a satisfactory legal and institutional framework, that is, an arrangement that would give EFTA the right to debate; (2) temporary exemptions for the application of appropriate, nondiscriminatory legislation; and (3) adequate safeguard mechanisms (*Agence Europe*, 23 November 1990).

[57] Progress had been achieved in the following areas: mutual recognition of the *acquis communautaire*; certain exemptions to this *acquis*, since EFTA members had demonstrated a willingness to reduce their demands; willingness to combine a high level of health and environmental protection with the establishment of the four freedoms; establishment of solid legal principles for flanking policies; and

but both sides lacked any better alternative to fulfill their objectives. For the EFTA countries, the EEA remained the best road to European integration, either because no membership negotiation would begin before 1993, or because it gave time for a progressive preparation of public opinion in favor of EC membership. For the EC, the EEA was still a useful device to take care of pan-regional stability and gain time before granting access to new members.[58]

Negotiators made little progress in January and February 1991. Persistent stalemate eroded even further EFTA countries' faith in the EEA and fueled tensions inside the two existing institutions. Among EFTA members, two major fault lines appeared. Both had to do with exemptions from the *acquis communautaire*. The first divided Alpine and Nordic countries on the transit issue. The EC had long demanded a removal of restrictions for the transit of its trucks through Austria and Switzerland, but the two Alpine countries had strongly opposed it. They were particularly concerned with the negative externalities of increased traffic on the environment, which was a politically sensitive issue in these countries. Under increasing EC pressure, however, bilateral talks had started prior to the EEA talks, and independently from them. But, once the EEA talks opened, the EC soon made an explicit link between them and the ongoing bilateral talks. As a consequence, the ongoing deadlock on the issue of transit threatened the whole EEA negotiation process—causing great strain among EFTA countries.[59] The second fault line was between Iceland and Norway over the issue of fisheries. Heavily dependent on the fishing industry, Iceland was eager to have its special position understood by the Community, and it feared that Norway's inflexible attitude could undermine its efforts.[60] Among EC members, Spain remained the most aggressive, and its stance contrasted greatly with countries like Denmark and Germany that found Spanish demands totally unacceptable. Spain did get support from Greece, Portugal, and Ireland, however, and thus maintained solid veto power inside the council.

Another consequence of the stalemate was the change of attitude among EFTA countries regarding the question of EC membership. By mid-April, all of the EFTA countries except Iceland had publicly stated their preference for EC membership, even if it would not be a viable alternative for at least three more

---

establishment of a system applicable to financial services. At the same time, dissension was still deep on issues such as the joint decision process, the agriculture sector, and fisheries (*EFTA Bulletin*, no. 1, 1991; *Agence Europe*, 20 December 1990).

[58] In addition, continuing deadlock in the Uruguay round of GATT talks strengthened the EC interest in an all-encompassing deal which would make it as big and powerful a bloc as possible. For a similar analysis, see *European Report*, no. 1644, 16 January 1991.

[59] On the issue of transit and its consequences, see *European Report*, no. 1655, 23 February 1991; *Agence Europe*, 22 February 1991; and *Die Presse*, 20 February 1991.

[60] *Aftenposten*, 11 April 1991.

years.[61] Even the Swiss Federal Council made adhesion a top priority.[62] But all of these countries reaffirmed that preparing for possible adhesion was not incompatible with the conclusion of a good agreement on EEA, which remained the best short-term solution. Accordingly, they were still willing to fight for a balanced accord.

Their show of unity began to induce some changes at the negotiating table. On May 14, 1991, both parties succeeded in coming to a general understanding on some thorny issues during a joint ministerial meeting. In particular, resolution was found on the issues of the judicial body, the opting-out mechanism, and agricultural products.[63] These positive elements prompted some relief, especially for EFTA countries, but compromise had been painful to Switzerland and Iceland.[64] Both countries were on the verge of quitting the process and had clearly reached their limit for an eventual participation in the EEA. Preparing for the next rounds of negotiations, EFTA countries strove to preserve their unity through the use of tactical linkages. They supported Austria and Switzerland on the transit issue and Iceland and Norway on fisheries. They restated their willingness to strike a balance between procedural and substantive issues.

Few disagreements were bridged in June.[65] The tug of war continued with each actor trying to force the other to back down. Consequently, on the eve of the summer recess at the end of July, both sides appeared less willing to search for compromise solutions than to fight. A last minute marathon failed to change the tide, and negotiations came to a halt with several unsolved issues, including fisheries and transit.[66]

Parties made use of the summer recess to prepare a more constructive attitude. In particular, the weaker side, EFTA, worked hard to find a politically acceptable way out of the deadlock. The seven countries made it clear, however, that they could not simply accept a bad agreement to save the process. They warned of the consequences of a failure, which would also be a "wrong signal to

---

[61] *Agence Europe*, 26 April 1991; *Financial Times*, 2 May 1991; *European Report*, no. 1675, 9 May 1991.

[62] "The prospect of adhesion to the EC now makes much more sense, but we should not rush into it. Adhesion has become an option we should consider with the closest attention" (press release from Swiss Federal Council, 10 May 1991; my translation).

[63] *EFTA Bulletin*, no. 2, 1991; *Agence Europe*, 15 May 1991; and *European Report*, no. 1676, 15 May 1991.

[64] Switzerland had to abandon its demand for an individual opting-out mechanism under combined pressure from the EC and the other EFTA members. Iceland remained highly critical of the "unholy trinity" that had been established, linking fisheries, the equalizing fund, and agriculture.

[65] The most important meeting in June was a joint ministerial meeting in Luxembourg on June 18, 1991. See *European Report*, no. 1687, 22 June 1991; and *Agence Europe*, 20 June 1991.

[66] *European Report*, no. 1698, 31 July 1991 and no. 1699, 3 August 1991; *Agence Europe*, 29–30 July 1991 and 31 July 1991.

those countries which expect to enter into closer relations with the countries of Western Europe."[67] But this did not have a significant impact on the process, mostly because in the EC attention was now markedly shifting away from the EEA talks to preparations for a treaty on political union. From this perspective, agreement on the EEA had to come soon to preclude indefinite delay. After yet another month of stalemate, progress could no longer be avoided.

Germany and Denmark took up the matter during a meeting of the General Affairs Council on October 1, 1991. They urged their EC partners to sign an agreement by the end of the month and pushed for the organization of two parallel meetings—one on transit and one on the EEA. Spain—with the support of the UK and Ireland—was still keen to get concessions on the issue of fisheries. The Netherlands and Greece emphasized the necessity for good bilateral agreements on transit as a precondition for an EEA agreement.[68]

The long hoped-for breakthrough emerged in the bilateral talks on transit. In Eindhoven on October 12, representatives of the EC, Austria, and Switzerland cleared the remaining hurdles for an agreement. As differences on transit narrowed, the situation looked ripe for a political agreement at the parallel ministerial meetings on October 21 in Luxembourg. The parties did not pass up the opportunity to put an end to such a difficult process. The final conclusion of this general agreement, however, depended upon the endorsement of the European Court of Justice (ECJ) over some procedural aspects of the treaty, as requested by the EC Commission on August 13, 1991. After hearing the member states' positions on the EEA, the court rejected the treaty on December 14, 1991. The court concluded that there was a fundamental contradiction in the objectives of the EC and the EEA. Because of this basic contradiction, the court stated that it was impossible to establish a common judicial body that would uniformly apply EEA law without infringing upon the legal autonomy of the Community.[69] In other words, the creation of the EEA Court was incompatible with EC law, and thus the political agreement reached on October 22 could not be signed in its current form.

The parties went back to the negotiating table, agreeing to focus only on the judicial mechanism and some minor points on competition rules. After some uncertainty in January 1992, both sides compromised on a new mechanism that replaced the EEA court with an EFTA court, which would settle disputes inside the EFTA, and conferred to the EEA Joint Committee the difficult task of preserving the legal homogeneity of the EEA. The ECJ found the new institutional

---

[67] *Agence Europe*, 11 September 1991.

[68] *European Report*, no. 1708, 2 October 1991.

[69] See Brandtner 1992 for a detailed analysis of the ECJ opinion.

framework compatible with EC law on April 10, and the EEA agreement was finally signed in Oporto, Portugal, on May 2, 1992.

Globally, the agreement allowed for a broad realization of the four freedoms and established several administrative and judicial bodies to monitor the implementation of the rules.[70] Goods, capital, services, and persons were to move almost freely inside a vast market of 376 million potential consumers. Social and environmental provisions would help the implementation of the four freedoms and ensure a harmonious life inside the area. Although providing benefits similar to EC membership, the EEA agreement fell short of it in many areas. It did not create a customs union but, instead, established a free trade area. Thus, it did not include a common external tariff, nor require the removal of border controls or the harmonization of indirect taxes. Moreover, it did not include participation in EC common policies (agriculture, fisheries, transport, and trade) nor in the European Monetary System.

Operationally, the agreement established organs and mechanisms to ensure a dynamic and homogeneous process.[71] It distinguished between decision-making procedures, on the one hand, and surveillance and enforcement mechanisms, on the other. The EC had the key decision-making role, the EFTA countries were left with few prerogatives. In the preparation phase, they could be informally consulted on an expert level with regard to some of the EC committees which assist the Commission in its executive functions. In the decision-shaping phase, they had an individual right to raise any matter of concern (*droit d'évocation*) and the option to collectively ask for the suspension of new rules (collective opting-out). They did not get any co-decision rights although they could unilaterally call for a general safeguard clause for some areas of vital interest.

Regarding surveillance and enforcement, provisions largely followed the two-pillar approach favored by the EC. The EFTA countries had to create an independent EFTA Surveillance Authority, the EFTA Court of Justice, and a Standing Committee. As can be seen in table 4.1, the EFTA Surveillance Authority mirrored the role of the EC Commission for surveillance of a legal nature, and the EFTA Standing Committee paralleled the task of the Commission and of the EC Council regarding surveillance of political nature. Judicial control was left to each pillar—the EFTA Court of Justice for the EFTA, and the EC Court of Justice for the EC. Joint action through the EEA Joint Committee was restricted to securing uniform interpretation of EEA rules and to settling disputes of a political nature between the signatories.

---

[70] For the full text of the agreement, see *Official Journal of the European Communities*, no. L1, 3 January 1994. For a useful summary of its provisions see *The EEA Agreement* (Geneva: EFTA, 1993).

[71] For a detailed description of the institutional mechanism, and of the problems around it, see Krafft 1992 and O'Keeffe 1992.

TABLE 4.1. Institutional structure of the European Economic Area

Functions	EFTA states	EEA	EC
General guidelines	EFTA governments	EEA Council	EC Council
Executive	EFTA Standing Committee	EEA Joint Committee	Commission and EC Council
Decision-making process leading to new rules	EFTA Standing Committee; EFTA governments and legislators	EEA Joint Committee	Commission and EC Council
Surveillance of a legal nature	EFTA Surveillance Authority and legal mechanisms of EFTA states		Commission
Judicial control	EFTA Court of Justice and jurisdictions of EFTA states		EC Court of Justice
Surveillance of a political nature	EFTA Standing Committee	Joint EEA Committee and EEA Council	Commission and EC Council
Dispute settlement			
Legal	EFTA Court of Justice	Arbitration limited to some disputes on safeguard measures	EC Court of Justice
Political	EFTA Standing Committee	EEA Joint Committee	
Parliamentary cooperation	Committee of Members of EFTA Countries' Parliaments	EEA Joint Parliamentary Committee	European Parliament
Cooperation of economic and social partners	EFTA Consultative Committee	EEA Joint Consultative Committee	Economic and Social Committee

Source: Translated from "Message relatif à l'approbation de l'Accord sur l'Espace Economique Européen," *Feuille Fédérale* 144, no. 4 (1992): 448a.

Away from the EEA and Toward EC Membership

The EEA Treaty failed to address the externalities of the collapse of the Communist world. In a rapidly changing European context, EFTA countries become dissatisfied with the new institutional arrangement and opted for a new course—EC membership. This option was financially more costly than the EEA, but gave full economic and political access to the Single Market. Under continuous pressure from Central and Eastern European countries, the EC became convinced that the only way to gain help from EFTA countries was to let them in rather than try to artificially keep the EEA alive.

The Impetus to Change: Failed Expectations from the EEA Agreement

Figure 4.3A depicts the bargaining game after the creation of the EEA. The key point here is that the newly created institutional setting failed to significantly improve the game payoffs, not only for EFTA countries but also for EC countries. This constituted a strong impetus for change and the search for a different solution.

On the EFTA side, the agreement was politically asymmetric and thus difficult to sell to domestic constituents. Economically, the agreement did not stop the erosion of national productive bases in EFTA countries. This erosion had more to do with the psychology of economic actors than with objective factors revealed both by academic research and by sharp differences between Sweden and Switzerland regarding FDI in the EC. A study by the London-based Center for Economic Policy Research concluded that moving from the EEA agreement toward EC membership would bring little economic gain for EFTA countries.[72] Regarding Switzerland and Sweden, both had externally oriented economies with strong multinationals, and both shared a high dependence on the EC market. Despite these commonalities, the outward flow of investments continued to

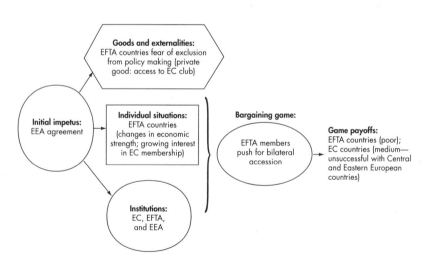

FIGURE 4.3A.   Toward EC membership

[72] CEPR 1992.

grow in Sweden after the conclusion of the EEA, whereas it significantly decreased in Switzerland. Differences in confidence in the respective national economies is surely one plausible explanation.[73] Finland's situation was different due to its need to compensate for the losses inflicted by the collapse of the Soviet market that had traditionally accounted for 15 to 25 percent of Finnish exports.[74]

On the EC side, the EEA failed to act as a magnet for Central and Eastern European countries, and thus the pressure did not lessen on the Community. In the course of 1990, all post-communist countries announced their willingness to join the Community. EFTA membership lost its appeal once EFTA members began to show less enthusiasm on the EEA process. Faltering concern in the West thus negatively influenced potential interest by Central and Eastern European countries and pushed them to lobby for a different structure of cooperation. Central and Eastern decision makers believed that EFTA would sooner or later disappear and that the EEA would go with it.[75] In addition, former communist countries were looking for a firm political anchor in the West rather than a kind of economic internship in the EEA. They thus pushed the Community to propose a new form of cooperation, the Europe Agreements. Poland, Hungary, and Czechoslovakia signed in December 1991.[76] These agreements on new forms of association gave priority to the political dimension of the relationship with the EC and included (1) association institutions, (2) political dialogue, (3) a free trade area in industrial goods, (4) economic and financial cooperation, and (5) cultural cooperation. They avoided the very process that the EC had hoped to impose on former communist countries, namely to put them in a "premembership" chamber where they would gradually adapt their economic systems in order to qualify for full membership. In their preamble, the agreements mentioned, albeit very cautiously, the ultimate objective as membership in the Community. The political dialogue and the technical assistance frameworks were designed to help the future applicants come closer to the conditions necessary for joining the EC.

The Response: Bargaining for Enlargement of the EC

Figure 4.3B depicts the institutional path toward a new arrangement between the EC and the four EFTA countries (Austria, Finland, Norway, and Sweden). These countries' first option was to use an existing institution, the EC, rather than to create a new one. By the end of 1992, all EFTA countries except Iceland

---

[73] This argument is made by Pedersen 1994, 124.

[74] Pedersen 1994, 98.

[75] See Nicolaïdis 1993.

[76] The agreement with Czechoslovakia was renegotiated in 1993 after the partition; during the same year agreements were signed with Romania and Bulgaria.

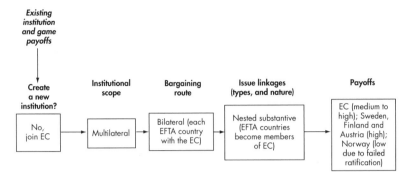

FIGURE 4.3B.   Bargaining for EC membership (Austria, Finland, Norway, and Sweden)

and Liechtenstein had officially submitted an application for EC membership: Austria in July 1989 (prior to the conclusion of the EEA), Sweden in July 1991 (during the negotiation process), Finland in March 1992, Switzerland in May 1992, and Norway in November 1992. As discussed in the previous section, this change of policy toward EC membership came when the EEA ceased to be tactically appropriate and thus lost its raison d'être for most EFTA countries. At a systemic political level, the deep transformation process in Central and Eastern Europe cleared the security-related hurdles toward EC membership. This was true for Sweden and Finland, but also for Switzerland. At the domestic political level, public opinion was still very skeptical toward European integration but the question was no longer taboo in any country. In addition, large numbers of political elites now favored adhesion. It was no longer necessary to disguise the desire for EC membership.

Overt support of EC membership was however not free of risks, as the Swiss case revealed. On December 6, 1992, the Swiss people turned down membership in the EEA. Voters did not react to the EEA per se but to the feared drift toward EC membership. Hence the debates focused on Swiss political institutions and values rather than on the economic benefits of joining the EEA.[77] Nationalists ably manipulated the agenda on highly sensitive political items and trapped the government, which could not agree on a unified stance on matters of European integration. Blocked by domestic constraints, the Swiss government had to return to its pre-1989 situation, a move that yielded an especially poor payoff.

On the EC side, member states decided during the European Council in Lisbon in June 1992 that widening the EC to include EFTA countries would again become possible after the ratification of the Maastricht treaty. They made clear

[77] See Kriesi et al. 1993 for a detailed analysis of the vote.

that the choice of enlargement negotiations would imply acceptance by the applicant countries not only of the traditional *acquis communautaire* but also the extensions contained in the Single European Act and in the Treaty on European Union. (See figure 4.3B.)

Negotiations were to be bilateral between each of the four applicants and the twelve EC members. The various bilateral processes would evolve in parallel within a common general framework. In contrast to the EEA process, the commission was not able to conduct the process on the EC side but, instead, simply assisted the Council of Ministers.

The new applicants would be substantively nested inside the European Union. No permanent exemptions from the *acquis* would be granted. The commission had previously evaluated the admissibility of each applicant under these terms, giving favorable opinions of the four candidates. Negotiations were aimed at establishing transitional periods to allow the incorporation of the *acquis communautaire* into the legislation of the four candidate states.

Talks officially opened on February 1, 1993, for Austria, Sweden, and Finland, and on April 5, 1993, for Norway. The parties agreed on March 1, 1994, as the deadline for finishing negotiations and submitting the results for ratification by the European Parliament so that the applicants could become members on January 1, 1995.[78] Progress was limited in 1993; parties quickly went over the chapters fully covered by the EEA but then stumbled over the difficult areas, some of them partially covered by the EEA Treaty (agriculture, fisheries, environmental protection) and some left out (state monopolies, regional and structural policy).[79] In December 1993, the four states declared their willingness to accept all the new provisions of the Maastricht Treaty on European Union and the EC granted them concessions on environmental protection.[80] Southern EC members did not welcome this progress because they feared that too easy a deal would move the momentum of European integration decisively to the north. Spain, in par-

---

[78] For a detailed chronology of the ministerial conferences throughout the process, see Granell 1995, 125–27.

[79] The EEA Treaty fully covered eleven out of twenty-nine chapter headings of the enlargement negotiations. In addition to the four freedoms, these chapters included transport policy, competition policy, consumer and health protection, research and information technologies, education, statistics, and company law. It partially covered five other chapters including social policy, environment, energy, agriculture, and fisheries. Among the remaining items, there were those covered by the EC prior to Maastricht, including customs union, external relations, structural instruments, regional policy, industrial policy, and taxation; there were those introduced by the Maastricht Treaty, including economic and monetary union, foreign and security policy, and justice and home affairs. Finally, among the general chapters, there were the key items of financial and budgetary provisions and institutions. See Granell 1995, 122.

[80] *Financial Times*, 22 December 1993; *Wall Street Journal*, 22 December 1993; *Journal de Genève*, 22 December 1993.

ticular, began to put the brakes on the process, first by requesting that the new members be denied early entry in the Economic and Monetary Union.[81] But bigger trouble came in January on the issues of fisheries, agriculture, and regional policy. Spain publicly disagreed with the Commission's position on fisheries and asked for higher quotas in Norwegian waters, a demand flatly rejected by Norway.[82] On agriculture, Austria, Norway, and Finland were greatly concerned with the proposals to align farm prices with EC levels upon entry into the union, and asked for transition periods.[83] On regional policy, Greece, Portugal, and Spain rejected the commission's proposal to apply the highest level of structural aid—the so-called objective 1 status—to the applicants' most disadvantaged regions.[84] Bargaining also hardened on Alpine transit through Austria. The Commission proposed to modify the bilateral treaty on transit and reduce the ban to three years instead of twelve years.[85] The disputes increased during February to include the amount of the financial contributions required by the applicants. On this issue, the poorer southern EC countries wanted to have most of the contributions of the new members go to them. And they opposed the demand by Sweden and Austria to be exempted from most of their contributions for the first three years on the ground that they needed the money to pay for the adjustment efforts for entry.[86]

With the March 1 deadline nearing, the stalemate endangered the whole political impetus in Western European integration. Some countries inside the EC were particularly worried about the bad consequences of a missed deal. Among them was Germany which put strong pressure upon Spain and the southern countries to stop making irresponsible demands. Germany also urged that financial concessions be granted to the new applicants so that they could sell the terms of entry to their domestic constituents.[87] Some countries were however more concerned about the establishment of a newly empowered minority that could block decisions made by a union of sixteen members. The UK and Spain threatened to oppose enlargement if the new blocking minority was changed, as planned, from 23 (out of 76 votes) to 27 (out of 90) votes. The UK complained about the loss of power of big countries, whereas Spain feared a weakening of the Mediterranean front.[88] They could not however block a first series of agreement with Sweden, Finland, and Austria on March 1, 1994. The EC made most

[81] *Financial Times*, 21 December 1993.
[82] The Royal Norwegian Ministry of Foreign Affairs, *Norway Daily*, no. 7/94, 11 January 1994.
[83] *Financial Times*, 13 January 1994.
[84] *Financial Times*, 18 January 1994.
[85] *Die Presse*, 21 January 1994.
[86] *Financial Times*, 22 February 1994.
[87] *Financial Times*, 28 February 1994.
[88] *Financial Times*, 28 February 1994.

of the concessions to ensure this outcome. Sweden got a budget rebate disguised as a farm adjustment payment. In order to facilitate Finland's participation in the Common Agricultural Policy at full price parity on entry, the EC stated that the entire land-area of Finland would be declared an Arctic region eligible for special agriculture support. Regarding Austria, in addition to declaring some regions eligible for structural support, the EC agreed to retain the restrictions on transit included in the existing bilateral treaty.[89] However, German pressure proved insufficient to push for a deal with Norway. The row over fisheries put an end to German hopes. Spain remained inflexible in its demand for additional fishing quotas, and Norway stuck to its "not a single additional fish" stance.[90]

The first breakthrough occurred on March 8 when Norway and the EC reached an agreement on agriculture. Special investment support would ease the process of readjustment during the first three years of Norwegian membership. Eighty-five percent of Norway's agricultural land was defined as disadvantaged and would be eligible for special support.[91] A second and decisive move on fisheries came on March 15. Norway slightly increased the fishing quotas agreed to under the EEA (from 11,000 to 14,000 tons of cod); in addition to these rights, Spain and Portugal were granted fishing rights from other EC members, and the EC promised to purchase quotas elsewhere in the world, including Russia and Canada.[92] The last hurdle to a successful completion of the negotiations was the institutional quarrel, pitching the UK and Spain against the other EC members. A last minute compromise emerged during a special meeting held in Ioannina (Greece) on March 29. The EC's new blocking minority was raised to 27 votes, but a "reasonable" delay was provided before calling a vote on a decision if 23 or more votes were opposed to it.[93] Spain immediately agreed to this compromise and the UK reluctantly accepted it two days later.

Successful ratification by the European Parliament occurred on May 4. The Parliament strongly endorsed the deal.[94] But the most difficult task remained: referendums had to be passed in the four applicant countries. The referendum passed in Austria on June 12 with 66.36 percent of the vote, in Finland on October 16 with 56.9 percent, and in Sweden on November 13 with 52 percent. It was defeated, however, in Norway on November 28 with 52.5 percent voting against

[89] *Journal de Genève*, 2 March 1994; *Financial Times*, 2 March 1994; *International Herald Tribune*, 2 March 1994.

[90] The Royal Norwegian Ministry of Foreign Affairs, *Norway Daily*, no. 43/94, 2 March 1994; *Financial Times*, 5–6 March 1994.

[91] The Royal Norwegian Ministry of Foreign Affairs, *Norway Daily*, no. 48/94, 9 March 1994.

[92] The Royal Norwegian Ministry of Foreign Affairs, *Norway Daily*, no. 53/94, 16 March 1994; *Wall Street Journal*, 17 March 1994.

[93] *Wall Street Journal*, 30 March 1994; *Financial Times*, 28 March 1994.

[94] The voting results turned out as follows: Norway, 376 for, 24 against, and 57 abstentions; Austria, 378-24-60; Finland, 377-21-61; and Sweden, 381-21-60 (Granell 1995, 123).

it. The Norwegian failure confirmed the doubts cast by the Parliamentary elections held the previous year on September 13, in which the anti-EC Center party was the biggest winner.[95] Despite all its efforts, the Labor-ruled government could not change the tide.

The Norwegian government suffered a blow from the "No" vote and thus received a bad payoff from the whole process. It lost credibility and restricted its margin for maneuver with the EC over the next decade. For the successful applicants, the payoffs were high. They could join the EC and still receive generous transition periods to adopt the *acquis communautaire*. Finally, for the EC, the successfully completed negotiation process sent a positive sign to possible applicants and to the rest of the world. However, not every EC member was pleased with the fiscal concessions given to the new members. France, the Netherlands, and Spain, in particular, found the terms to be too generous, and blamed Germany for this.[96] More generally, the negotiations over the entry of these four countries revealed the fault lines that had appeared earlier in the Maastricht Treaty negotiations, divisions between a rich north and a poor south, between big and small members, between supporters of a tight federation and supporters of a loose one.[97] This resurfacing of conflict gave support to those who resented the idea of pressing ahead with enlargement rather than attending to institutional reforms. Hence the payoffs of the new institutional setting were medium-to-high inside the EC.

The story of the EC-EFTA institutional relationships since the mid-1980s is one of both institutional creation and institutional decay. In the mid-eighties, the institutional bargaining game between the EC and the EFTA entered a new era. EFTA countries were the first to try to promote change after the EC adopted the Single European Act. They feared loosing private goods from their privileged relationship with the EC. The EC, however, became interested in major change only after the collapse of the communist bloc. To preserve pan-regional stability and prosperity and avoid the crowding-out of its club, the EC proposed to closely work with the EFTA and create a new institution, the EEA. Despite a common interest in promoting such a change, parties got bogged down during the negotiation process due to a mixture of severe domestic constraints, the high salience of the EC to its members, and sharply asymmetric power relationships. The result was an asymmetric new institution that proved to be attractive only to very few EFTA members. Most other members rushed toward EC membership, which provided these countries with more political rights and more economic

[95] *Arbeiderbladet,* 15 September 1993; *Financial Times,* 15 September 1993.
[96] *Financial Times,* 2 March 1994.
[97] *Financial Times,* 14 March 1994.

goods than the EEA at only a somewhat higher price. They thus had no reason to stick with the EEA. By the same token, this decision also fatally rocked the EFTA boat.

The experience of the EFTA-EC institutional relationships is suggestive of several elements and hypotheses presented in the introductory chapter of this volume. First, it shows how the high salience of existing institutions makes nesting difficult, if not impossible. Even though there was an inherent ground for a substantive nested linkage in the case of the EEA, EC countries only accepted partial tactical nesting of their institution for fear of diluting their prerogatives. This partial acceptance predetermined the choice of a bilateral bargaining route and bilateral decision-making and monitoring structures, and it laid the ground for an extremely asymmetrical new institution. Second, the experience highlights how crucial the link is between the nature of the good and the type of institution. In particular, it shows that hegemony is not sufficient to force other actors to participate in the provision of CPR goods. The EC failed to secure, through the EEA, active cooperation of EFTA countries vis-à-vis developments in Central and Eastern Europe, mostly because the new institution did not give the right incentives to them. They had no reason to care about an institution that offered them few net benefits. Third, and pointing to more detailed research on negotiation processes, the case of the EEA emphasizes how asymmetric power, and stringent domestic constraints, can quickly transform negotiations into nasty fights under situations of incomplete information. Weak actors may try to exploit incomplete information in order to extract concessions on the basis of domestic constraints. When facing a much more powerful actor, one runs a high risk that a strategy of inflating demands will backfire and result in poor consequences for both parties, but especially bad consequences for the weaker party.

From the substantive perspective of regional integration processes, my analysis of the EEA builds useful bridges for comparative work on regional integration in Europe, Asia-Pacific, and North and Latin America. In other work, I have shown how the focus on institutional bargaining games can shed new light on cross-national comparison, and I mention here two policy-relevant implications of the EEA case.[98] First, the historical experience should be a warning to those who want to engage in the creation of ambitious pan-regional institutions in other parts of the world. Such efforts have been on the drawing board both in the Asia-Pacific region within the Asia-Pacific Economic Cooperation (APEC) forum, and in the Western Hemisphere with the idea of a Free Trade Area of the Americas (FTAA). The high salience of existing institutions in these two regions—in particular ASEAN, Mercosur, and NAFTA—precludes substantive nesting for the moment. Second, given the CPR nature of some of the most im-

[98] See, for instance, Dupont 1998.

portant goods that the pan-regional institutional setting should provide, it would be illusory to rely on power alone to impose new institutions. From this perspective, US actions have been more promising than declarations about the need to move quickly. A careful and selected issue focus is a more promising—and institutionally safer—path than the kind of organizational focus that the EEA took in Western Europe.

References

Antola, Esko, 1990. "Finnish Perspectives on EC-EFTA Relations." In Finn Laursen, ed., *EFTA and the EC: Implications of 1992* (Maastricht: European Institute of Public Administration).

Bachmann, Hans et al., eds., 1970. *EWG and EFTA am Scheideweg.* (Zürich: Polygraphischer Verlag).

Baldwin, Richard E., 1994. *Toward an Integrated Europe* (London: Center for Economic Policy Research).

Berglund, Sten, 1991. "The Finnish Parliamentary Election of March 1991." *Scandinavian Political Studies* 14, no. 4.

Binswanger, Hans Christoph, and Hans Manfred Mayrzedt, eds., 1972. *Europapolitik der Rest-EFTA-Staaten Oesterreich, Schweden, Schweiz, Finnland, Island, Portugal.* (Zurich: Schulthess Polygraphischer Verlag).

Brandtner, Barbara, 1992. "The 'Drama' of the EEA: Comments on Opinions 1/91 and 1/92." *European Journal of International Law* 3, no. 2.

Brauchlin, Emil, 1989. "Comment les entreprises suisses se préparent-elles à la CE de 1992?" In Roland Ruffieux and Annik Morier-Genoud, eds., *La Suisse et son avenir européen* (Lausanne: Payot).

Cameron, David, 1992. "The 1992 Initiative: Causes and Consequences." In Alberta M. Sbragia, ed., *Euro-Politics: Institutions and Policymaking in the "New" European Community* (Washington, D.C.: Brookings Institution).

CEPR, 1992. *Is Bigger Better? The Economics of EC Enlargement* (London: Centre for Economic Policy Research).

Church, Clive, 1990. "The Politics of Change: EFTA and the Nordic Countries' Responses to the EC in the Early 1990s." *Journal of Common Market Studies* 28, no. 4.

Corbett, Richard, 1989. "Testing the New Procedures: The European Parliament's First Experiences with Its New Single Act Powers." *Journal of Common Market Studies* 27.

Dupont, Cédric, 1994. "Domestic Politics and International Negotiations: A Sequential Bargaining Model." In Pierre Allan and Christian Schmidt, eds., *Game Theory and International Relations* (Cheltenham: Elgar Publisher).

———, 1998. "European Integration and APEC: The Search for Institutional Blueprints." In Vinod K. Aggarwal and Charles Morrison, eds., *Asia-Pacific Crossroads: Regime Creation and The Future of APEC* (New York: St. Martin's Press).

Dupont, Cédric, Pascal Sciarini, and Derek Lutterbeck, 1997. "Views from the Small: Common Shocks and Divergent Responses; Autria, Belgium and Switzerland in Comparative Perspective." Paper presented at the European Consortium for Political Research Annual Meetings, Bern, 28 February–2 March.

Granell, Francisco, 1995. "The European Union's Enlargement Negotiations with Austria, Finland, Norway and Sweden." *Journal of Common Market Studies* 33, no. 1.

Gstöhl, Sieglinde, 1994. "EFTA and the European Economic Area or the Politics of Frustration." *Cooperation and Conflict* 29, no. 4.

Haaland, Jan I., 1990. "Assessing the Effects of EC Integration on EFTA Countries: The Position of Norway and Sweden." *Journal of Common Market Studies* 28, no. 4.

Hamilton, Carl B., 1991. *The Nordic EFTA Counties' Options: Seeking Community Membership or a Permanent EEA-Accord.* Discussion paper series (London: Center for Economic Policy Research).

Hauser, Heinz, 1991. *Traité sur l'EEE, adhésion à la CE, course en solitaire: Conséquences économiques pour la Suisse* (Berne: Office Fédéral des Questions Conjoncturelles).

Krafft, Mathias-Charles, 1992. "Le système institutionnel de l'EEE: Aspects généraux." *European Journal of International Law* 3 no. 2.

Kriesi, Hanspeter, et al. 1993. *Analyse de la votation fédérale du 6 décembre 1992* (EEE). (Geneva: Department of Political Science/GFS-Forschungs institut, Analyse-Vox No. 47).

Laursen, Finn, 1990. "The Community's Policy Towards EFTA: Regime Formation in the European Economic Space (EES)." *Journal of Common Market Studies* 28, no. 4.

Luif, Paul, 1990. "Austria's Application for EC Membership: Historical Background, Reasons and Possible Results." In Finn Laursen, ed., *EFTA and the EC: Implications of 1992* (Maastricht: European Institute of Public Administration).

Moravcsik, Andrew, 1991. "Negotiating the Single European Act: National Interests and Conventional Statecraft in the European Community." *International Organization* 45.

Nell, Philippe G., 1990. "EFTA in the 1990s: The Search for a New Identity." *Journal of Common Market Studies* 28, no. 4.

Nicolaïdis, Kalypso, 1993. "East European Trade in the Aftermath of 1989: Did International Institutions Matter?" In Robert O. Keohane, Joseph S. Nye, and Stanley Hoffmann, eds., *After the Cold War: International Institutions and State Strategies in Europe. 1989–1991* (Cambridge: Harvard University Press).

O'Keeffe, David, 1992. "The Agreement of the European Economic Area." *Legal Issues of European Integration,* no. 1.

Ostrom, Elinor, 1990. *Governing the Commons: The Evolution of Institutions for Collective Action* (New York: Cambridge University Press).

Pedersen, Thomas, 1994. *European Union and the EFTA Countries: Enlargement and Integration* (London: Pinter).

Saeter, Martin, 1990. "Norway: An EFTA Road to Membership?" In Finn Laursen, ed., *EFTA and the EC: Implications of 1992* (Maastricht: European Institute of Public Administration).

Sciarini, Pascal, 1992. "La Suisse dans la négociation sur l'Espace Économique Européen: De la rupture à l'apprentissage." *Annuaire Suisse de science politique* 32.

Valen, Henry, 1990. "The Storting Election of 1989: Polarization and Protest." *Scandinavian Political Studies* 13, no. 3.

Wieser, T., and E. Kitzmantel, 1990. "Austria and the European Community." *Journal of Common Market Studies* 28, no. 4.

Williamson, Oliver E., 1985. *The Economic Institutions of Capitalism: Firms, Markets, Relational Contracting* (New York: Free Press).

Wörlund, Ingemar, 1989. "The Election to the Swedish Riksdag 1988." *Scandinavian Political Studies* 12, no. 1.

CHAPTER FIVE

When Giants Clash:
The OECD Financial Support Fund and the IMF

BENJAMIN J. COHEN

What happens when one large multilateral organization threatens to encroach directly on the central and long-established role of another? This, in effect, was the question posed back in 1975 when, in the wake of the first oil shock, the twenty-four members of the Organization for Economic Cooperation and Development (OECD), a regional institution based largely in Europe, resolved to create a $25 billion financial "safety net" for mutual balance-of-payments support. The goal of the initiative, dubbed the Financial Support Fund (FSF), was to help OECD countries in their efforts to cope with the impact of sharply higher energy prices—under the circumstances, an entirely understandable ambition. The consequences for global institutional arrangements, however, could have been dramatic—particularly for the International Monetary Fund (IMF), which had previously enjoyed universal recognition as the central source of payments financing for national governments. With $25 billion at its disposal, the FSF threatened to eclipse the activities of the IMF, whose loanable resources at the time were nearing exhaustion. The IMF suddenly faced the prospect of a formidable regional rival.

The content of this chapter is based on verified historical documentation, some publicly available, some graciously provided from the archives of the OECD Secretariat, and some provided during interviews initiated while I was still personally involved as a consultant to the OECD in 1976–77. All opinions, however, are mine alone. The OECD bears no responsibility for any of the analysis in these pages. I am grateful to Paul Boeker and Emile Van Lennep as well as to Vinod Aggarwal and my other colleagues in this collective project for helpful comments and suggestions. The able assistance of Lynne Bernier is also gratefully acknowledged.

In principle, OECD governments intended to nest the FSF firmly within the broader structure of international monetary relations first established at Bretton Woods—a straightforward substantive linkage. In practice, however, the FSF was seen by many as a direct challenge to the authority of the Fund and wholly inconsistent with the unitary design of the postwar monetary regime. The stage was set, therefore, for a clash of giants—two major organizations, the OECD and IMF, each with its own distinct interests and preferences, and each with its own powerful allies and protagonists. Ultimately opponents of the FSF prevailed, despite vigorous lobbying by the OECD and support from many of its members. The critical battleground, ironically, turned out to be the United States, where in the end the FSF foundered when it failed to achieve formal legislative ratification. Washington had originally sponsored the initiative and had led the negotiations for its creation.

What caused the FSF to be stillborn? Why did the clash of giants end with total victory for one side, utter defeat for the other? Was the FSF a bad idea, a good idea badly conceived, or simply an idea whose time had come and gone quickly? These questions form the central analytical focus of this chapter. Although structured as an historical study, the chapter's aim is prospective: to draw lessons from this now-forgotten episode about conditions that may or may not favor a successful nesting of comparable institutions in the future.[1] In short, what can we learn from the FSF experience about how to make regional organizations institutionally compatible with broader global accords?

The discussion will examine the FSF story as a drama in three acts: an initial exploratory phase, which opened with the frantic search by Western nations for appropriate responses to the Oil Shock of 1973, culminating with the proposal for a Financial Support Fund at the OECD; the (successful) negotiation phase, which began in late 1974 and climaxed with the signing of the FSF agreement in April 1975; and the (unsuccessful) ratification phase, which closed anticlimactically a couple of years later when it became evident that the scheme had irrevocably lost the support of the United States.[2] In reviewing each phase, use will be made of the consolidated analytical framework for the study of institutional bargaining games developed by Vinod Aggarwal in chapter 1 of this volume. Drawing on a wide range of traditions in international relations theory, Aggarwal identifies several key factors that may be thought to drive the creation of regional organizations and their likely relationship with broader institutional arrangements. In the

---

[1] Remarkably little has been written about the Financial Support Fund. The only serious full-length study that I have been able to locate is an early analysis, in French, by Belgian scholar Jean-Victor Louis (1975). More cursory comments may be found in Camps 1975, De Vries 1985, and James 1996.

[2] Characterization of the first phase as successful is intended only in the narrow sense to mean that the FSF negotiations managed to achieve formal accord. The question of whether, in view of the subsequent failure to achieve ratification, the first act can truly be described as successful will be postponed until later.

FSF drama, three elements highlighted by Aggarwal stand out as pivotal: cognitive considerations, structural factors, and, within the United States, domestic politics. The influence of all three elements will be examined closely.

We begin with a brief synopsis of the FSF episode. The three acts of this play are then explored in more detail in the next three sections, which are then followed by a review of analytical findings and implications. The chapter concludes with an outline of lessons for the challenge of institutional reform in the future.

Synopsis

The FSF drama began with the first oil shock in the fall of 1973. Following the outbreak of Arab-Israeli hostilities in early October, world energy prices soared, provoking widespread fears of impending economic calamity for oil importers. The Organization of Petroleum Exporting Countries (OPEC), with a near monopoly of oil exports and reserves, suddenly seemed in the driver's seat. Energy-dependent nations worried not only about where the money would come from to pay for more costly imports, but even more acutely, they worried about their growing vulnerability to future shocks or shortages in what now appeared to be very much a sellers' market. Governments around the globe scrambled feverishly to line up financial resources and secure adequate access to oil supplies.

In this atmosphere of crisis, the United States government—guided by the strategic instincts of Secretary of State Henry Kissinger—saw an opportunity for collective action that might counterbalance the emerging power of OPEC. For Kissinger the real problem was the threat posed to the unity of the western anti-Soviet alliance, already frayed by growing commercial strains and the corrosive effects of the Vietnamese war. Efforts to reinforce transatlantic solidarity earlier in 1973, which Kissinger had ambitiously designated the "Year of Europe," had ended in division and acrimony over a wide range of economic and security issues. But here now was a new chance to mobilize and reinvigorate the industrial nations under firm American leadership. In December 1973, speaking in London, Kissinger called for comprehensive collaboration on all aspects of the energy problem. And in the ensuing Washington Energy Conference two months later, oil consumers were urged to match OPEC's cartel-like behavior with an effective coalition of their own. Ultimately, under U.S. prodding, negotiations led to creation of the International Energy Agency (IEA), linked to the OECD, in November 1974. The goals of the IEA, which were to include an emergency oil-sharing scheme and an energy information system as well as development of a long-term cooperative plan to reduce oil dependency, were ostensibly economic. In fact, its raison d'être was plainly political—in the words of one commentator, its purpose was "to erode the political and economic power of the oil cartel" (Scheinman 1976, 11).

Precisely for that reason, however, support for the IEA was not easy to muster. Several European nations, as well as Japan, were wary of a confrontational stance that might jeopardize access to OPEC production in the future. Some also resented what seemed a blatant attempt by Washington to reassert U.S. influence at a moment of relative weakness for its more import-dependent allies. For Kissinger, therefore, the challenge of the IEA negotiations was to offer supplementary incentives of sufficient allure to attain his desired response—in effect, to win support, or at least buy off resistance, by adding reliable side-payments for reluctant nations. Along one track, this led the secretary eventually to accede to European demands for a simultaneous—and, in principle, more conciliatory—strategy of dialogue between consumer and producer nations, later broadened into what came to be known as the North-South dialogue.[3] Along a second track, this led to creation of the Financial Support Fund.

The case for a financial initiative of some sort was clear. Most OECD nations, being oil importers, were hard hit by OPEC's higher prices and quickly found themselves facing sizable external deficits. In time, of course, adjustments might be possible, even with inelastic energy demand, to close the gap in the balance of payments. Other imports could be squeezed, or exports promoted. But in the short term governments had little choice. The current deficits had to be financed, either from a country's own monetary reserves or by borrowing. For nations with limited liquidity, the question was: Borrow from whom?

In the aggregate, the answer was evident. Borrowing would be from OPEC itself, since the oil exporters' profits had to go somewhere. To the extent that burgeoning "petrodollar" revenues were not immediately spent on imported goods and services, they had to be invested in foreign assets or otherwise lent back to oil consumers as a group. OPEC's combined surpluses, by definition, had to be offset by an equivalent capital transfer to the rest of the world. At a more disaggregated level, however, the answer was not so evident, since what was true for consumers as a group would not necessarily be true for each country individually. In fact, there was no reason at all to assume that OPEC reflows would match up neatly with the distribution of current deficits among oil importers. Quite the contrary, while some countries could look forward to healthy external accounts owing to their ability to attract OPEC investments, others were bound to face severe stresses. The

---

[3] Kohl 1976. In fact, Kissinger's concession was less conciliatory than it seemed to the Europeans, who hoped that a dialogue might ease tensions between oil producers and consumers. For Kissinger, according to one highly placed State Department source, the dialogue would provide one more opportunity to erode OPEC's power, much of which derived from its solidarity with other Third World governments. By highlighting the adverse effects of higher oil prices for non-oil-developing economies, Kissinger hoped to drive a wedge between OPEC and the other countries of the south.

challenge, therefore, was not to encourage a *primary* recycling of petrodollars from OPEC to oil importers; that would occur automatically. The problem was to ensure a satisfactory *secondary* recycling of petrodollars—an appropriate allocation of loanable resources within the group of consuming countries. How could nations with overall deficits be assured access to sufficient financing at reasonable terms?

Eventually, as we know, the problem was resolved—more or less by default, and certainly not without difficulties—by the private markets. In ensuing years Western banks and other financial intermediaries, mobilizing OPEC's surplus revenues, became the principal source of payments support for a diverse array of countries, in the process effectively "privatizing" the global regime for liquidity creation (Cohen 1981). In 1974, however, all that still lay in the future. At the time, elite opinion was sharply divided. No one could yet be sure that the markets were up to the challenge, and policymakers were still accustomed to looking first to public rather than private sources for the bulk of their external finance. Attention therefore focused on the feasibility of creating some new intergovernmental recycling mechanism—in effect, a common pool resource to help underwrite the deficits of oil importers. The climate was ripe for some attractive new balance-of-payments initiative.

The breakthrough finally came in another speech by Secretary Kissinger, this time in Chicago on November 14, just one day prior to formal creation of the IEA. Kissinger was well aware of lingering opposition to his consumer cartel strategy; of the OECD's twenty-four members, fully one-third—including, most prominently, France—refused initially to participate. To sweeten the deal, therefore, he now proposed to supplement the IEA with a new "safety net" to promote the "financial solidarity" of Western nations.[4] As spelled out four days later by Treasury Secretary William Simon, the net would take the form of a joint loan and guarantee facility, with total funding amounting to some $25 billion, to be administered by the OECD and available only to OECD members. Participation, Simon insisted, "should be linked with a commitment to cooperate in reducing dependence on oil imports"—obvious code for an obligation to join, or at least not oppose, the operations of the IEA.[5]

The linkage between the safety net and the IEA was obviously tactical. In practice, however, Washington never did insist on a formal oil commitment of any kind. Instead, the proposal quickly took on a life of its own, quite

---

[4] According to a well-placed OECD official (interview, July 1977), the term "safety net" was first suggested by Paul Volcker, then Under Secretary of the Treasury, at a meeting of an OECD working party in Tokyo in April 1974. The same official also expressed confidence that Volcker was the chief author of Secretary Kissinger's speech in November, although other sources credit Assistant Secretary of State Thomas Enders.

[5] In the words of the *Financial Times*, "Mr. Simon's speech leaves little doubt that it is part of a coordinated effort to break the OPEC cartel" (20 November 1974).

independent of Kissinger's broader geopolitical designs, owing to the pressing need many governments (including the French) felt for assured access to payments support. Once the proposal was placed on the table, it in fact became linked to a quite different set of questions involving the broad structure of international monetary relations—a linkage that was truly substantive rather than tactical.

Negotiation of the FSF was remarkably swift. Within a week, a working group, chaired by Jacques Van Ypersele of the Belgian Finance Ministry, was established by the Group of Ten industrial nations (G-10) to study Washington's initiative.[6] Within two months, preliminary agreement was reached on the broad outlines of a plan embodying most of what Secretaries Kissinger and Simon had proposed, including quotas for the commitments of individual governments. And by the end of March final details were hammered out by the Van Ypersele group, now reconstituted as an ad hoc working party of the OECD. On April 9, 1975, the "Agreement Establishing a Financial Support Fund of the Organization for Economic Cooperation and Development" was duly signed by all twenty-four member governments—including those, like the French, that were still resistant to full participation in the IEA.[7] In diplomatic terms this was an extraordinary achievement, given the highly politicized and sensitive issues involved. As one source observed, "Rarely has a negotiation of such complexity and importance been conducted with such speed."[8]

Implementation, on the other hand, ultimately proved impossible, despite rapid ratification by twenty-one of the OECD's twenty-four members.[9] The critical battleground, as indicated, was the United States, where the necessary enabling legislation was first postponed and then, in the summer of 1977, finally withdrawn by the new Carter administration. On August 29, 1977, the OECD was formally informed by letter that "the Administration does not intend to seek ratification of the OECD Financial Support Fund. . . . Our embassies in OECD countries are informing their host governments of this position." Without the support of the project's biggest and most influential member, there seemed little point to going on. The FSF was allowed to pass quietly into history.[10]

---

[6] The G-10, formed in 1963, initially included Belgium, Britain, Canada, France, Germany, Italy, Japan, the Netherlands, Sweden, and the United States, plus Switzerland on an ex officio basis. Though Switzerland now participates officially and Saudi Arabia has become formally affiliated as well, the group continues to be known as the Group of Ten.

[7] OECD 1975. For technical reasons the signature of one member, Turkey—which was then in the middle of a transition between governments—was actually delayed until May.

[8] Louis 1975, 368. In the original French it reads: "Rarement, une négociation portant sur un accord aussi complexe et aussi important aura été menée à ce rythme."

[9] The only exceptions, apart from the United States, were Finland and Luxembourg.

[10] Parallels with the International Trade Organization, a post–World War II American initative that was also ultimately killed for lack of U.S. ratification, are of course striking. For more on the ITO experience, see Gardner 1969, esp. chap. 17.

ACT ONE

How could a proposal like the FSF be negotiated so quickly only to be later rejected so decisively? In an effort to answer that question, we begin with the initial exploratory phase in 1973–74, as OECD nations hastened to respond effectively to the dramatic acceleration of energy costs. The essential elements of the bargaining game during this phase are highlighted in figures 5.1A and 5.1B.

Two issues at the time were paramount. The first was uncertainty at the level of elite beliefs: a lack of consensus over the financial consequences to be expected

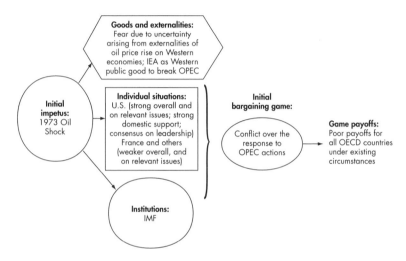

FIGURE 5.1A.   Responding to the 1973–74 Oil Shock

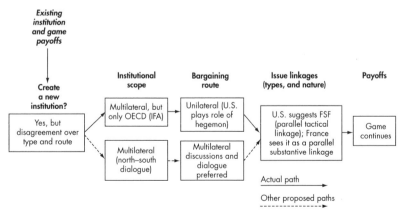

FIGURE 5.1B.   Dispute over institutional responses to the Oil Shock

from higher oil prices, compounded by parallel fears generated by the abandonment of pegged exchange rates earlier in 1973 and by the worldwide recession that set in during 1974. Under the circumstances, it was not surprising that governments would feel impelled to do something—anything—to help protect themselves against the unknown. The second issue was power politics at the level of interstate relations: heightened tensions manifested through political conflict and bargaining. At the time two dimensions of conflict ultimately proved critical—one between the newly assertive OPEC and the energy-hungry OECD nations, and the other among OECD members themselves.

The Impact of Uncertainty

In the wake of one of the most unprecedented events in economic history, the Oil Shock of 1973, uncertainty reigned in financial circles. Would oil-importing nations be bankrupted by OPEC greediness, or were fears of a lasting collapse overblown? Could the private markets and IMF be relied upon to successfully recycle petrodollars to where they were most needed, or would additional support be required to prevent desperate governments from resorting to mutually destructive "beggar-thy-neighbor" currency or trade practices? In retrospect, the answers are clear. Financing needs, while serious, turned out for the most part to be manageable. The markets and IMF did prove to be more or less up to the job; and governments did resist the illusory temptations of competitive depreciation or import restraint. At the time, however, there was no convergence of views at all about either the magnitude or duration of the financial challenge at hand. Specialists differed wildly in both diagnoses and prescriptions. As one observer commented, "There is argument rather than agreement among the experts. . . . [T]his absence of a guiding 'concept' is not a trivial problem" (Camps 1975, 19). The attractiveness of some new balance-of-payments initiative, therefore, was understandable. The FSF could be viewed as a kind of mutual insurance policy in an atmosphere of emergency and incalculable risk.

A measure of the degree of uncertainty prevailing in 1974–75 can be found in the wide divergence among projections of OPEC earnings that were in circulation at the time (Cohen 1976). In 1974, the combined surpluses of OPEC's members approached $70 billion, up from a mere $7 billion in 1973. Authoritative estimates of future transfers varied enormously, from an early World Bank suggestion of some $650 billion (in current dollars) through 1980 to later calculations running as low as $165–190 billion. Comparable discord marked debate over other related issues as well, such as how OPEC's investable surplus might be distributed among alternative investments and which economies were most likely to benefit from the primary recycling of petrodollars. Facing future imbalances, few governments were prepared to put themselves entirely in the hands of the private markets, which at the time were still largely untested as a secure source of balance-of-payments support, and the loanable resources of the IMF were known to be limited relative to potential need, amounting to less than $12 billion.[11] The risk of a disorderly scramble of deficit-reduction measures, therefore, was real. The only real certainty, it seemed, was that some new way had to be found to ensure adequate financing when needed.

Over the course of 1974, proposals for new recycling mechanisms thus sprouted like mushrooms. As early as January, IMF Managing Director Johannes Witteveen initiated discussions leading in June to creation of a special oil facility at the fund, open to all IMF members and funded mostly by loans from oil producers (De Vries 1985, chap. 17). However, with total resources of only some $3½ billion, the facility clearly amounted to not much more than a drop in the bucket. During the summer, therefore, OECD Secretary General Emile Van Lennep began campaigning for an additional arrangement to be funded by borrowing from the private markets—though, like Washington's later proposal, to be managed by the OECD rather than the IMF and to function solely for OECD members.[12] And in September, at the IMF–World Bank annual meeting, Witteveen called for another and larger IMF oil facility for 1975, modeled along the lines of the 1974 arrangement—an initiative enthusiastically backed by a number of national leaders, including especially Britain's Chancellor of the Exchequer Denis Healey, who proposed not only to greatly increase the facility's scale of lending to as much as $25 billion annually, but also to make it permanent. All these plans were already the subject of public discussion when Secretary Kissinger introduced his own idea for a supplementary safety net in November.

Ironically, some of the stiffest resistance to extensive new official support schemes had come initially from the U.S. Treasury, led by Secretary Simon, who as late as October still seemed rather sanguine about the capacity of the private markets to effectively recycle petrodollars to needy governments (De Vries 1985, 335–36). It was only when Simon, in tandem with Kissinger, changed his tune in November that serious intergovernmental negotiations were able to get under way. However, even then it was clear that no one was quite sure just how serious the problem was or what approach might offer the best solution.

---

[11] The total resources of the Fund, including all member currencies and gold holdings, were of course considerably larger. But Fund gold could not legally be disposed of; and most member currencies, being inconvertible, were unavailable for lending purposes. Only the currencies of a small number of industrial countries were technically classified as "usable."

[12] Specifically, the Van Lennep proposal would have authorized the Bank for International Settlements, acting as financial agent of the OECD, to raise funds directly from international and national financial markets under a collective OECD guarantee for lending to individual OECD members as needed. First sketches of the plan were circulated within the OECD as early as July 1974. A chief author of the proposal was Stephen Marris, Van Lennep's economic advisor.

BENJAMIN J. COHEN

The Impact of Power Politics

Given all this uncertainty, which was quite understandable under the circumstances, how did the Kissinger safety net manage so quickly to become the main focus of institutional bargaining? The answer, clearly, has to do with structural factors reflecting state capabilities and international political relationships. Though its conception could well have been justified solely on technical grounds—particularly as a means of averting "beggar-thy-neighbor" responses to emerging oil deficits[13]—the FSF was first and foremost a by-product of power politics. Without the sponsorship of the United States, still plainly the most powerful actor in the interstate system, it might never have prevailed in the proliferation of contending proposals.

In fact, strategic considerations dominated from the start. Led by Secretary Kissinger, who was determined to organize an effective Western response to OPEC's producer cartel, the U.S. government began early to press for some kind of counterpart cartel of consumers, eventually resulting in creation of the International Energy Agency. The safety-net initiative was an integral part of Kissinger's grand strategy—a side-payment offered to overcome the reluctance of key OECD members, many of whom viewed the secretary's anti-OPEC stance as risky and overly provocative. In effect, Washington was obliged to fight two battles at once, one with OPEC and the other with its own allies.

That Kissinger's motivations were confrontational was never in question. For him, preservation of the anti-Soviet alliance was paramount. From the outset, therefore, he made clear his determination to neutralize any threat from OPEC to the unity or self-confidence of the West. The vulnerability of OECD nations to energy shocks or shortages simply had to be contained. The immediate price increases should be moderated or even rolled back. Oil dependency should be reduced. And effective defenses should be established to alleviate any risk of political manipulation of oil supplies in the future. The key was to reaffirm the solidarity of the industrial world, preferably in some institutional form, in order to maximize diplomatic leverage. For Kissinger, there was no alternative to a policy of collective resistance to OPEC's new assertiveness.

For some of Washington's allies, on the other hand, there *was* an alternative—not confrontation but, rather, dialogue and conciliation designed to appeal to OPEC's own long-term economic interests. Why risk needless antagonism, it was argued. Why not seek instead to cultivate harmonious trade and financial

[13] Earlier, in a formal declaration adopted in May 1974 (the Trade Pledge), the members of the OECD had unanimously promised to refrain from introducing or intensifying trade restrictions in response to the Oil Shock. By the fall of 1974, however, according to a knowledgeable OECD official, some governments were threatening to rescind their pledge unless assured additional financial assistance in some form (interview, July 1977).

relationships that, over time, would deepen the stake of oil producers in the stability and prosperity of the West? OPEC members, after all, had their own vulnerabilities to worry about, which might be alleviated by offers of assured access to markets for their energy exports, financial outlets for their surplus revenues, or advanced technologies for their industrial development. A foundation existed for building a mutually beneficial "positive interdependence." Why use vinegar when more flies could be attracted with honey?

Most resistant was France, which had long pursued its own unilateral policies of friendship and cooperation with key OPEC governments. The French had no desire to jeopardize the "special relationships" they had so laboriously constructed in the Arab World, intended at least in part to ensure privileged access to scarce energy supplies. They were also deeply suspicious of any scheme that might help revive America's postwar dominance of Europe. Paris was acutely conscious of the divergence of state capabilities in this arena. As a major oil producer with, in addition, massive reserves of coal and natural gas, the United States was far less vulnerable to OPEC pressures than most of its allies in Europe or Japan. A consumer cartel, therefore, might simply consolidate America's influence over its more energy-starved partners. In French eyes, the Kissinger strategy seemed to point to "a new Atlantic structure designed to link French and European economic security to the United States, thus opening the way for renewed American hegemony over the Continent" (Kohl 1976, 248). Throughout 1974, accordingly, France (along with several smaller OECD nations) made clear its persistent opposition to what eventually became the IEA. Not even Kissinger's safety-net proposal in November would suffice to persuade the French to join (though it did help ensure that Paris would do nothing to thwart the operations of the IEA).

In fact, initial responses to the FSF initiative were very much the same as to the IEA: too confrontational and, potentially, too hegemonic. Since the safety net would work exclusively through a secondary recycling of petrodollars by oil consumers, by-passing OPEC altogether, it in effect "directly snubbed the oil producers."[14] Less provocative, many thought, would be something like the Van Lennep or Healey plans, which by calling for more reliance on primary recycling implied greater cooperation with OPEC nations. Likewise, since a direct pooling of resources would naturally give weight to potential creditors—and, in particular, to the United States, which was one of the countries best placed to attract surplus oil revenues—it threatened to add to Washington's influence over

[14] Hager 1976, 44. Snubbing OPEC, of course, was precisely what Kissinger had in mind. As *The Economist* wrote, "American global strategy demands that the Arabs not be given too easy, too safe a home for their surplus petrodollars [which] could underwrite yet higher oil prices" (11 January 1975, 49).

its allies, thus reinforcing fears of renascent American hegemony as well.[15] More reassuring would be something like the first oil facility, which was managed through the less politicized procedures of the IMF.

Despite such objections, however, the FSF proposal quickly moved to stage center, reflecting America's continuing predominance in the Western alliance. Overall superpower status as well as specific advantages as an energy producer and potential creditor gave the United States more than enough leverage to set the agenda for financial negotiations. The Europeans and Japanese may have had their doubts, but none—not even France—was prepared to openly defy the wishes of the U.S. government on an issue of such vital importance. Once Washington made its preferences clear, and stated them unequivocally, others felt they had little choice but to accept the idea as a focal point for subsequent bargaining.

ACT TWO

The brief negotiation phase, which climaxed with the signing of the FSF agreement in April 1975, was dominated overwhelming by structural factors: the direct distribution of state capabilities in the bargaining game. Figure 5.2A and 5.2B outline the key elements of this stage. Most critical to the outcome now was the evident determination of the United States to do whatever was needed to gain the agreement of its allies.

Initial reactions to the Kissinger proposal were generally cool—not least because of lingering doubts about the need for such massive intervention in the recycling process. In Europe, most opinion favored the kind of approach embodied in the Van Lennep and Healey proposals, as well the IMFs 1974 oil facility, which envisioned borrowing from either oil producers or the private markets (backed if necessary by official guarantees) to raise funds for deficit countries. The West German government, in particular, was critical of Washington's alternative strategy for a direct pooling of resources by oil consumers, which would have obliged Germany, as a major creditor country, to make one of the biggest commitments.

On the U.S. side, in contrast, there was rising skepticism about the reliability of OPEC's surplus earners. Could they always be counted upon to lend to such schemes in the magnitudes likely to be required, particularly if better investment returns might be expected elsewhere? Washington was evidently concerned that oil producers would demand special interest rates or exchange guarantees for

---

[15] France, for example, was reported to be opposed because, among other things, "the U.S. plan would give Washington too great a say as to whom the funds would go and when" (*International Herald Tribune*, 9 December 1974).

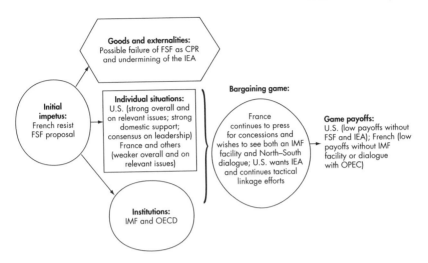

FIGURE 5.2A.   Negotiating to create the FSF

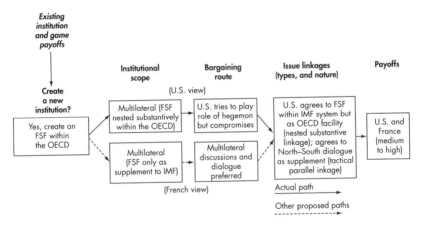

FIGURE 5.2B.   Negotiating the nesting of the FSF

their cooperation in any primary recycling scheme. There was also a fear that OPEC might attach political conditions to its cooperation, thus turning such arrangements into a sort of "money weapon" to reinforce its "oil weapon." Nor, U.S. officials argued, could the private markets necessarily be counted on to fill any remaining gap, no matter what guarantees might be available. Only a jointly funded intergovernmental arrangement could manage to produce the needed financing quickly and with appropriate terms and certainty.[16]

[16] *The Times* (London), 30 December 1974; *Financial Times*, 10 January 1975.

But why lodge a new recycling mechanism in the OECD rather than in the IMF? For the United States, two considerations dominated. First, given the safety net's origins as an adjunct of the IEA, a home in the OECD seemed natural—all part of Henry Kissinger's grand strategy of unified Western opposition to the OPEC cartel. And second, Washington had little interest in sharing either decision-making or financial resources with the multitudes of oil-hungry developing countries, all of whom would have a voice in the governance of any initiative within the Fund. The issue that mattered most to U.S. policymakers was the fate of the anti-Soviet alliance, not the financial health of the Third World.

Finally, after much bargaining, the two sides essentially agreed to split the difference. At a meeting in Washington on January 16, G-10 finance ministers formally endorsed both approaches—the Witteveen proposal for a second oil facility as well as the Kissinger safety net (now to be blended with the Van Lennep proposal)—in effect opting for two insurance policies (*IMF Survey*, 20 January 1975, 17). The oil facility, along with the IMF's other loanable resources, would be a first line of defense; the FSF became a supplementary last-resort source of help for deficit countries. With a touch of hyperbole worthy of Richard Nixon, Chancellor Healey declared this to be the "most successful meeting ever held" to reform the international monetary system despite the fact that his own more ambitious suggestions had been decisively rejected.[17] More prosaically, the result could be described as an old-fashioned horse trade: Washington got what it wanted by giving the Europeans what they wanted.[18] The 1975 oil facility, with projected resources of some $6 billion, was officially approved by the IMF Executive Board within three months, on April 4, five days before the formal signing of the FSF agreement.[19]

Other objections, likewise, were rather quickly resolved through artful negotiating compromises. Fears about the risks of confrontation with OPEC had already been allayed by a deal announced at a summit meeting of President Gerald Ford (who had taken office following the resignation of Richard Nixon in mid-1974) and Valéry Giscard d'Estaing on the French island of Martinique in December, where the U.S. promised to take part in an early conference of oil-consuming and producing nations (Kohl 1976, 250–52). In return for this paral-

---

[17] *The Times* (London), 17 January 1975. Earlier, in December 1971, Nixon had described the realignment of exchange rates agreed on by the G-10 at a meeting in Washington—the so-called Smithsonian Agreement—as "the greatest monetary agreement in the history of the world."

[18] Chancellor Healey credits himself with personally persuading the American side to accept the two-sided bargain (Healey 1989, 425–26).

[19] *IMF Survey*, 14 April 1975, 97; De Vries 1985, chap 18. A ceiling of $6 billion, considerably less than the $7–10 billion first suggested by the IMF, was reportedly demanded by the United States as a condition for its acceptance of the 1975 oil facility in addition to the FSF (*The Banker*, February 1975, 116).

lel, and ostensibly more conciliatory, approach—later broadened into a North-South dialogue on a broad range of development issues[20]—Paris agreed to drop its formal opposition to the IEA, with which it would now maintain a form of liason, and to actively support the FSF.[21] France's *volte-face,* in turn, persuaded others to come on board as well. Likewise, concerns about potential U.S. dominance of the FSF were eased once Washington agreed to a limited share of no more than 28 percent of total voting power, well below what would be required to dictate lending policy.[22] Additional safeguards for smaller countries were provided by a provision that no decisions would be adopted without at least half the member countries participating in a majority vote (OECD 1975, article 16).

Compromises were also successful in surmounting more particularistic obstacles to accord. In January, Britain was won over by the G-10 decision to endorse Johannes Witteveen's proposed second oil facility as well as the FSF. London's early reaction to the Kissinger initiative had been distinctly negative, in large part because it threatened to overshadow Denis Healey's own earlier suggestions. However, once Washington agreed to split the difference, the chancellor was able to declare victory for what he continued to refer to as the "Healey Plan" even while surrendering to U.S. preferences (*The Times [London]* 17 January 1975). And subsequent West German resistance was overcome by a U.S. concession on the form of funding for the FSF. Germany, as indicated, was concerned about the potentially high budgetary cost of a direct pooling of resources. In the words of Jacques Van Ypersele, the Germans were "fearful of becoming the insurance company of the rest of the Western world."[23] But those worries, too, were allayed once Washington agreed to an optional alternative method of FSF financing, permitting members to make commitments in the form of a loan guarantee (for borrowing by the FSF) rather than by cash contribution (OECD 1975, article 7).

In short, agreement on the FSF was quickly made possible by a series of critical concessions by the United States. Why was the United States so accommodating on so many issues? Quite clearly, the battle with OPEC took precedence. Disagreements among friends could not be allowed to distract attention from

---

[20] The North-South dialogue, formally labeled the Conference on International Economic Cooperation, met intermittently for the next three years before ending inconclusively.

[21] France was able to participate indirectly in the IEA, although not as a formal member, through the mechanisms of the European Community (now European Union), which was permitted to sit in the IEA as an observer. Members of the EC/EU typically have consulted among themselves before taking positions within the IEA.

[22] OECD 1975, article 16. Specifically, votes were to be determined in proportion to member quotas, which were denominated formally in Special Drawing Rights (SDRs). Of aggregate quotas amounting to 20 billion SDRs, Washington accepted a quota of SDR 5.56 billion, equal to 27.8 percent of the total (OECD 1975, article 3).

[23] Interview, September 1977.

the real enemy, which in this arena remained the oil cartel. Flexibility was therefore called for to maintain Western solidarity. In the end, Washington was able to attain both its strategic objectives: the IEA as well as the financial safety net. The rare speed with which the FSF agreement was negotiated was a direct reflection of foreign-policy priorities then prevailing in the United States.

ACT THREE

Despite Washington's negotiating success, however, implementation of the FSF proved elusive—most importantly, because of a change of mood in the United States itself. After so swiftly shepherding its allies to agreement, the Ford administration subsequently chose to procrastinate, preferring to push other legislative priorities instead. For the next year, the ratification process remained stalled on Capitol Hill. By the start of the national election campaign in 1976, it was clear that the FSF no longer enjoyed active support in the U.S. government. Once the Carter administration came into office, formal endorsement gave way to determined hostility.

What explains the anticlimactic outcome of the ratification phase? As in the initial exploratory phase, both cognitive considerations and structural factors once again played a critical role. At the intellectual level, in contrast to the earlier uncertainty of 1973–74, a new consensus of elite opinion was finally beginning to develop by the spring of 1975 which, unfortunately for supporters of the Kissinger initiative, did not happen to be favorable to implementation of the FSF. At the structural level, a new dimension of conflict now took center stage: competition between the OECD and the IMF—the clash of giants. Together these two elements, mediated through domestic U.S. politics, ultimately determined the evolution and finally the denouement of the FSF story, as can be seen in figures 5.3A and 5.3B.

A New Emerging Consensus

In the atmosphere of crisis generated by the Oil Shock, it was understandable that governments might not thoroughly examine all potential consequences of their decisions for existing institutions. Their main concern was the unknown (and unknowable): how much financing would be needed in the future. Their immediate objective was self-defense: to avert the risk of illiquidity. In the circumstances, therefore, more seemed preferable to less. If one lending scheme was good, two would be better. Who had time to worry about more distant implications for the structure of international monetary relations?

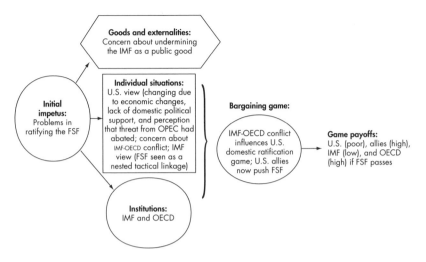

FIGURE 5.3A.　Clash of giants: Struggles over the FSF

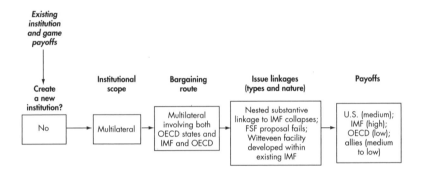

FIGURE 5.3B.　Failure of the FSF

Even as the ink dried on the FSF agreement, however, it was becoming evident that the financial challenge was less dire than many had feared. OPEC surpluses declined throughout 1975 (though rising again temporarily in 1976), while market financing increased; and with the easing of the world recession, most oil consumers were finding their external payments a lot easier to manage than expected (De Vries 1985, 357). Policymakers' sense of urgency, therefore, started to recede—and as it did, second thoughts began to emerge about the FSF. The problem lay in the expected linkage between the FSF and the IMF. The global monetary regime already had one center of decision making in the Fund. Was a second agency really needed, even if conceived solely as a lender of last resort?

The advantages of a supplementary safety net were clear. But what about the possible disadvantages of divided authority in the management of monetary affairs?

To some extent the issue had been anticipated by FSF proponents, who from the start posed the idea strictly as a back-up to the IMF rather than as an alternative. Later critics who characterized the initiative as "short-sighted" or "hastily conceived" were a bit unfair.[24] Linkage was, in principle, to be strictly hierarchical: the FSF was clearly structured to nest snugly under the IMF's wing. Kissinger himself, in his November 1974 speech, spoke of an initiative to "augment and buttress," not displace or rival, existing financial arrangements. And in his follow-up remarks four days later, Secretary Simon explicitly insisted that "what we are suggesting is in no way intended to replace the International Monetary Fund as the permanent institution providing the basic financial support for a well functioning world economy." During the ensuing months IMF representatives were involved as full participants in the deliberations of the Van Ypersele working group, and in the final agreement signed in April 1975 the FSF's objective was clearly limited to serving "to supplement, in exceptional cases, other sources of credit" (OECD 1975, article 1). A government would be eligible to borrow only if it "has made the fullest appropriate use of other multilateral facilities" and would be subject to policy conditions comparable to those applied by the IMF (OECD 1975, article 5).

Most importantly, the FSF would be *temporary*—a short-term expedient, not a long-term structural reform. Two years after its activation, the FSF would be liquidated unless extended by a 70 percent majority vote of its members (OECD 1975, article 19). Explained Charles Cooper, Assistant Secretary of the Treasury, in Congressional testimony a month after the agreement was signed, "There was a great deal of concern both in the United States and on the part of some other countries that we not be creating a new permanent institution. . . .We wanted to make it very clear that this was a transitional and a temporary institution, and for that reason we thought we should put a limitation on the period it could operate."[25]

Nonetheless, fears were soon roused regarding the future role of the IMF. No one could be sure how matters might work out in actual practice. After all, even with the second oil facility, the Fund's loanable resources were nearing rock bottom. Larger OECD governments, confronted with serious payments problems,

---

[24] The quotes are from an interview with an IMF official who was closely involved with these events (September 1977).

[25] U.S. House of Representatives 1975a, 12. This theme was echoed by U.S. Government officials privately as well as publicly. As late as the summer of 1977, a ranking official of the U.S. mission to the OECD insisted that "the FSF is an insurance policy, a bridging operation. . . . No one would think of giving these functions permanently to the OECD" (interview, July 1977).

might have no choice but to go first to the FSF, with its rich endowment of $25 billion. Moreover, who was to determine when a country "has made the fullest appropriate use of other multilateral facilities" or whether OECD conditionality was fully compatible with IMF practice?[26] And who could predict how participants, after two years of operation, would feel about simply letting the FSF lapse?[27] Ultimately—diplomatic language notwithstanding—the operation and duration of the FSF would in practice be decided by the OECD alone, not anyone else. The IMF, observers began to worry, might be condemned to growing irrelevancy, at least for countries eligible to borrow from the new FSF.

Typical were the remarks of economist Fred Bergsten, testifying before the Senate Banking Committee in June 1976: "Today's balance-of-payments problems within the OECD area derive from shortcomings in general economic policy rather than the price of oil. . . .Hence they should be handled through the normal international lending institutions, notably the IMF, rather than any new oil-related facility. . . .[B]y creating a new international financial mechanism, [the FSF] would weaken the International Monetary Fund, just at a time when the United States has a major interest in strengthening that institution" (U.S. Senate 1976, 26–27).

Gradually, such fears coalesced into a new mainstream consensus among specialists on both sides of the Atlantic. Wrote British economist John Williamson, "analysis has not suggested that there is a compelling need for the creation of any new intermediation agency such as the $25 billion OECD safety net" (Williamson 1975, 220). Milton Godfrey, an American business consultant echoed that view: "the proposed support fund has no real justification" (U.S. Senate 1976, 35). By mid-1976, even the FSF's most ardent advocates were beginning to acknowledge the possible risks to the IMF's central role and to search for new ways to more securely nest the two institutions. In July, for example, Illinois Senator Adlai Stevenson, though a firm supporter, felt impelled to introduce an amendment "to insure that the Financial Support Fund is a lender of last resort by requiring that the IMF . . . first determine that the applicant is unable to obtain all or a part of any loan which it seeks from the IMF."[28] But not even last-ditch efforts like these sufficed to turn the tide of opinion. In October the *New York Times*, which less than two years earlier (21 January 1975) had hailed "[t]he breadth of vision in this extraordinary project," now concluded that "the

---

[26] A hint of the kind of problems that could arise was suggested inadvertently by Jacques Van Ypersele who, even while insisting that "the IMF must have a say on establishing loan conditionality," added that "the OECD need not follow its advice one hundred percent" (interview, July 1977).

[27] Cooper admitted in the same Congressional testimony that "at the end of two years, of course, circumstances may show that we have been too optimistic and the life of the Fund should be extended [though] that does not appear likely at this stage" (U.S. House of Representatives 1975a, 4).

[28] *Congressional Record—Senate*, 94th Cong., 2d sess., 29 July 1976, S 11031.

oil safety net is dead. . . .[T]he scheme may just as well be given a quiet, respectful burial" (4 October 1976).

By early 1977, when Bergsten and such like-minded colleagues as Anthony Solomon and Richard Cooper came to power with the new Carter administration, the handwriting was on the wall.[29] Little would be done to promote any initiative that threatened to dilute the pivotal authority of the IMF. Working group chair Jacques Van Ypersele attributed the subsequent loss of momentum for ratification directly to the "change of personalities" in the executive branch.[30] More bluntly, one high OECD official privately blamed the "one-world philosophy" of the new administration's top officials—"proponents of a one-world concept in the financial sphere, who feel that the IMF can do no wrong."[31] Hence, despite determined lobbying by the OECD, the FSF was put on hold, in effect allowed to linger in legislative purgatory until it simply faded into ignominious oblivion.

The Clash of Giants

As critical as cognitive considerations may have seemed, however, they tell only a part of the story. Washington's change of heart can hardly be attributed to improving economic conditions or the evolution of expert opinion alone. There was also another factor, involving issues of fundamental institutional structure, that figured at least as prominently in the minds of U.S. policymakers: that was the increasingly effective opposition of the IMF.

The Fund, at the time, was an institution in search of a new mission. Its role at the center of global monetary relations had been severely compromised by the shift to currency floating in 1973 as well as by Richard Nixon's earlier suspension of the dollar's gold convertibility in 1971. Subsequently, the failure of the so-called Committee of Twenty (which was formally concluded in June 1974) to agree on any significant measure of systemic reform had only added to the organization's growing sense of impotence and frustration (Williamson 1977). Even at the best of times, the IMF was bound to view proposals for a new deep-pocketed rival like the FSF with suspicion—and these were clearly not the best of times. During 1973–74, institutional weakness made it difficult for IMF officials

---

[29] Bergsten was named Assistant Secretary of the Treasury for International Affairs. Solomon, an investment banker, became Treasury Under Secretary; Cooper, an economics professor, became Under Secretary of State for Economic Affairs.

[30] Interview, September 1977. This view was also expressed by Secretary General Van Lennep himself in private correspondence to me in 1995 (reprinted with permission): "I, personally, still believe that the strong publicly stated opposition of Fred Bergsten combined with the fact that the IMF is based in Washington were decisive in turning the U.S. position around."

[31] Interview, July 1977.

to counter the rush of ideas for new recycling facilities at the OECD or elsewhere.

By 1975, on the other hand, international conditions were beginning to improve and signs of progress were finally becoming evident in the deliberations of the Interim Committee (the successor to the Committee of Twenty), ultimately leading to accord on the Second Amendment of the Fund's Articles of Agreement in January 1976. IMF officials, therefore, now felt better positioned to fight back. Their aim was to reassert the Fund's pivotal authority at the peak of decision making on monetary matters. The catalyst was Johannes Witteveen, who first took over as managing director from a disappointing predecessor in September 1973. In the words of the Fund's official historian:

> [Some initiative] was important for the Fund as the organization responsible for international monetary arrangements and for cooperation in the international monetary field. . . .[I]t was essential that the Fund take some action. Already the Fund's influence and functions had been reduced by the collapse of the par value system and the introduction of floating rates earlier in 1973. By the middle of 1973, the Fund's image had also suffered by the failure of world officials to agree on a reformed system. Thus . . . Mr. Witteveen pushed the Fund into action.[32]

Action did not take the form of a frontal assault on the FSF. Though clearly unenthusiastic about the prospect of a new deep-pocketed rival to his organization's primacy, Witteveen never directly challenged Washington's initiative. A skilled politician, who had previously served as finance minister and deputy prime minister of the Netherlands, he knew better than to publicly oppose the IMF's largest and most powerful member. Rather, his strategy was to emphasize the undoubted strengths of the Fund—for example, its universality, experience, and proven expertise—as well as, more subtly, its essential neutrality in any confrontation between oil producers and consumers. The erosion of the organization's relevancy was not denied. But the problem, he maintained, was financial, not institutional. The only threat that was openly acknowledged was the depleted level of the Fund's usable resources. The main solution, therefore, was a major increase in financing for the IMF. The public message was, "The Fund still has a job to do." The implied message was, "Give us the money to get the job done, and we won't need any sort of supplementary safety net in the OECD."

Beginning with the battle for a second oil facility, which was effectively won at the G-10 meeting in January 1975, the campaign moved into high gear over the

---

[32] De Vries, 1985, 359. Another source puts the point more bluntly: Witteveen "turned out to be very much in favor of reasserting the IMF's power" (Ehrbar 1977, 101).

course of the next two years—first with a proposed increase of IMF quotas, which was formally approved in March 1976; and then with a plan for a Supplementary Financing Facility (SFF), also known as the Witteveen facility, which came into existence in 1977 (De Vries 1985, chaps. 27–28). By focusing attention on replenishment of its own resources, the Fund in effect deflected attention from the FSF, which was gradually relegated to a back burner in policy discussions. By mid-1977 it was the FSF, not the IMF, that now appeared condemned to irrelevancy.

The FSF did not go down without a struggle. Behind the scenes, led by Secretary General Van Lennep, the OECD Secretariat continued to argue energetically for its ratification, focusing increasingly on the unexpected emergence of second thoughts in the United States. Confidential briefs were prepared responding point by point to objections raised by the safety net's American critics. Private meetings were arranged with legislators and policy officials on both sides of the Atlantic. And public backing was sought, whenever possible, from European governments and other interested organizations like the Bank for International Settlements (BIS). As late as the spring of 1977, the FSF was still being actively promoted by a majority of Washington's allies. At a G-10 meeting in Paris in April, the United States was reported to have received "tough criticism" for its failure to ratify its own early initiative (*The Times* [London], 18 July 1977). And in June the influential chairman of the BIS, Jelle Zijlstra, appealed for immediate activation of the FSF, even without U.S. participation if necessary.[33] "The new IMF capability at present is likely to be inadequate compared to the scale of the problem we face," he declared bluntly (*International Herald Tribune*, 14 June 1977).

By this time, however, support for the FSF in the United States had dwindled to the vanishing point, to the immense relief of the IMF. A prominent business publication in the summer trumpeted that "Witteveen's success at repositioning the IMF at the center of the world economy has been a tonic for the morale of the Fund's staff" (Ehrbar 1977, 99). The risk of eclipse had been averted. Even in the cautious wording of the IMF's official historian it is possible to detect some note of celebration and self-congratulation: "One result of the Fund's supplementary financing facility was that the financial support fund in the OECD, extensively discussed in 1975 and 1976, never came into being. This was an understandable disappointment to Mr. Van Lennep, who had initiated the idea independently of U.S. officials, worked hard in developing the

[33] As indicated, twenty-one of the twenty-four members of the OECD had ratified the FSF agreement by the spring of 1977, representing 71.3 percent of total voting power. This was more than enough for formal activation of the plan, which legally could have been accomplished by a decision of as few as fifteen members holding as little as 60 percent of total quotas (OECD 1975, article 23).

plan, and hoped that the OECD would, for the first time, have ample funds available to it.[34]

The Witteveen facility was formally adopted by the Fund's executive board on August 29—not by coincidence, the very same day that the OECD was formally informed by Washington of its withdrawal of support for the FSF.

The Mediating Role of Domestic Politics

This brings us, finally, to the role of domestic politics. Washington's reversal of preferences over the course of the drama was striking. Although much can be explained by shifts in the cognitive and economic environment and the opposition of the IMF, these are in a sense all "external" variables—factors that influence the attitudes and calculations of policymakers from the "outside in." Even with them, the picture remains incomplete unless we take account of "internal" variables, too—factors that make their influence felt from the "inside out," through political conflict and bargaining *within* the country rather than abroad. In practice, external variables are unlikely to exercise much impact at all except as they are mediated through the domestic political process.

During the exploratory and negotiation phases of the FSF drama, Secretary Kissinger's anti-OPEC strategy encountered little domestic resistance. Americans, shaken by the perceived threat to their energy security, required little urging to support a confrontational or even aggressive posture in relations with oil producers. Kissinger never even felt the need to consult with Congress before launching his safety net initiative. Apparently the only serious bargaining sparked by the idea took place within the executive branch, between the Treasury and State Departments, starting soon after Secretary Simon was appointed in April 1974. Simon was too new to his post, however, and as yet too unsure of his place in Washington's power structure to offer much resistance to Kissinger's then dominant voice within the administration. Although never fully persuaded that the markets were incapable of handling the recycling problem, the Treasury Secretary was nonetheless receptive to contingency planning within the government as well as at the OECD and, by the autumn, was persuaded to agree, albeit with some reluctance, to go public with the joint Treasury-State proposal.[35]

---

[34] De Vries 1985, 459. The disappointment may have been more than just professional. According to at least one informed source, running through the whole episode was an underlying personal rivalry between Witteveen and Van Lennep, both of whom had previously served for many years in the Dutch government (interview, July 1977). Washington insiders spoke of the "Double-Dutch rivalry"—Witteveen vs. Van Lennep as well as the clash between the IMF and OECD.

[35] Reportedly, as early as July 1974 during a stopover at OECD headquarters in Paris, Simon privately encouraged the Secretariat in its preparation of the Van Lennep proposal. According to a well-placed OECD official, this was "the first sign of official endorsement" of an OECD-administered safety net (interview, July 1977).

Whatever reservations Simon may have held in private about the safety net, no substantive differences could be detected between the rough idea sketched out by Kissinger on November 14 and the more detailed version that Simon elaborated four days later. As Assistant Secretary Cooper, Simon's deputy, insisted the following spring: "There are no differences of any significance at all between us and the State Department on this. This is something we worked very closely on and I am pleased to say this is an area where cooperation between State and Treasury is complete and full and there are no serious disagreements" (U.S. House of Representatives 1975a, 15).

Apparently, there were also no serious disagreements between the executive branch and Congress—at least, not at first. Testimony by administration officials soon after the FSF agreement was signed encountered little criticism on Capitol Hill, and no evidence exists to indicate that ratification would have been unusually difficult had State and Treasury pushed for immediate action.[36] Nothing was done, however, to promote Congressional consideration for over a year, beyond routine submission of draft legislation in June 1975, allowing opposition ample opportunity to emerge and mobilize (U.S. House of Representatives 1975b). By the time formal hearings got under way in mid-1976, the FSF agreement was plainly in trouble (U.S. Senate 1976). Once the changeover of administrations occurred in early 1977, its fate was essentially sealed.

Several factors seem to have contributed to the change of heart in Washington. Of considerable importance was the improving economic climate, as adjustments to the 1973 Oil Shock finally began to take hold. With the public's sense of urgency slowly receding, it became correspondingly more difficult to sustain domestic support for a seemingly radical and potentially expensive financial initiative—particularly as even more demanding emergencies, such as the looming bankruptcy of New York City, began to appear on the horizon.[37] Of some salience as well were personal frictions generated by Henry Kissinger's abrasive and muscular style of policymaking. On Capitol Hill, the Secretary of State was resented for neglecting the usual courtesies of prior consultation before formally announcing the U.S. plan.[38] In the executive branch, Secretary

[36] Quite the reverse in fact. Most sources suggest that ratification was indeed feasible at the time. In the words of one IMF official, who was no friend of the FSF, "The administration might have gotten the FSF through the Congress in 1975 had they moved quickly" (interview, September 1977). See also U.S. House of Representatives 1975a.

[37] New York's financial difficulties were cited in particular by Jacques Van Ypersele—"a condition," he suggested, "which made anything that resembled foreign aid look questionable" (interview, September 1977).

[38] One Congressional staffer referred to the safety net initiative as "one of those grandiose Kissinger schemes" (interview, September 1977).

Simon was reportedly piqued by Kissinger's heavy-handed dismissal of his own private reservations about the safety net idea.[39]

Also important was a bureaucratic turf war between the State Department and Treasury triggered by the Kissinger initiative. While the Treasury had always enjoyed authority over U.S. representation at the IMF, the State Department was the lead agency for the OECD. Treasury officials, worried that a successful FSF would force them to share their traditional primacy in international financial policymaking with their counterparts at Foggy Bottom, therefore became the Fund's natural allies in its competition with the OECD.[40] And then of course there was the Federal electoral cycle, which had a major impact on the calculations not only of legislators but of two successive administrations as well. Domestic political weakness made the incumbent, President Ford, increasingly hesitant to push for controversial legislation of any sort.[41] His defeat brought to power an opponent, Jimmy Carter, who naturally had little interest in sustaining or promoting key policies of his predecessor.

Most important of all, though, was the overarching clash with the IMF, whose campaign for renewed relevancy was notably successful in diverting attention from the FSF. First came a review of Fund quotas—the formal basis of regular financial contributions by member governments—which had already begun in early 1974. In January 1975, Managing Director Witteveen engineered agreement in principle on a quota increase of nearly one-third (SDR 10 billion). Although final details were not worked out for another fourteen months, that prospect alone sufficed to delay consideration of the FSF, since the U.S. share (roughly SDR 1.7 billion) would require Congressional authorization. Treasury officials argued, with some reason, that legislators were unlikely to approve both financial initiatives simultaneously. In fact, Congress at the time exhibited little interest in even a single new program of costly foreign assistance, let alone two.[42]

---

[39] In fact, according to one highly placed State Department source, Simon was "regularly humiliated by Kissinger power plays" and "was never convinced the FSF was needed or that useful" (confidential correspondence).

[40] Indeed, for some key players this seemed the real clash of giants, not the Double Dutch rivalry of Witteveen's IMF and Van Lennep's OECD. One State Department official recalls a European minister saying that "we Europeans can only hope for peace between the world's two superpowers—the U.S. Treasury and the U.S. State Department." The State Department, of course, remained the natural ally of the OECD, but by 1976, with the OPEC threat fading, its influence over financial matters was clearly on the wane.

[41] Political weakness also made Ford increasingly attentive to the views of Secretary Simon, who carried much weight in the Republican party. In the words of one Washington source, "Ford, facing an election, needed Simon more than he needed Kissinger." Simon's reservations about the FSF were well known inside the beltway.

[42] Interviews, September 1977.

And then, in early 1977, came Witteveen's proposal for his Supplementary Financing Facility, which from the start was seen as a direct rival to the FSF. The idea of a new arrangement at the IMF was warmly supported by the incoming Carter administration, partly because it would rely on financing from oil exporters as well as industrial nations (thus making the scheme more palatable to potential donors like Germany) and partly because its resources would be available to all governments, not just members of the OECD (thus making it attractive to developing countries as well).[43] In both respects, the Witteveen facility thus seemed more consistent with a "one-world philosophy" than did the FSF. It would also restore the Treasury to primacy in international financial policymaking in Washington.

In another irony, officials now also began to make the argument that two schemes were too many. With oil deficits shrinking, activation of both initiatives might actually create too much liquidity, they contended, and given the demonstrated capabilities of the IMF as a lending institution, the SFF seemed preferable. Washington's new attitude was concisely summarized in a brief colloquy between Illinois Senator Stevenson and Treasury Under Secretary Anthony Solomon in August 1977 (U.S. Senate 1977a, 38):

SENATOR STEVENSON: With this addition [the Witteveen facility], if the resources would be adequate, then it follows that the administration does not support an OECD support fund. Is that correct?

MR. SOLOMON: If the Congress gives approval to this and the facility is established, then we would not expect to return to the Congress for any contribution to the Financial Support Fund.

In effect, the executive branch, under two successive presidents, felt compelled to make a choice—and elected to give priority to the IMF.

REVIEW

What can we learn from the FSF experience, either about how actors make their choices or about how the outcomes of bargaining games are determined? It is evident that salient roles were played by each of the key elements highlighted by this historical drama: cognitive considerations, structural factors, and domestic politics. Much useful insight can be gained from a review of all three, first singly and then in combination.

---

[43] De Vries 1985, 548–49. See, for example, the statements by Carter Under Secretary of the Treasury, Anthony Solomon, in U.S. House of Representatives 1977, 56, and U.S. Senate 1977b, 33.

Cognitive Considerations

Insofar as cognitive considerations are concerned, the message of the FSF episode seems straightforward. Ideas do matter—both as stimulus and as constraint. Ideas may be understood as "shared beliefs" (Jacobsen 1995) or "consensual knowledge" (Rohrlich 1987). Most relevant for our purposes are ideas understood as *causal beliefs*, that is, "beliefs about cause-effect relationships which derive authority from the shared consensus of recognized elites" (Goldstein and Keohane 1993, 10). Causal beliefs provide guides for individuals on how to achieve specified objectives, serving both as "road maps" to help shape strategies for the attainment of goals and as "focal points" to help coordinate action and bond together effective coalitions. Ideas in this sense can be a powerful force for initiative and innovation, particularly in an emergency when actors feel least certain about the prospective consequences of alternative actions. But they can also be a stubborn barrier to change to the extent that they put effective blinders on decision makers, acting to limit imagination and restrict the number of acceptable outcomes. Both types of influence were evident in the FSF drama.

During the exploratory and negotiation phases, when governments were still reeling from the shock of sharply higher oil prices as well as the earlier abandonment of pegged exchange rates, consensus over the management of international monetary relations effectively broke down. No one could be sure that the multilateral structures established at Bretton Woods were up to the job of coping with prospective recycling needs. Minds were open to new suggestions about how to cope with impending payments imbalances. In this climate, the perception of dramatically altered economic circumstances produced an intense demand for institutional reform of some kind. Out of the ensuing competition of ideas, the FSF proposal emerged a viable contender, in part precisely because it seemed to offer both a clear road map at a time of uncertainty and a potentially effective focal point for collective action. Quite clearly, the initiative would never have received the attention it did—even apart from the power of its sponsor, the United States—had there not been, in effect, a severe jolt to the prevailing cognitive order.

During the ratification phase, by contrast, as the general sense of urgency abated, more traditional notions began to reassert themselves—particularly regarding the crucial issue of where institutional authority should properly reside in the global regime. Most recognized experts continued to hold to the view that monetary affairs are best managed in a unitary fashion. Just as national money systems are governed by a single central bank, the international system should have just one center of decision making: the IMF. At the level of elite opinion, therefore, opposition to implementation of the FSF agreement began to build up, ultimately prevailing despite conciliatory efforts like those of Senator Stevenson.

Here, too, ideas had a powerful impact, aided by the existence of an articulate and far-flung network of knowledge-based experts—an "epistemic community"[44]—with access to key policymakers and a comparatively uniform point of view. It helped as well that some of the most prominent members of the community actually became policymakers themselves, with positions of real political authority in the U.S. government, during the period that the issue of ratification was still pending. In the end, the same idea that had seemed so attractive under conditions of worrisome uncertainty came to be precluded once normal times returned.

Structural Factors

The message here, too, seems fairly straightforward. Power also matters—like ideas, both as stimulus and constraint. The role of power in determining the shape of global institutional arrangements has long been emphasized by students of world politics: most generally in the well-known theory of hegemonic stability, but more specifically in that strand of the literature labeled by David Lake (1993) "leadership theory," which highlights the impact of dominant powers ("hegemons") on the production of an "international economic infrastructure." The patronage of the powerful is clearly critical to effective organizational reform. On the one hand, significant regime transformation is less likely to be attempted without the active support or sponsorship of one or more leading governments. On the other hand, major reform is more likely to be rejected if that support or sponsorship is withheld. Both types of influence were evident in the FSF drama.

The OECD safety net represented a potentially dramatic change in global institutional arrangements. Looking back, it seems improbable that such a grave challenge to the IMF would even have been contemplated without the explicit intervention and forceful diplomacy of the United States. Few governments paid serious attention to Secretary General Van Lennep's proposal when it was first floated in the summer of 1974. A financial facility at the OECD, with resources to rival the IMFs, became a plausible possibility only when it was promoted by Washington. Plainly evident throughout the exploratory and negotiation phases was what Scott James and David Lake term the first "face" of hegemony: the overt "use of positive and negative sanctions aimed directly at foreign governments in an attempt to influence their choice of policies" (James and Lake 1989, 4). Some use, in addition, was also made of hegemony's third face—the projection of ideas—to legitimate the Kissinger proposal.[45] In effect, Washington took

---

[44] The term comes from John Ruggie (1975) and has been popularized by Peter Haas (1992).

[45] The second face of hegemony, the influence of the hegemon's international market power on incentives and interests in foreign countries, does not appear to have played a major role in the story.

advantage of the uncertainty generated by the oil problem to promote its own conception of an appropriate solution. But most vital to the rapid success of the FSF negotiation, quite clearly, was an unabashedly open exploitation of power by the U.S. government.

Washington's power also proved decisive during the ratification phase—by its lack of use—as the executive branch first procrastinated and then turned actively hostile to the FSF. Despite appeals from figures as prominent as Jelle Zijlstra, no government was prepared to activate the safety net without participation by the OECD's richest member. Despite efforts by Van Lennep and his Secretariat to continue the fight for ratification, few wished to cross swords with the IMF without Washington's blessing. The Fund and OECD were two giants locked in combat. But neither could prevail except through the influence of the United States. In effect, having changed its mind, Washington exercised a veto over the whole process. What the hegemon wrought, the hegemon then discarded.

Domestic Politics

Once again, the message here seems straightforward. Domestic politics matters, too. As Robert Putnam (1988) has reminded us, international diplomacy is a game played at two levels, not just one—within countries as well as between them. At the international level, negotiators seek accord through mutual accommodation and compromise. But agreements reached abroad must also be capable of winning political support at home, particularly when formal legislative ratification is called for. At the domestic level, key constituencies must be satisfied that their interests, or their conception of the public interest, are being adequately served. No inter-governmental negotiation, however artfully conducted, can be considered truly successful if implementation is subsequently blocked by domestic discord.

In this sense the FSF initiative was obviously *not* a success, despite Henry Kissinger's best efforts. In the rush to win over governments in Europe and Japan, little was done to gain hearts or minds on Capital Hill or neutralize potential opposition. The legal requirement of ratification, apparently, was not expected to be much of a problem. No special effort was made to cultivate key Congressional figures or mobilize public opinion; nor was anything done to mollify critics at the Treasury, from Secretary Simon on down. Instead of moving rapidly to organize a winning coalition, backers allowed the agreement to linger in the legislative hopper while, over time, preferences gradually shifted in favor of the IMF alternative. In the end, the FSF failed because its sponsors neglected to tend their own backyard. The game that was won at the international level was thus lost at the domestic level.

Implications

Several implications emerge from this analysis, both concerning causal linkages among the three key elements in the story and confirming the validity of some of the hypotheses on game-change efforts suggested by Vinod Aggarwal in his introductory essay.

Among the three elements, one stands out clearly as decisive: the role of power, both at the structural level and at the level of domestic politics. Ideas may have mattered as "road maps" and "focal points" in the climate of uncertainty generated by OPEC's oil shock, but the choice among ideas plainly depended on the relative strength of their respective sponsors. Opposition at the level of elite opinion may ultimately have helped kill the FSF proposal, but the influence of the relevant epistemic community would have been far less had key members not been appointed to positions of formal authority in Washington. The FSF, as negotiated, might have taken a different shape, more like the original Van Lennep or Healey plans, but not given the distribution of state capabilities in the bargaining game. The OECD might have prevailed in its clash with the IMF, but not once the patronage of the United States was withdrawn. Ratification by the U.S. Congress might have been possible, but not without the requisite effort to capture the domestic political process. In every act of the drama, manifestations of power took center stage.

To put the point simply, other considerations may have been necessary to the development of each act, but without the exercise of material capabilities they were insufficient to explain outcomes. Many factors set the agenda, but power was the final arbiter.

Among the hypotheses proposed by Aggarwal (see chapter 1, this volume), several are confirmed by this experience. First is his suggestion that provision of a common pool resource may well be stimulated, rather than inhibited, by large numbers of actors. Following the rise of oil prices, available liquidity sources were clearly at risk of being overwhelmed. A disorderly scramble for financing, which might have triggered a self-destructive conflict of protectionism or other deficit-reduction measures, was a real threat. In these circumstances, the question was not *whether* to act, but rather *how* and *on what scale*. Governments knew they had to restrain their own worst impulses.

Likewise, regarding institutional choice, it is evident that the first instinct of all concerned was to utilize or modify an existing institution rather than pursue the more difficult path of creating a wholly new organization. The only question was *which* existing institution, the IMF or OECD? Henry Kissinger preferred the latter because it fit better with his grand geopolitical designs. William Simon, as well as the later Carter team, was far more partial to the former because of its pivotal role at the center of the international monetary system.

Third, regarding both type of institution and bargaining route, the choice of multilateral approaches was manifestly affected by the type of institutions already in existence. No one (save possibly the French government) seriously questioned the need to act together rather than separately, though there was of course much room for disagreement over specifics. Should the collective response of oil importers be confrontational or conciliatory? Should there be one new recycling mechanism or two? How firmly should any safety net be nested under the wing of the IMF? Answers to these questions were heavily influenced by power considerations. But as Aggarwal suggests, the use of material capabilities in such a highly institutionalized context was bound to be constrained by existing institutional power resources as well as by the initiatives of existing organizations and bureaucracies.

Finally, on the specific issue of linkages, attitudes clearly were dependent on how threats were perceived by key actors, again as Aggarwal suggests. Early in the drama, when OPEC's oil weapon seemed by far the most salient issue, the U.S. naturally put most emphasis on the parallel tactical linkage between the FSF and IEA. Possible conflict with the IMF seemed less important than reinforcing transatlantic solidarity through the regionally based OECD. Later, however, as OPEC's surpluses started to decline and Western economic conditions improved, the need for a strong OECD correspondingly faded. As a result Washington's preferences shifted, now stressing the safety net's substantive linkage to the IMF instead. Ultimately, the Fund's triumph in the clash of giants reflected the broader transformation of policy perceptions that occurred once the atmosphere of crisis began to recede.

LESSONS FOR THE FUTURE

The FSF was not a bad idea. Given the atmosphere of crisis prevailing in 1974–75, it made perfectly good sense for governments to take any precautionary action possible. Nor was the safety net poorly conceived. Proponents were well aware of the need to ensure institutional compatibility with the operations of the IMF. Yet despite careful crafting and the patronage of a powerful sponsor, the FSF foundered—an enterprise left stranded by time. The experience suggests several lessons for comparable future efforts to nest regional initiatives within broader global structures.

First, there must be a perceived *need* for any such project—a cognitive consensus that institutional reform is indeed called for. Key actors must be persuaded, and remain persuaded, that existing structures may be inadequate to cope with present or prospective challenges.

Second, the project must be *credible.* Proponents must be able to make a convincing case for the effectiveness of the proposed reform—that it should indeed be capable of achieving its declared objectives and can potentially be implemented at acceptable cost. In a world of imperfect information, no argument can be absolutely irrefutable. But it must be plausible.

Third, the project must be *non-threatening*—posed as a supplement rather than as a substitute for prevailing global structures. Every effort should be made to avoid institutional rivalries, particularly in circumstances where existing organizations already have reason to feel weak and challenged (as the IMF did in 1973–74). Useful steps might include inviting representatives of existing organizations to participate at the negotiation stage, incorporating the policy frameworks of relevant global institutions into the new initiative's own legal framework, and perhaps even providing for regular consultations or standing joint committees.

Fourth, the project must have an influential *sponsor*—the backing of one or more governments with sufficient clout to gain formal international agreement.

Fifth, state sponsors in turn must be able to assure the project's necessary *ratification,* formal or informal, at home. Domestic political support must be actively cultivated and mobilized.

And finally, a high priority must be placed on *speed,* both in negotiation and in ratification of an agreement. While time may be needed to build a credible case for the proposed reform, it also creates an opportunity for a buildup of opposing forces. In politics, it is always advantageous to strike while the iron is hot.

None of these six conditions, by itself, is likely to ensure a successful nesting of regional and global institutions. But judging from the FSF experience, they would certainly all appear to be necessary, and in combination, might prove sufficient as well. The FSF itself was both a product and a victim of contingency—conceived in response to a perceived threat, abandoned after it was felt that the crisis had passed. But even if the safety net did turn out to be an idea whose time had come and gone, its story is instructive as a cautionary tale. From its failure, much can be learned for comparable circumstances in the future.

REFERENCES

Camps, Miriam, 1975. *"First World" Relationships: The Role of the OECD,* Atlantic papers, no. 2 (Paris: Atlantic Institute for International Affairs).

Cohen, Benjamin J., 1976. "Mixing Oil and Money." In J. C. Hurewitz, ed., *Oil, the Arab-Israel Dispute, and the Industrial World: Horizons of Crisis* (Boulder, Colo.: Westview Press).

———, 1981. *Banks and the Balance of Payments: Private Lending in the International Adjustment Process* (Montclair, N.J.: Allenheld, Osmun).

De Vries, Margaret Garritson, 1985. *The International Monetary Fund, 1972–1978: Cooperation on Trial,* vol. 1 *Narrative and Analysis* (Washington D.C.: International Monetary Fund).

Ehrbar, A. F., 1977. "The IMF Lays Down the Law," *Fortune*, July.

Gardner, Richard N., 1969. *Sterling-Dollar Diplomacy: The Origins and Prospects of Our International Economic Order,* rev. ed. (New York: McGraw-Hill).

Goldstein, Judith, and Robert O. Keohane, 1993. "Ideas and Foreign Policy: An Analytical Framework." In Judith Goldstein and Robert O. Keohane, eds., *Ideas and Foreign Policy: Beliefs, Institutions, and Political Change* (Ithaca, N.Y.: Cornell University Press).

Haas, Peter, ed., 1992. "Knowledge, Power, and International Policy Coordination." Special issue of *International Organization* 46 (Winter).

Hager, Wolfgang, 1976. "Western Europe: The Politics of Muddling Through." In J. C. Hurewitz, ed., *Oil the Arab-Israel Dispute, and the Industrial World: Horizons of Crisis* (Boulder, Colo.: Westview Press).

Healey, Denis, 1989. *The Time of My Life* (London: Michael Joseph).

Jacobsen, John Kurt, 1995. "Much Ado about Ideas: The Cognitive Factor in Economic Policy." *World Politics* 47 (January).

James, Harold, 1996. *International Monetary Cooperation since Bretton Woods* (New York: Oxford University Press).

James, Scott C., and David A. Lake, 1989. "The Second Face of Hegemony: Britain's Repeal of the Corn Laws and the American Walker Tariff of 1846." *International Organization* 43 (Winter).

Kohl, Wilfrid L., 1976. "The International Energy Agency: The Political Context." In J. C. Hurewitz, ed., *Oil, the Arab-Israel Dispute, and the Industrial World: Horizons of Crisis* (Boulder, Colo.: Westview Press).

Lake, David A., 1993. "Leadership, Hegemony, and the International Economy: Naked Emperor or Tattered Monarch with Potential?" *International Studies Quarterly* 37 (December).

Louis, Jean-Victor, 1975. "Le Fonds de Soutien Financier de l'O.C.D.E.," *Studia Diplomatica* 28, no. 4.

OECD, 1975. *Agreement Establishing a Financial Support Fund of the Organization for Economic Cooperation and Development.* Paris, 9 April.

Putnam, Robert D., 1988. "Diplomacy and Domestic Politics: The Logic of Two-Level Games." *International Organization* 42 (Summer).

Rohrlich, Paul Egon, 1987. "Economic Culture and Foreign Policy: The Cognitive Analysis of Economic Policy Making." *International Organization* 41 (Winter).

Ruggie, John Gerard, 1975. "International Responses to Technology: Concepts and Trends." *International Organization* 29 (Summer).

Scheinman, Lawrence, 1976. "US International Leadership." In J. C. Hurewitz, ed., *Oil, the Arab-Israel Dispute, and the Industrial World: Horizons of Crisis* (Boulder, Colo.: Westview Press).

U.S. House of Representatives, 1975a. *The OECD Financial Support Fund ($25 Billion Safety Net).* Hearings before the Subcommittee on International Trade and Commerce of the House Committee on International Relations. 94th Cong., 1st sess., 5 May.

U.S. House of Representatives, 1975b. *United States Participation in the Financial Support Fund.* Communication from the President of the United States Transmitting a Draft of Proposed Legislation to Provide for the Participation of the United States in the Financial Support Fund. 94th Cong., 1st sess., 6 June.

U.S. House of Representatives, 1977. *U.S. Participation in the Supplementary Financing Facility of the International Monetary Funds.* Hearings before the Subcommittee on International Trade, Investment and Monetary Policy of the House Committee on Banking, Finance, and Urban Affairs. 95th Cong., 1st sess., 20, 29, 30 September.

U.S. Senate, 1976. *Financial Support Fund Act.* Hearings before the Senate Committee on Banking, Housing, and Urban Affairs. 94th Cong., 2d sess., 4 June.

U.S. Senate, 1977a. *International Debt.* Hearings before the Subcommittee on International Finance of the Senate Committee on Banking, Housing, and Urban Affairs. 95th Cong., 1st sess., 29, 30 August.

U.S. Senate, 1977b. *The Witteveen Facility and the OPEC Financial Surpluses.* Hearings before the Subcommittee on Foreign Economic Policy of the Senate Committee on Foreign Relations. 95th Cong., 1st sess., 21, 23 September and 6, 7, 10 October.

Williamson, John, 1975. "The International Financial System." In Edward R. Fried and Charles L. Schultze, eds., *Higher Oil Prices and the World Economy: The Adjustment Problem* (Washington, D.C.: Brookings Institution).

————, 1977. *The Failure of World Monetary Reform, 1971–74* (London: Thomas Nelson).

CHAPTER SIX

Institutional Nesting: Lessons and Prospects

VINOD K. AGGARWAL

The tension between globalism, regionalism, and sectoralism has continued to challenge both policymakers and analysts. Can these different modes of organization in the world system be reconciled with each other? Is there an inevitable conflict between global arrangements on the one hand, and regional or sectoral arrangements on the other hand? This volume has sought to examine these questions by developing the notion of an institutional bargaining game and examining how such games might evolve through actors' institutional strategies.

Existing approaches to examine the development of international institutions have contributed much to our understanding of institutional change. Each of the three schools reviewed in chapter 1—neorealist institutionalism, neoliberal institutionalism, and the cognitive approach—provides us with a different analytical lens on the problem of understanding institutional changes. In brief, the neorealist approach emphasizes the role of power and control in influencing the rise and fall of international institutions. The neoliberal school focuses on transaction costs and the importance of existing institutions in constraining and motivating the development of new ones. And the cognitive approach emphasizes the role of scientific consensus and the interaction of "epistemic communities" with interest groups in affecting the course of institutional development. As I suggested, however, the leading contenders do not adequately capture important aspects of the phenomena of institutional evolution. In particular, standard analytic approaches do not adequately address the problem of how actors attempt to nest or develop parallel institutions as they engage in the modification of existing institutions or the innovation of new ones.

The introductory essay provided a comprehensive framework to capture the institutional bargaining process. The task of this chapter is to assess the utility of the framework in enhancing our understanding of the conditions under which institutional reconciliation might be possible. In particular, it examines the empirical contributions of the chapters in this volume from an analytical perspective, with an eye to investigating the fit between theory and practice.

The first section considers the extent to which the notion of an institutional bargaining game—based on the interplay of goods, individual situations, and institutions—helps us to structure the bargaining setting observed in the various empirical chapters. The second section then turns to an examination of the factors that best explain the process of institutional change. The third section focuses on the key issue of institutional reconciliation resulting from actors' use of nested and parallel linkages and examines the lessons that we might glean from the theoretical and empirical analysis. In the concluding section, I point to theoretical and empirical avenues for future research on the evolution and nesting of institutions.

THE INSTITUTIONAL BARGAINING GAME

The introductory chapter identified two distinct phases in the institutional bargaining process—an initial bargaining game and a game change phase. With regard to the initial game setting (see figure 1.3A in the introduction), I argued that actors respond to an initial impetus, conditioned by the "goods" involved in the resulting negotiations, actors' individual situations, and the institutional context. In turn, the payoffs of this bargaining game provide a stimulus to the institutional game change phase (discussed below and schematized in figure 1.3B in the introduction).

To what extent does the bargaining construct depicted in figure 1.3A help to illuminate the choices faced by actors in the empirical cases? To examine this question, we must examine the factors that define the initial bargaining game for the four empirical papers. (See table 6.1.)

In the ten empirical cases examined in the four studies, the initial impetus varied considerably. Changes in interactions played a key role in the European Monetary System (EMS) crisis (speculation against non-German European currencies) and in the Financial Support Fund (FSF) case (the Oil Shock of 1973–74). Domestic changes were crucial in creating the initial problems in the EMS and FSF ratification. In the first case, German unification and monetary policies led to pressure on the currencies of other European states. In the FSF debate, U.S. domestic opposition undermined the proposed fund. International factors were important in the remaining cases, with international institutional changes being crucial in the two of the three European Economic Area (EEA)

TABLE 6.1. The process of institutional formation: The bargaining games

Chapter and Type of case	Initial Impetus	Externalities and goods	Individual situations	Institutions	Bargaining game
EMS Crisis (Chap. 2 Weber)	2.1) German unification and GEMU	German policy on monetary stability (CPR)	Germany strong; elite belief in need to fight inflation; all others weak	EU and EMS	Germany vs. other Europeans over bearing adjustment burden
Region	2.2) Speculation against UK pound, Italian lira, and French franc	Undermining of EMS (damage to CPR)	No change	EU and EMS	Struggle over amount of realignment needed in return for Bundesbank interest rate reduction
Bosnian crisis (Chap. 3, Crawford)	3.1) End of Cold War and beginning of civil war in Yugoslavia	Fear of spillover to broader European theater; interest in European security region (public good)	German ideological view on self-determination and political differences	WEU and CSE	Conflict over recognition of Croatia
Region/issue-area	3.2) Entry of U.S., Russia, and UN; onset of Bosnian war	Concern for preserving multilateralism (public good); threat to Western values	U.S. overall strong with domestic pressures; German support for Croatia; Russian domestic pressure for support of Serbs	UN and NATO	Dispute over dealing with Serbs in Bosnian War

TABLE 6.1. Continued

Chapter and Type of case	Initial Impetus	Externalities and goods	Individual situations	Institutions	Bargaining game
EEA creation (Chap. 4, Dupont)	4.1) Single European Act	EFTA Fear of Being left out (private good)	Variation in EFTA countries situations, but overall weak; EC strong	EFTA, EC, Luxembourg framework	Conflict over going beyond the Luxembourg process
Region	4.2) Call for closer relations by East and Central Europeans after collapse of SU	EC fears job hindered deepening process (private and limited club good); pan-regional stability (CPR); EFTA fear of being left out (private good)	No change in IS	EFTA, EC, Luxembourg framework	EFTA presses for better EC link; EC worries about widening and deepening
	4.3) EEA agreement	EFTA countries' fear of exclusion from involvement in policymaking (private good; access to EC club)	Changes in economic strength and growing domestic opposition to EEA in EFTA states; interest in EU	EC, EFTA, and EEA	EFTA push for bilateral accession

TABLE 6.1. Continued

Chapter and Type of case Issue-area	*Initial Impetus*	*Externalities and goods*	*Individual situations*	*Institutions*	*Bargaining game*
FSF creation (Chap. 5, Cohen)	5.1) 1973–74 Oil Shock	Fear of effect on Western economies; creation of IEA to break OPEC (Western public good)	U.S. strong overall; domestic support and consensus on leadership; France and others weaker overall	IMF	Conflict over response to OPEC actions
	5.2) French resist FSF	Failure to create FSF (CPR) undermining of IEA	No significant changes	IMF and OECD	U.S. wants IEA: France presses for North-South dialogue
	5.3) Ratification problems	Concern about (IMF) (public good)	Changing U.S. view due to economic changes; changing domestic political situation; concern about OECD-IMF conflict	IMF and OECD in conflict	IMF-OECD conflict influences ratification

cases. Thus, this survey suggests that institutional bargaining games can be set in motion by changes in interactions, domestic politics, or international institutional changes, as depicted in the overarching framework presented in figure 1.1 of the introduction.

These initial stimuli led to a variety of externalities and implications for goods. Externalities proved particularly important in the FSF Oil Shock case, the civil war in Yugoslavia, the Single European Act (which threatened EC-EFTA agreements), and German unification and economic policymaking.

Concern about the undermining of public goods played a role in several cases. These include the U.S. attempt to use the 1973–74 Oil Shock as a means to bolster the public good of the Western alliance, the concern that the IMF as a public good was threatened by the FSF, and the fear that both the public goods of a European security region and of multilateralism were being undermined in the Bosnian crisis.

Common pool resources (CPRs) were involved in the French resistance to both the FSF and IEA (whose resources were available only to developed countries who were members of these groups). Similar concerns about the impact of CPR provision were raised in the EMS case.

Finally, EFTA-EC negotiations are best characterized as a mix of CPR, limited inclusive club goods, and private goods. Pan-regional stability to be provided by the EEA was a type of CPR. The inclusive club goods were limited by fears of crowding the EC club with too many new members, particularly the East Europeans. And there were also elements of private goods in the negotiations, because the EC could selectively grant access to its single market.

The empirical studies clearly show that actors' preferences over outcomes also varied based both on the existing institutional context and their individual situations. To give a few examples from the cases, in the EMS crisis, Germany's economic position—combined with the presence of the EU as an institution that no one wished to undermine—proved to be a critical factor in determining national policies. Thus, the bargaining games in both of the cases discussed by Steven Weber were strongly constrained by concern about the need to reconcile any changes in the EMS with the broader objective of preserving the EU.

Variation in individual situations proved particularly significant in the struggle over how to deal with both the civil war in Yugoslavia and the Bosnian war. While Beverly Crawford argues that differences in countries' overall capabilities in the decision to recognize Croatia were not significant, she suggests that domestic politics, particularly in the context of a weak set of institutional norms, prompted the ensuing conflict over recognition. Later, the sharply differing individual situations of the United States, Germany, and Russia led to the eventual decision to actively use NATO to implement the Dayton Plan.

In the EEA debate, wide variation in EFTA countries' views stemmed from their individual situations—particularly their relative dependence on the EC market. Moreover, important differences in EFTA countries' domestic political situations, together with the impact of changing economic circumstances on these states, led to problems with the EEA. These in turn led to varying EFTA states' preferences about acceding to the EU. The importance for the EC of preserving its institutional autonomy also undermined the prospects for the EEA.

Finally, in the aftermath of the 1973–74 oil crisis, the relative strength of the United States (both overall and with respect to energy issues) led it to take a considerably more aggressive stance toward OPEC than France and other weaker European countries. In addition, the existence of the IMF and opposition from this institution greatly affected actors' calculations about the value of the FSF. In the end, economic and political changes in the United States, combined with this IMF opposition, led to the demise of the FSF.

The framework outlined here provide a means of capturing the most significant issues involved in defining the initial bargaining games discussed in the empirical cases. The focus on stimuli, combined with attention to their effect on externalities and goods, actors' individual situations, and the institutional context, helps to set the stage for the process of possible institutional innovation—the topic to which we now turn.

INSTITUTIONAL CHANGE EFFORTS: CREATION, TYPE, AND BARGAINING ROUTE

Faced with favorable or unfavorable payoffs, actors have the option of promoting changes in the game they are playing. Of the three strategies available—the direct manipulation of goods, changing individual situations, or institutional innovation—this book has concentrated on institutional changes. As depicted in figure 1.3B in the introduction, if actors choose to go down this road, they must agree on either a multilateral or bilateral institutional scope and pursue either a multilateral, bilateral, or unilateral bargaining path toward this end. During the bargaining process, actors can then engage in linkage bargaining as they face the problem of institutional reconciliation. These linkages can be either nested or parallel, either substantive or tactical, and can connect either issues or institutions. The effect of these institutional change efforts and various linkage strategies may lead to a new game structure with a different set of payoffs for actors (examined in detail in the next section).

In each of the observed game change efforts (see table 6.2), I depict the steps involved along with the factors that proved most significant in view of the hypotheses presented in the introduction. In the discussion that follows, rather

TABLE 6.2. Institutional change efforts

Cases	Create a new institution?	Institutional scope	Bargaining route	Linkages (type, and nature)
EMS/Crisis				
1) Coping with German unification and GEMU	No, use existing institutions; cognitive consensus on preserving EMS and legitimacy of commitment to integration; constraints of EU	Multilateral because of institutional constraints	Multilateral with German unilateral threats	Nested substantive link to Maastricht; see as tactical by some non-Germans
2) Coping with speculation	No view prevails, but sharp debate; cognitive dissensus on appropriate mechanism; differences on control	Multilateral or bilateral because of institutional constraints and control concerns	Multilateral; constrained by multiple overlapping institutions	Deeper nested substantive link to EMU and EU
Bosnian crisis				
1) Croation recognition	No, use existing institutions; control of warring parties and institutional strengthening	Multilateral because of cognitive consensus	Multilateral with a few exceptions (institutional constraints)	Nested substantive to UN and linkage to U.S.; seen by non-Germans as nested-tactical
2) Bosnian war	No, use existing institutions; constraints of existing institutions	Multilateral because of cognitive consensus	Multilateral (institutional constraints) for all options	Parallel substantive reconciliation among existing institutions

TABLE 6.2. Continued

Cases	Create a new institution?	Institutional scope	Bargaining route	Linkages (type, and nature)
EEA creation				
1) Response to Single European Act	No, use existing institutions; cognitive consensus in EC on deepening; among EFTA members, concern with control based on domestic coalitional factors and institutional density	Multilateral because of transaction costs and existing institutions	Different routes: unilateral, bilateral, and multilateral with cognitive concern for advancement on multilateral deepening	Parallel substantive link between EFTA and EC (functional cooperation)
2) EEA development	Yes, reconcile; cognitive agreement on limits to Luxembourg; concerns about policy control and transaction cost among EFTA members	Two pillar vs. true multilateralism; transaction costs, existing institutions, and control issues	Dispute over EC and EFTA relationship (institutional constraints)	Nested substantive: EU and EFTA within EEA within GATT; some tactical linkages by member states
3) Erosion of EEA	No, join existing EU; loss of control for EFTA countries; EC fails to control pressure from Eastern and Central Europe	Multilateral because of existing institution	Bilateral route	Nested substantive with EFTA members joining EU

TABLE 6.2. Continued

Cases	Create a new institution?	Institutional scope	Bargaining route	Linkages (type, and nature)
FSF creation				
1) IEA proposal	Yes, de novo; cognitive consensus on need to respond; for U.S. creation of regime and control of OPEC	Dispute over scope of multilateral institution; need for control	U.S. plays a hegemonic role; side payments of FSF; North-South cooperation	U.S. suggests FSF as parallel tactical link; seen as parallel substantive link by France
2) FSF development	Yes, reconcile; nested concern because IEA within OECD; control of financial fund	Multilateral FSF within OECD (nested)	U.S. as hegemon; concern over nested systems by U.S., USSR, and OPEC	Nested substantive within broadly defined IMF system, but lodged within OECD
3) FSF failure	No, use existing institution; new cognitive consensus: no need for FSF; institutional struggle: IMF-OECD	Multilateral because of existing institution	Multilateral as U.S. shifts view; OECD-IMF institutional conflict	Nested substantive with IMF (Witteveen facility)

than focusing on each case individually, the key elements are summarized in the aggregate.[1] Of the ten cases summarized in the table, three involved the development of new institutions. Seven involved situations where actors responded to problematic payoffs by attempting to rework the relationship among existing institutions. Of the three institutional creation efforts, two of these—the development of the EEA and the FSF—were marked by efforts to create a new institution and reconcile it with existing ones. In the first of these cases, the EEA case, a supra-institution was created within which existing institutions were to nest. In the second case, the FSF was to be nested within the broader financial institutional setup. Finally, in one case, the creation of the IEA, an effort was initially made to establish a new institution without concern for existing arrangements. In the other seven cases involving the restructuring of relationships among existing institutions, actors engaged in some type of linkage effort (generally nested substantive, but sometimes parallel substantive) to tie together some group of arrangements.

How do the hypotheses fare in view of the empirical cases? We begin with the choice between creating a new institution or modifying or using existing ones. Cognitive consensus was the primary driving force in this decision, and a cognitive dissensus also created either conflict or limited institutional creation efforts (the failure of the FSF, the division between joining the EU versus supporting the EEA, the problems in institutional reconciliation in the Bosnian case, and the conflict over the response to speculation-against non-German currencies in the EMS). "Control" was the next most important factor in the institutional modification option. This factor proved decisive in efforts to control OPEC via the IEA, to control the FSF, to negotiate decision making authority concerns in the EEA, to control the warring parties in Bosnia through institutions, and to resolve currency speculation in the EMS crisis. Moreover, these choices were seen to have important distributional consequences. Also critical, in most of the cases, was the existence, salience, and density of preexisting institutions, which served as a key constraint on the decision to create new institutions or work with existing ones. By contrast, transaction cost issues played a relatively minor role and appear to have been a significant influence only in the development of the FSF and somewhat less so in the creation of the EEA.

Turning next to institutional scope (bilateral or multilateral arrangements), inertia and transaction costs appear to have been the most important factors, followed by cognitive concerns, and control considerations. Institutional density and institutional nesting concerns seem to have been crucial factors in the EMS members' response to speculation. They also played a role in the organizational

---

[1] I postpone the bulk of the discussion about linkages to my examination of bargaining outcomes below.

structure of the EEA and the latter stages of the FSF case. Transactions cost arguments do not appear to have been significant in the FSF cases, but they did play a role in the development of the EEA. Cognitive considerations were particularly important in the Bosnian case and drove the concern for preserving multilateralism. Finally, in the IEA case, control concerns led the United States to favor "minilateralism,"[2] with the United States pressing to exclude OPEC and other third world countries from participating in the management of energy issues.

With respect to the bargaining route, we see a full panoply here of unilateral, bilateral, and multilateral efforts. The formation of the IEA seems to have been driven by the hegemonic role of the United States, with nested systemic concerns involving the Soviet Union. While some bilateral paths were taken within institutions, the most common route was a multilateral one. Actors appear to have been constrained by the presence of a host of existing institutions and to have been concerned that these institutions might be undermined by unilateral or bilateral actions.

This review of the empirical analysis has provided us with a different perspective on institutional change than the standard approaches provide. The hypotheses developed in the first chapter, which drew on these approaches, work with varying efficacy in predicting patterns of institutional change. The empirical analysis—while not definitive because of the relatively small number of cases—suggests that our study of institutional change can be enriched if differentiated by bargaining phases. Specifically, we have seen that cognitive approaches and power considerations are most important in explaining decisions on creating new institutions, whereas transaction costs arguments fare best in explaining institutional scope, and neoliberal institutional arguments, combined with power considerations, best account for the bargaining route. In short, one size does not fit all with respect to explaining the process of institutional change.

Linkages and Institutional Reconciliation

We now turn to the key question of using linkages in the process of institutional reconciliation. Tables 6.3A and 6.3B allow us to examine the evolution of institutions discussed in the four case study chapters (see also the last column of table 6.2). By tracing the evolution of the cases in these chapters, we can gain some sense of the dynamics of institutional change.

In the cases involving problems with the EMS, the dispute over who would bear the burden of adjustment involved with German unification was handled

[2] Yarbrough and Yarbrough 1992.

TABLE 6.3A.   List of all bargaining linkages

Linkage abbreviation	Linkage description
Chapter 2: European Monetary System	
EMS 1a	German link monetary cooperation to maastricht objectives
EMS 1b	Other European countries view German effort as tactical one to maintain dominant monetary position
EMS 2a	Dissolution of the ERM and delinking from the EU
EMS 2b	Restricted French-German monetary cooperation in lieu of ERM
EMS 2c	Widening the bands in the ERM
Chapter 3: Bosnian Security Institutions	
Bosnia 1a	German nesting of EC actions in broader UN context
Bosnia 1b	Non-Germans see German effort as tactical one to force recognition of Croatia
Bosnia 2	Reaffirmation of multilateralism commitment involving partial reconciliation of various institutions under the Dayton agreement
Chapter 4: EC, EFTA, and the European Economic Area	
EEA 1	EC-EFTA functional cooperation
EEA 2a	EC-EFTA integration based on substantive agreement in principle
EEA 2b	EC also sees EEA as leverage against U.S. in GATT negotiations; EFTA view that EEA was a step toward adhesion to EC
EEA 3	Majority of EFTA members seek complete EC membership
Chapter 5: Financial Support Fund, OECD, and the IMF	
FSF 1a	U.S. agreement to participate in North-South dialogue
FSF 1b	French view of U.S. linkage to FSF as parallel substantive
FSF 2a	Nesting of FSF within existing institutional framework
FSF 2b	IMF rejection of U.S. attempt to substantively nest FSF within the OECD
FSF 3	U.S. abandonment of the FSF and agreement to the Witteveen facility that would be substantively nested within the IMF

within an EU context. When the Europeans were forced to match a rise in German interest rates with hikes of their own, much debate took place over a deal that would lead to some type of realignment within the ERM in order to avoid an exit of the pound and possibly other currencies. Although the pound and lira did, in fact, leave the ERM, considerable policy coordination continued and the Germans linked cooperation in monetary matters to broader Maastricht objectives (EMS 1a). Some saw this linkage as a tactical effort by the Germans to maintain their monetary policy and their dominant position in the monetary system (EMS 1b). In the next round, speculation continued against the pound, franc, and lira, and alternatives to the ERM were hotly debated. These alternatives included dissolution of the ERM (EMS 2a) and delinking it from the EU, some type of restricted French-German monetary cooperation in lieu of the

TABLE 6.3B. Empirical summary of bargaining outcomes

LINKAGE TYPE			Reconciliation of new institution with old institution	Use or modification of existing institution(s)
			Independent institutions (no concern for compatibility)	Institutionally based negotiations on single issues [EMS 2a]
No linkage		Substantive	1. Stable, compatible inter-institutional link for related issues 2. Temporary, inter-institutional compatibility between issues (if target does not correctly perceive link)	1. Stable, institutional link between related issued [Bosnia 2] [EEA 1] 2. Temporary, institutional solution to externalities (if target does not correctly perceive link)
Parallel linkage		Tactical	1. Contingent, inter-institutional compatibility for all issues (independent of or in conflict with power change) [FSF 1a] 2. Unstable, inter-institutional compatibility for all issues (if target does not correctly perceive link) [FSF 1b]	1. Contingent, institutional link between issues (independent of power change) 2. Unstable, institutional link between issues (if target does not correctly perceive link)
Nested linkage		Substantive	1. Stable, hierarchically compatible institutions for related issues [EMS 2b] [EEA 2a] [FSF 2a] 2. Temporary, hierarchically compatible institutions for issues (if target does not correctly perceive link)	1. Stable, hierarchical link between issues within existing institution(s) [EMS 1a] [EMS 2c] [Bosnia 1a] [EEA 3] [FSF 3] 2. Temporary hierarchy between issues within existing institution(s) (if target does not correctly perceive link) [EMS 1b] [Bosnia 1b]
		Tactical	1. Contingent, hierarchically compatible institutions for all issues independent of or in conflict with power change) [EEA 2b] [FSF 2b] 2. Unstable, hierarchically compatible institutions for all issues (if target does not correctly perceive link)	1. Contingent, hierarchical link between issues within existing institution(s) (independent of or in conflict with power change) 2. Unstable, hierarchical link between issues within existing institution(s) (if target does not correctly perceive link)

Note: Institutional scope (multilateral and bilateral) and bargaining route (multilateral, bilateral, and unilateral) are not illustrated as outcomes on this chart.

ERM (EMS 2b), or widened bands in the ERM (EMS 2c). In the end, the last option was chosen, with the establishment of 15 percent bands. In the process, a deeper nested substantive connection was made to the EMU and the broader EU, and the ERM survived.

The analysis of the EMS crisis provides evidence of a cognitive agreement on the connections between the EMS and EU. Some power considerations were undoubtedly also important, with German actions often being perceived as bullying. What is most striking, however, is the role of nested institutions in constraining German behavior. By contrast, in this instance, transaction and organizational costs seem to be considerably less significant.

The debate over Croatian and Slovenian recognition following the breakup of Yugoslavia presents us with an instance of nested efforts within an existing institutional context. While all EC members wished to pursue a multilateral approach to the issue of successor-state recognition in order to control defectors, the WEU (the regional security institution in Europe), did not prove to be up to the task. In addition, the norms of the CSCE also failed to serve as a sufficient guide for decision making. The Germans sought to nest EC actions within a broader international context of the United Nations to encourage U.S. participation—a move they viewed as a logical substantive connection (Bosnia 1a). Non-Germans, however, viewed this effort as a tactical move to pressure them into recognizing Croatia (Bosnia 1b). In the end, the outcome was as the non-Germans feared, with Germany moving ahead with unilateral recognition and the others being forced to follow. In the next phase of negotiations, this action led to the involvement of the United Nations, the United States, Russia, and NATO, and a reduced role for EC-based institutions. In the Bosnian negotiations, the major participants agreed only on a commitment to multilateralism, rather than a complete nested institutional security architecture. Thus, after significant debate over the respective role of NATO, the United Nations, and other organizations, the participants could only manage to develop a division of labor involving a parallel substantive reconciliation among these institutions as part of the Dayton Agreement (Bosnia 2).

This case demonstrates the difficulty that may arise in attempting to reconcile existing institutions that wish to preserve their autonomy. As a consequence, the effort to nest proved unsuccessful, and the participants who had a strong cognitive commitment to multilateralism could only agree to a potentially unstable, thin, parallel, substantive reconciliation.

The EEA cases involved the institutional relationship between the EC and EFTA and the procedures that EFTA members would use to deal with these institutions. Following the Single European Act (SEA) that set the EC members on the path to European Union, the EFTA members began to worry about their position vis-á-vis the EC. Still, for the most part, they continued to emphasize the parallel substantive linkage between the two existing organizations and pursued functional cooperation with the EC (EEA 1). After Central and Eastern European states called for closer economic relations with the EC, the EFTA and the EC moved toward development of an overarching institution to manage the relationship between these two institutions. This effort resulted in the formation of the EEA with the EU nested partially (because some policy domains remained outside the EEA) and the EFTA nested fully within this broader arrangement, and the EEA in turn being nested firmly within GATT. There was, however, disagreement on the nature of this nesting, with substantive reasons for the relationship based on integration principles (EEA 2a). But a tactical logic for members of these organizations was also at work: the EC saw this relationship as a way of leveraging the EEA so as to stand against U.S. demands in GATT, while EFTA members saw the EEA as a step toward eventual adhesion to the EC (EEA 2b). Because of the way the EEA was negotiated, some EFTA members began to worry about their ability to influence EC policy, and the EEA began to face difficulties. In the end, the outcome was a partial defection from EFTA as the majority of EFTA's member states sought complete EC membership—thus leading to an outcome of a nested substantive connection of membership in the EC (EEA 3). In sum, despite considerable time and effort, the creation of a new nested substantive institution proved to be a failure.

In the EEA analysis, multiple elements explain the choice of the type and nature of the linkage. Cognitive considerations, control of policymaking in the broader EEA, and the presence of existing institutions and transaction cost issues all combine to explain the varying fortunes of the EEA. Often, the cognitive consensus on the benefits of nested institutions ran into power considerations and concerns about both domestic and international control that varied depending on the actors' individual situations. Moreover, the context of the existing institutions of EFTA and the EC sharply affected the course of bargaining and eventual outcomes.

As we have already seen in the FSF story, the U.S. effort to develop the IEA to counter OPEC was resisted by the French (among others) primarily due to their more vulnerable economic position. The United States responded to these concerns with a parallel tactical linkage to the FSF and to an agreement to participate in a North-South dialogue (FSF 1a). The French appear to have seen this as a parallel substantive linkage (FSF 1b), but in any case (however perceived), this concession appears to have done the trick. However, the differing views of these linkages opened up the possibility of institutional instability. As French resistance to the IEA diminished, the actors turned to the question of how the FSF would fit into the existing international financial infrastructure. Major institutions, including the OECD and IMF, already existed in the area of financial management. Thus, it was not surprising that the participants chose to nest the FSF in an existing institution (FSF 2a); but the debate over whether such nesting would take place within the OECD or IMF now became prominent. When the United States decided to substantively nest the FSF within the OECD, even with some deference to the IMF's wishes, the IMF and its supporters rejected this substantive link to prevent its own authority from being undermined (FSF 2b). Although one might have envisioned a scenario whereby the United States pressed on with its vision and engaged in tactical linkages to pressure the IMF and its supporters, a changing U.S. domestic situation led it away from supporting an FSF that would be nested within the OECD. Instead, the United States abandoned the FSF and agreed to a financial support arrangement (the Witteveen facility) that would be nested substantively within the IMF (FSF 3).

As in the EEA cases, a combination of cognitive factors, together with power and preexisting institutional constraints best explain the creation, evolution, and demise of the FSF proposal.[3]

What factors proved most significant in reconciling institutions, and particularly for nesting institutions? Turning first to examples of institutional adaptation, we have seen that a strong cognitive consensus owing to the high salience of the EU had a salutary effect on cooperation in the EMS case. Indeed, the depth of commitment to the EU combined with highly institutionalized mechanisms to overcome bickering that arose from differences in objectives and power. In the absence of such cognitive commitment or agreement on a hierarchy of goals, countries could only muster a division of labor among institutions in the Bosnian case. This proved to be a relatively positive outcome, despite criticisms that there was a lack of clear ordering of roles among institutions. Put differently, a division of labor through parallel linkage would appear to be preferable to conflict over nesting. These lessons can be seen in the failure to successfully develop either the EEA or the FSF. In both cases, negotiators did not correctly anticipate the depth of opposition provoked by the perceived challenge of new institutions. While power could substitute for cognitive consensus as in both the EEA and FSF cases with a dominant role being played by the EU and the United States, respectively, the linkage reconciliation efforts proved to be fleeting.

A RESEARCH AGENDA ON INSTITUTIONAL RECONCILIATION

This book has provided an analytical approach the analysis of institutional reconciliation efforts. It argues that by focusing on the concept of development

---

[3] For example, Cohen's rich multicausal account of the development of the IEA and FSF provides little evidence for Keohane's (1984) claim of the central role of transaction costs in explaining the formation of the IEA.

and change in "institutional bargaining games," which draw systematically from neorealist institutionalist, neoliberal institutionalist, and cognitive approaches, we can better understand the bargaining and linkage process involved in the formation of institutions. In thinking about directions for future research, it is worth reviewing both the broader theoretical lessons of the analysis as well as the policy implications of the empirical insights from the cases in this book.

Two avenues for moving beyond the framework applied in this book are worth considering. First, it would be useful to formalize the interaction among goods, individual situations, and institutions to better understand their contributions to setting up game payoffs. This is a somewhat daunting task, but one that should prove rewarding and enhance our understanding of institutional evolution.[4] Second, it is worth recalling that in attempting to promote game change, we have focused on *institutional strategies* to the relative exclusion of direct attempts to manipulate goods or actors' individual situations. This is, of course, not necessarily the most powerful way to manipulate games, and thus attention to how institutional bargaining games are transformed by direct manipulation of goods and individual situations is worthy of serious examination.[5] By pursuing these two avenues of research, we should be able to further our understanding of institutional bargaining games and more precisely assess the importance of variables drawn from different schools of thought.

Turning to empirical and policy considerations, while successful nested and parallel institutional reconciliation can have important advantages for cooperation in the international system, this is not an easy objective to realize. Both the EMS crisis and the Bosnian cases illustrate the importance of coordination among institutions along these lines. In the EMS case, strong connections between the European Union program and monetary arrangements prevented what might otherwise have been a total collapse of the ERM. Thus, broader institutional constraints facilitated the resolution of a crisis in a way that in this case would have been unlikely to occur in its absence. In the Bosnian case, initial conflict over German recognition of Croatia gave way to consideration of how actors could cooperate multilaterally in resolving the Bosnian crisis. Although the actors could not agree on the more substantive norms that they wished to implement, they were at least able to come up with a division of labor among various international and regional institutions (parallel substantive linkage) that allowed the parties to cope with the crisis. This operational arrangement demonstrates the possibility of actors agreeing on how existing institutions might successfully work together.

---

[4] See Aggarwal and Dupont, forthcoming, on a more formal treatment of the relationship between goods, individual situations, and institutions.

[5] I have examined actor's efforts to manipulate goods and individual situations for the empirical case of debt rescheduling in Aggarwal 1996.

The EEA and FSF chapters tell a less optimistic story. In these cases, we have seen the difficulties involved in creating new institutions and nesting them within existing ones. In the EEA case, Cédric Dupont argues that the participants faced a rapidly changing international environment and were not able to sufficiently cope with changing domestic pressures from their constituencies. Thus, this effort to nest existing institutions within a broader institution actually harmed the existing EFTA arrangements—although one might argue that defection from EFTA and adhesion to the EC was inevitable in the long run. Cohen's analysis discusses the benefits that might have come from a new financial fund within the OECD-IMF broad apparatus. But he also points to the difficulties in creating new institutions that are seen as threats to existing ones. Among other findings, he notes that cognitive changes, the inability of the proponents of the FSF to carefully specify how this organization would fit with the IMF, and a lack of speed in ratifying the arrangements led to the FSF's demise.

For policymakers, the temptation to create new institutions as a solution to new problems may be a perilous illusion.[6] As we have seen, reconciling new and old institutions is not an easy task. Indeed, it may be best to work to restructure existing institutions to accomplish one's policy goals. As policymakers face the difficult task of working with each other in different regions and on different issues, we hope that they may be able to learn from the analysis and experiences discussed in this volume.

[6] See Dupont 1998 on this idea.

REFERENCES

Aggarwal, Vinod K., 1996. *Debt Games: Strategic Interaction in International Debt Rescheduling* (New York: Cambridge University Press).

Aggarwal, Vinod K., and Cédric Dupont, forthcoming. "Goods, Games, and Institutions," Unpublished manuscript.

Aggarwal, Vinod K., and Charles E. Morrison, eds., 1998. *Asia-Pacific Crossroads: Regime Creation and the Future of APEC* (New York: St. Martin's Press).

Dupont, Cédric, 1998. "European Integration and APEC: The Search for Institutional Blueprints," in Aggarwal and Morrison, *Asia-Pacific Crossroads*.

Keohane, Robert O., 1984. *After Hegemony: Cooperation and Discord in the World Economy* (Princeton: Princeton University Press).

Yarbrough, Beth V., and Robert M. Yarbrough, 1992. *Cooperation and Governance in International Trade: The Strategic Organizational Approach* (Princeton: Princeton University Press).

Index